# Helping Parents Understand Schools: A Different Perspective on Education and Schooling in America

# Helping Parents Understand Schools: A Different Perspective on Education and Schooling in America

Lyndon G. Furst
*Andrews University*

INFORMATION AGE PUBLISHING, INC.
Charlotte, NC • www.infoagepub.com

**Library of Congress Cataloging-in-Publication Data**

The CIP data for this book can be found on the Library of Congress website (loc.gov).

Paperback: 9781681236858
Hardcover: 9781681236865
eBook: 9781681236872

Printed in the United States of America

# CONTENTS

### P A R T   I

## INTRODUCTION

### P A R T   I I

## SCHOOLS AND THE PEOPLE IN THEM

PART III

# MATTERS OF PUBLIC POLICY

PART IV

# SENSITIVE ISSUES IN PUBLIC SCHOOLS

# FOREWORD

### Bruce S. Cooper

As the title *Helping Parents Understand Schools* suggests, this book is written for parents and other folks who may have some parenting role or have an interest in American public education. The book is filled with useful ideas, insights and wisdom about learning and life—based in part on the author's experiences and observations over the last 50 years or so. The author, Dr. Lyndon G. (Jerry) Furst, constructed this volume, using selected essays, published in his local hometown newspaper during the past 20 years to provide the underlying structure of the book. Thus, the concepts that he suggests have been subjected to public scrutiny and tested in the local "market-place of ideas."

The conceptual framework approaches education and schooling as a crucial part of human and community life. The book is designed mostly for parents to help them understand the experiences their children go through in schools, and to suggest some ways parents can work in collaboration with teachers to help their kids be successful in school—and beyond. Therefore, the book is written in language that can be understood by most people and families.

Furst frequently illustrates his conceptual train of thoughts with personal experiences drawn from his lifetime as an educator. He is careful to avoid educational jargon, although his ideas are well documented. The author has carefully crafted his work to be related to his published editorials, illustrated through personal ex-

*Helping Parents Understand Schools: A Different Perspective on Education and Schooling in America,* pages vii–xi.
Copyright © 2017 by Information Age Publishing

periences, and grounded in the professional literature, making it acceptable to the community of scholars.

His 19 years as an elected member of his local public school board provided Furst, with an up-front view of public school policy-making, its formation, implementation, and effects-effectiveness. Those observations helped him to understand the inner-workings of a public school and provided the basis for many of his newspaper *Perspectives* and his thinking on public policy. Even though his professional career was in private schools, he starts the book with a strong defense of *public* education. Five chapters are dedicated to describing the schools, and especially the people in them—while another four chapters deal with matters of public policy related to public education.

This book, *Helping Parents Understand Schools*, provides a timely, rich and powerful basis for understanding issues and problems that have challenged observer's thinking over time. Using his weekly editorials, the author identifies the flow of changes in his own thought processes. His willingness to share those personal transitions provides much value to the book.

It's so wonderful to read a chapter, and see Furst quote his previous work and then integrate these ideas into the current publication that is further strengthened by his commentaries and references to applicable professional literature. He has thus effectively used years of experience as well as the findings of other educators to illustrate and elaborate on the main points in this book.

## TESTING KEY ISSUES IN EDUCATION

In Part Two, "Schools and People in Them," he focuses the entire Chapter 4 on the use and misuse of standardized testing in the public schools. Thus, he exposes the idiocy of testing and over-testing children in schools, with little benefit to the kids or their classroom teachers. He unravels the mysteries of interpreting scores derived from standardized tests. Furst helps place meaning to the numbers generated by the testing companies so that parents can get a better picture regarding their children's progress in school.

Further, Furst examines the problem of, and effects of, "Test-All," where kids, teachers, and community are often judged by the outcomes of education testing. Right at the start of Chapter 4, he points out the uses and overuses of testing to judge everyone and everything in education. As he explains, "People place labels on children based on the results of their test scores, or their grades in school. Such statements as 'she is an A student" or "He is only average in musical skill," are examples of ways we identify people."

The use and misuse of the "testing" of kids and schools—and teachers—are serious problems, and this chapter gives us a nice balance, between the usefulness and abuses of testing. In his words, "Test scores and grades can be useful tools in understanding a person's educational attainment, but they can also be improperly used in determining an individual's value as a person."

## SCHOOL CHOICE AND ITS ADVANTAGES

In Part Three of this book, Matters of Public Policy, Chapter 8 analyzes the educational reforms known collectively as "school choice." Furst goes on to discuss the advantages to families who have *choices* when making the selection of a school for their children. I like this chapter because Dr. Furst cites and quotes my own research on homeschooling, private and religious schools, and choice in education (see Cooper, 2005; Cooper, Spielhagan, & Ricci, 2016; Weinberg & Cooper, 2004).

Let's take one of Dr. Furst's ideas—and walk it from idea and issue, to opinion and beliefs, as expressed in his weekly editorials in the local paper. The process makes understanding and purposive ideas very clear and convincing, chapter-by-chapter, issue-by-issue. As the Table of Contents shows, the book covers the world—and horizon—of key education issues today. As we take Chapter 8, for example, on "School Choice" as a key issue in U.S. education, Furst explains how he had serious doubts about any possible benefits from the various "choice plans" being discussed at the time.

He then explains the transformation in one of his published editorials that he shares in the book: "However, my thinking shifted over time as I saw the rise of the public school academies (charter schools) throughout the state and the effect of such competition on my fellow board members in our public school district. Thereafter, it seemed that almost every change proposed was prefaced with somebody stating, 'We've got to stay competitive!.'"

The chapter on school choice is not presented in isolation, as it is preceded by a rather comprehensive chapter on the topic of school reform. Thus, school choice is seen in the context of the larger paradigm of school reform. This placement positions school choice proposals in a more useful vantage point.

Dr. Furst then goes on to analyze the issues of choice and competition (C & C) in a critical context and quotes from several of his newspaper editorials. As he explained in his book, "Some educators fear that the rough and tumble of the business world would destroy the democratic values taught in the public schools. I do not discount that possibility." And another *Perspective*, published a decade ago, speaks to that concern. "From my perspective, no benefit accrues when supporters of the three approaches to schooling feud among themselves."

They should consider that they all have the same goals—the education of children. Thus, "if they see themselves involved in education rather than schooling, they will find much common ground." The author openly supports public schools, private and religious schools, and homeschooling. But he acknowledges that a spirit of competition will naturally follow any choice program; so he appeals to educators in all venues to moderate that spirit.

Furst offers not only a philosophical defense to the concept of school choice but also an example from his hometown school district where he served for 17 years as a locally-elected member of the school board. While this district's success may not be easily replicated everywhere, it does identify the distinct possibilities that occur when innovative school administrators team up with a supportive, knowledgeable school board. This chapter thus identifies and analyzes several options available to parents as they make choices regarding the "educational journey" of their offspring.

In Chapter 10, Furst tackles perhaps the toughest issue in education: *school finance* in terms of levels of *equity* based on sources of revenue. Should schools be locally or state and/or nationally funded, or perhaps all three levels of government contributing—and even *private* sources. We have become so used to a high level of service from the government and we feel abused when we get less than what we normally expect. Maybe it is time for Americans to get used to doing with less. Our public institutions can no longer cater to our every whim.

Furst goes on to explain just how important *equitable funding* is to schools, and the appropriate roles of Federal and State governments in equalizing local property-based funding. He then provides the example from his home state of Michigan: e.g., that went through a rather strange political confrontation in the early 1990s resulting in a complete redesign of the system for funding public education; this change resulted in a much more equitable system.

## CONCLUSION

The book is a miracle; and the author, Dr. Jerry Furst, is thus a miracle-writer. He places himself at the center of U.S. education—with its problems, issues and strengths—and he then writes a positive, creative critique that includes a useful set of solutions for these issues and shortcomings. And perhaps the greatest miracles in this book are the perspectives and years of writings that are harnessed to this end. We thus benefit from Furst's key issues, his personal views, and his wisdom. He reaches an important conclusion: *That our education system begins, moves, and ends with the parents.* In fact, it appears that parents—and even grandparents—are key factors in bringing overall harmony to the school community.

After all, parents are usually the *first, primary* "teachers" of their children; and their influence is ever-present in the children's lives. Thus, as pointed out in Chapter 11, fathers and mothers are well advised to exercise a degree of care about subtle expressions of racial and social antagonism. Children are very quick to pick up on the signals adults send and make these beliefs a part of their own persona. A short paragraph quoted in the book is the author's final word on the sensitive issue of race relations.

"We can enjoy humor and still show concerns for the racial sensitivities of all Americans. We need to stop looking for an excuse to label every little misstatement 'racist.' And we especially need to stop letting the media do our thinking for us. We need to make more progress in improving race relations. America is a multiracial society and we might as well learn to live with each other."

Bruce S. Cooper, Ph. D.
Professor Emeritus, Fordham University

## REFERENCES

Cooper, B. S., Spielhagen, Francis R., & Ricci, C. (2016). *Home schooling in new view.* Charlotte, NC: Information Age Publishing.

Cooper, B. S. (2005). *Homeschooling in full view: A Reader.* Charlotte, NC: Information Age Publishing.

Weinberg, L. C., & Cooper, B. S. (2007). What about religious charter schools? *Education Week Commentary, 26*(42), 39–40.

# PREFACE

### Lyndon G. Furst

This book is written for parents, although others who are interested in the phenomena of schooling and educating children in formal settings might also find something of interest in the book. This work is fashioned around the weekly essays I write for our hometown newspaper, *The Journal Era*. It is not just a cut-and-paste job or an accumulation of those previous writings. I have merely used them as structural foundation to guide my way through the complexities of the educational system.

I see the world from a different point of view than many other people. I do not do that on purpose, it just happens that way. Thus, the readers of this book will not find a repetition of what is common to other authors who write about American education, although I am not too far outside the mainstream of current thought. I had never expected that the newspaper columns I wrote would ever become a full-length book.

My first task was to pull from approximately 1,000 articles, all those related to some aspect of education and schooling, and then find some organizing principle as I prepared them for inclusion in this current publication. Though I had not planned it that way, the assembled articles fell neatly into 12 categories which form the chapters in this book.

The reader should keep in mind that each chapter is formed by the various short newspaper publications over a period of 20 years. Thus, they may not all be

*Helping Parents Understand Schools: A Different Perspective on Education and Schooling in America,* pages xiii–xv.
Copyright © 2017 by Information Age Publishing

consistent, as my thinking is always subject to change over time. The reader will have the advantage of my in-the-classroom observation as I scrutinized children and their instructors in real classrooms in real schools. After each visit, I had time for serious reflection on what I had just witnessed. The writing that followed was informed by both my observation and my knowledge of the current professional literature on public education. The reader will get, not merely a theoretical point of view, but one that is seen through the lens of real events happening on a daily basis in a public school.

In addition, my position as an elected member of the public school board, gave me a front row seat to view the development and implementation of public policy at the local, state and national levels of governance. Soon after I took my place around the table in the Boardroom, my colleagues elected me to the position of Treasurer of the board. It is mostly an honorific title, but it did place me at the center of much controversy at a time of tight budgets. While I had done my doctoral research on a topic related to public school finance, the present realities of competing public demands for the scarce dollars available, was an entirely different experience.

I was spared some of the usual expected agony when the Michigan legislature in a most bizarre series of events eliminated the entire school funding mechanism for the state's public schools. This gave me a chance to see public policy being made as the legislature designed a new school finance system from start to finish. That story is told in more detail in chapter 10. However, the experience of watching the political process at work and seeing from the perspective of local board member, the impact of each legislative enactment on the operation of public schools, gave me some valuable insight into the policymaking process. The influence of these perceptions no doubt is noticeable in Part Three of this book.

From my experience, the average American citizen has never given much thought to the business of public policy. In fact, I would guess that very few parents are aware of how public policy plays out to the advantage or disadvantage of their own children. It is with that thought in mind, that I devoted 4 chapters to various aspects of educational policy. From my perspective, parents should take note of the policymaking process and not feel intimidated in making their own voices heard when they think things are getting off track. They have a vested interest in the education of their children and they can only protect that interest, as they are knowledgeable about the competing voices that speak to educational issues. Hopefully this book will have a positive influence on parents as they consider their proper role in public education and encourage them to be actively involved.

The last section of the book introduces two touchy issues affecting public schools, race relationships, and religion. My experience of living in a community that holds organized religion in high regard has affected my perspective on the topic. The same is true for issues of race. The community where I have resided for more than twenty years is noted for the high level of racial and ethnic diversity among the residents. These two factors have no doubt affected my perspective on both subjects. I present them with a degree of faith in the goodness of parents and others who read this book, to keep an open mind on the issues. I believe those who peruse the pages of this tome will find my different perspective a refreshing read.

# DEDICATION

This book is dedicated to parents. Not only to biological parents, but also those who carry the responsibility of parents, are included in the focus of this dedication. That includes a wide range of people, such as adoptive parents, foster parents, stepparents, grandparents, uncles, aunts, older brothers and sisters, the neighbor next door, close friends, or even the kind stranger who sees a child in need and performs a random act of kindness in response.

Parenting is an awesome responsibility for which there is very little preparation available. Of course, I am aware of the numerous books, videos, seminars, and workshops on how to function as a successful parent. Some of them have good counsel, while others are void of wisdom. No amount of training or reading can contain everything one needs to know about filling the role of a parent.

Every child is different and it takes a great deal of wisdom to modify one's knowledge base and apply it in such a way as to meet the needs of the individual child. With this in mind, I have tried to fashion the content of this book in such a way that it stays focused on the schooling side of parent's responsibility.

Parents do not carry this burden alone, for there is a Higher Power that has given a promise of hope, "I will contend with him that contendeth with thee, and I will save thy children." Isaiah 49:25 (KJV)

# PART I

INTRODUCTION

# GENESIS

## In the Beginning

Early in the year 1995, the first *Perspective* was published in *The Journal Era,* a small town weekly newspaper, in Southwest Michigan. I had recently been elected a trustee of the public school district to fill out the term of a board member who had been defeated in a recall election. I frequently have a different viewpoint on things than others. I do not do differ on purpose; it just naturally seems to happen. There are times when I am not hesitant to express my different perspective on issues. This variation is true for almost any topic under discussion, but it is especially true when it comes to matters of education.

One night after a particularly contentious board meeting, the editor of *The Journal Era* approached me and said, "You have some interesting ideas about the public schools. Why don't you write them up into an article and I will publish them in the paper." Taking the challenge, my first article was entitled, "Prayer in the Public Schools." (*Perspective*, 1995, February 15)

My article expressed a somewhat different viewpoint than was most common in our area of the state. The editor liked it and encouraged me to write some more. I had no idea when I first started that I would be writing what would eventually become a weekly column that I would continue to pen, for 20 years.

*Helping Parents Understand Schools: A Different Perspective on Education and Schooling in America,* pages 3–7.

## MISINFORMED PUBLIC

Of special concern, as I began to write the *Perspectives,* was the general misinformation as to how the public schools function and what outside forces influence their operations. I found the public was sorely lacking in knowledge about the public schools and how they operated. Even many parents seemed uninformed about what was taking place in the schools their own children attended. While the *Perspectives* published each week reflected my unique perspective on the issues at hand, the more important goal was to describe, to the best of my ability to be accurate, what actually transpires in the teaching/learning process that is the core function of the school.

The business, and it is a business, of schooling is much more complex than most people recognize. This is especially true for the older generation who remember when life was less complicated and fewer outside demands were placed on school personnel. For example, at one time, little federal law applied to the public schools. By contrast, now, the federal finger seems to touch just about every aspect of public school operations. The *Perspectives* attempt to unravel, or at least identify, the complexities public school personnel face on a daily basis. Admittedly, I put my own spin on it and the writing is influenced by my own viewpoint. Those two decades of sometimes stable and sometimes shifting perspective, form the conceptual foundation for this book.

In each chapter, I take a major issue schools face as they continue operations. The perspective I bring to the public forum is unique insofar as almost my entire professional career has been with the private religious schools. However, I am a strong supporter of public schools as evidenced by the articles I have published in the newspaper. This view gives a different perspective to the issues confronting public education.

While the *Perspectives* I present in this volume are the same as were published in the newspaper, seldom is the entire essay reproduced. To do so would make the present work overly cumbersome and difficult to construe. Further, I have taken editorial liberties on occasion to make the reading smoother and to correct grammatical errors. In addition, an effort was made to protect the identity of certain people who might not wish to be named.

I present my different perspectives with a warning to readers: do not attempt to identify a political pattern in my writing because there is none. I have, on occasion, been accused in the Letters to the Editor section of the newspaper of being a "far left Liberal." Yet, liberal friends have at other times told me "You are certainly not a Liberal. I offer no apology for what some readers might view as frustrating inconsistency. After all, I have clearly identified my unusual combination of viewpoints by the title of my weekly column: *A Different Perspective.*

## RESEARCH METHODOLOGY

This book contains the observations of the author over a lifetime of involvement in education at one level or another. Its foundation is more than mere observation; it rests on the written record of those observations over a 20-year period. In this respect, it is not a typical research-based book in that no hypothesis was tested nor was any statistical analysis conducted as is typical in quantitative research. However, the book is not merely the undisciplined musings of a casual bystander reported herewith. This work falls within the realm of "qualitative research" based on a disciplined approach to inquiry (Watras, 2009).

There is value in descriptive work as one attempts to convey to readers an explanation of the public school system and its contribution to the strength of our cultural heritage (Eisner, 1997). A good description helps to form a picture in the mind of recipients and is an effective method of communication. In this book, the *Perspectives* form the primary data set, augmented by a narrative account of accumulated personal experience. Any validity depends on faithfulness of the author in keeping the narrative as true to the actual event as possible. The written *Perspectives* have been tested in the open marketplace of ideas by being published in the newspaper and subject to public responses.

Like any other academic work attempting to be informative, this book does not stand-alone. Rather, it rests on the massive amount of literature in the field of education produced by the community of scholars. I did not intend to write a strictly academic book. Instead, my goal was to produce a volume that was academically sound and would be acceptable in the scholarly world, while still being useful to the primary audience, which is constituted by parents and other members of the general public. My goal, then, is to help clear up some of the uncertainties existing with regards to public schools.

There is one major caveat of concern primarily to researchers from the empirical tradition, namely the absence of documentation in a number of the *Perspectives*. Originally, I wrote for the public where strict adherence to the rules of research is inapplicable. Where possible I have searched the archives of available publications, but especially in the older *Perspectives*, I was frequently unable to access the original documents. Throughout the book, I have identified the instances where the reference work is not available.

## THE ROAD AHEAD

This section provides a roadmap of the entire book and the structure of the topics it discusses. The book is divided into four major sections as follows:

Part One Introduction Matters contains this un-numbered chapter as well as Chapter 1. It identifies the origin of the book and establishes the basic premise upon which the book was written—that America is very blessed with its system of public schools. However, there seems to be a continual attack on the schools by local critics as well as those who speak from a broader stage. This chapter provides not only a defense of public education, but also a positive perspective to assist parents and others get a balanced picture of public schools in America.

Part Two: Schools and the People in Them comprises five chapters. These chapters focus on how people influence school operations and how schooling influences the lives of people. Chapter 2 considers why children misbehave. It offers some insight into school discipline, although that is not the prime focus of the chapter. Next, Chapter 3 recognizes the important knowledge, skills, and attitudes acquired in the school that fall outside of the formal curriculum and seldom provide testable outcomes.

Educational policy makers tend to be very fond of testing students. Chapter 4, Testing and Other Such Foolishness, then, identifies some of the technical aspects of the testing "game." Recognizing that parents play an important role in the formal education of their children, Chapter 5 makes suggestions on appropriate parental involvement in the educational process. The final chapter in Part Two is the very heart of the book. It is in the classroom that the life of the school will be found. Chapter 6, Life in the Classroom, provides illustrations of what should be considered the central focus of public education.

The third section, Matters of Public Policy, is comprised of four chapters. Chapter 7 deals with school reform, a seemingly ubiquitous process in American education. One of the reforms that has been popular is School Choice, the subject of Chapter 8. Chapter 9 is a reaction to the reform movement and expresses concern about Federal Involvement and the Centralization of Schooling. The final chapter in this section, 10, deals with School Finance and Financial Management.

The final Section introduces two sensitive issues in American education. Chapter 11 provides a perspective on racial issues while Chapter 12 looks at some of the controversy surrounding religion in the public schools. Both topics are widely misunderstood throughout America. The challenge in both chapters is to clear up some of the confusion so parents can communicate intelligently about these two topics about which Americans find it difficult to converse.

The chapters follow a set pathway. Each chapter begins with an introductory section, frequently a personal experience from my work as an educator. The next section is "The Road Ahead" that provides a structural map of the chapter. Some "Final Thoughts" close out each chapter. The *Perspectives* I use are listed separate from other sources that are identified in the bibliography. A short Epilogue following the last chapter ties it all together with one final *Perspective* that provides a summation of the book.

## LIST OF *PERSPECTIVES* REFERENCED

Published in *The Journal Era*, Berrien Springs, Michigan.

1995, February 15. Prayer in the public schools.

## REFERENCES

Eisner, E. W. (1997). *The enlightened eye: Qualitative inquiry and the enhancement of educational practice* (2 ed.). New York: Macmillan.

Watras, J. (2009). Historical perspectives towards qualitative research. *Journal of Ethnographic & Qualitative Research, 4*(1), 1–8.

CHAPTER 1

# IN DEFENSE OF PUBLIC SCHOOLS

## THE SETTING

A tense atmosphere pervaded the college lecture room. Yet, it was not an academic matter that caused the angst among those present. Instead, a group of people from the surrounding community came to hear the public school superintendent present reasons why they should vote "yes" on a tax proposal on the ballot for the next election. In that state, the system of financing public education depended quite heavily on property tax. Local school boards were required by law to determine the rate of taxation that would bring sufficient revenue into the school system to provide an adequate education for the young people who live within the district.

### An Angry Crowd

It is very difficult to convince people that they should raise their taxes. It was even more difficult in the district at hand because of the low value of real property within its boundaries. There was very little commercial or industrial property in the district that usually have much higher taxable value than single-family housing. At the meeting, the superintendent, a mild-mannered soft-spoken man, did his

*Helping Parents Understand Schools: A Different Perspective on Education and Schooling in America,* pages 9–22.

best to make a case for a "yes" vote when Election Day arrived. The crowd did not accept the argument. One after another, speakers rose to make speeches against the requested rate of taxation. Most of the anger was turned against the superintendent and his fellow administrators in the district. Why did the school district need more money? If this passes, the schools will be back next year asking for even more money. One vocal person stated emphatically, "We do not really have to vote yes on this request, because if the millage proposal does not pass, the state has to make up the difference and provide the funds needed to run the schools."

The crowd seemed pleased with the possibility of the state being forced to finance the cost of operating the schools in their district. However, when the moderator suggested that was not the case, one irritated citizen stated emphatically, "Oh yes they will. I read it in the newspaper and if it were not true, they would not have printed it." That seemed to put an end to the discussion and the crowd began to disperse. However, many of them lingered on, comparing the various options available to them. Emotion still flowed freely as individual homeowners shared the burden of high taxes on their modest homes.

The consensus throughout the entire community seemed to coalesce around the belief that the public schools spend too much money and they need to be more frugal. There was especially strong resentment that the teachers' union had outsmarted the administration during the last negotiation session and teachers were given a pay scale that was too rich for this community.

### A Misinformed Public

A few days after the events described in the previous section, an acquaintance of mine who had been at the meeting regarding the upcoming school tax election, discussed with me her response to the school superintendent's explanation of the need for a higher tax rate. "I think the public schools spend too much money," she stated emphatically. "They need to cut back on their expenditures." I knew that arguing with her would be futile. So, I merely asked her a simple question, "How much money do they spend?" At first, she was puzzled by my inquiry, but then she realized that she had been basing her opinion on a mere assumption rather than solid facts. She admitted that she did not know how much money the public schools spend each year. Further, she did not know how the local school budget compared with other schools in the area. The only thing she knew for sure was that she felt her taxes were too high and put too much strain on the family budget. This taxpayer is not alone in her lack of knowledge about the public schools.

It is not only financial matters where there is much misunderstanding, but also a myriad of other things remain a puzzlement to the average property owner from whom a large portion of the school revenues are derived. For example, I frequently hear the complaint that, "They have taken God out of the public schools." Another statement I often hear, "You cannot even pray in public schools anymore." Both of these statements are incorrect as will be discussed in much more detail in

Chapter 12 (Flowers, 2005). I only offer them here as examples of misinformation about the public schools that flows so freely throughout our society.

## THE ROAD AHEAD

This chapter provides the foundation for the broad topic of the book. It is all about public schools, how they function, and the contribution they make to the larger community. In the short vignette at the opening of the chapter, the stage is set for what is to come. The chapter has five major sections, the first of which has already been presented. Next, the continuing attack on public education is described through several *Perspectives* that were written over the past 20 years. This is followed by a defense of public schools and then a positive view of these schools as presented in various *Perspectives*. In Some Final Thoughts, I present the suggestion that the public education community take proactive steps to ward off some of the criticisms that come to them.

## THE ATTACK ON PUBLIC EDUCATION

Public schools in America are under constant attack by a variety of entities and from various directions (Sackler, 2013). It is doubtful that any other public agency faces the continuous flow of criticism that America's schools must endure. Of course, the public schools, like other institutions, have their flaws. The success of public schools depends on a number of factors, some of which are outside the school's control, to achieve the goal of an adequate education for all students under their care.

In many cases where a public school system comes under fire from critics, a multitude of problems not susceptible to school control are present. This is especially true in large cities and poverty-stricken areas of the nation (Ullucci, 2015).

School personnel face intractable problems with the result being the children under their care tend to score poorly on standardized tests. These low test scores form the basis for much of the criticism aimed at American public education. However, from my perspective, the American public schools do a magnificent job of educating a multi-cultural population in the basic foundations of knowledge necessary for survival in today's rapidly changing world.

### Local Critics

For some 20 years, a variety of *Perspectives* have been written in response to criticism of the public schools. The critics come from a variety of viewpoints and range from local self-appointed antagonists to nationally-recognized pundits. First, consider charges against school leaders by a resident of a local school district in Southwestern Michigan described in a *Perspective*.

Education leaders ignore facts in defense of monopoly," stated the headline in a local newspaper recently. I could not resist reading the article even though I have grown weary of attacks on the public schools in our local papers. I wanted to find the answer to questions hinted at in the headline: which education leaders, what facts do they ignore, and what monopoly do they defend?

Written by a local businessman who is billed as an "Opinion Maker," the article is typical of the conservative mantra characterizing much of the continued attacks on public education. It chooses only "facts" which support the notion that public schools are failing and ignores those that confirm the success of our schools. In business parlance, the author truly starts with the end in mind and chooses only to accept data that supports it.

The education leaders referred to are two public school superintendents from Southwestern Michigan. Rather than ignore facts, these educators reported data supporting the work of the schools. They cited a book that claims the crises in American education was manufactured as part of a political agenda (Berliner & Biddle, 1995). The author of the opinion article ignored these. (*Perspective*, 1997, April 16)

The Opinion Maker continued to expand on his accusation against the local educators. The monopoly he referred to is the public schools. What he seems to ignore is that a number of private schools in the area, as well as charter schools, are available to the public. In addition, Michigan has minimal restrictions on home schools. In the area where Opinion Maker resides, at least two, and possibly more, home school circuits provide support for parents who take on the responsibility for the formal education of their children. If the public schools ever had a monopoly, it certainly is a very weak one now.

Opinion Maker made an astounding observation regarding the failure of public education. He stated that a negative relationship existed between the cost of education and the amount of learning that resulted. Similar statements have appeared periodically in the media. However, a closer look at some examples would show that it does not make any sense. The assertion implies that if less money were spent on public education, better results could be expected. Taking that idea to its logical end, the best education would be one where no money is spent. If such a situation were true, parents who reside in wealthy districts would demand that their budgets be traded with more poorly funded school systems.

The *Perspective* concluded with strong support for continued public debate on matters of public policy such as education. However, it is not useful to distort the facts and ignore rational thought as was done in Opinion Maker's attack on the schools. Unfortunately, I am not able to provide a proper citation for the source, insofar as the newspaper's electronic archives do not extend back to that date.

## Nationally Distributed Essay

Another *Perspective* dealt with a more comprehensive broadside against public education. Other newspapers throughout the nation published a strongly worded negative opinion of public schools authored by a well-known pundit. (I was unable to retrieve the original document.) The call for Christians to take their children out of public schools and put them in religious schools or home school them, provided a catalyst for my perspective on the matter. While my *Perspectives* have consistently supported public education, they have also given strong support to both private education and home schools. The *Perspective* provides a close look at the disparagement of publically funded education:

> The unfavorable view of the public schools is well known by those who read this column on a regular basis. It is written in a manner that evokes a sense of anger at the public schools for a number of reasons. First, they are operated by the government and are therefore automatically suspect. The conservative tradition is generally opposed to social programs funded by tax dollars. Such ventures are in the purview of political liberals. The commentary expresses a good deal of angst regarding a line of court decisions that prohibit religious ritual (public prayer) and indoctrination (Bible reading) in the public schools.

> This is followed by a grievance against public schools over their teaching of toleration for people who live a bit out of the mainstream of conservative America. The particular target in the recent column is homosexuals. That the schools would encourage toleration for such people is repulsive to the conservative mind. Thus, the plea for an exodus from the public schools. (*Perspective*, 2004, June 23)

## The Accountant's Report

The attack on public education takes many different shapes. Usually, about the time school starts, the media will notice events or public statements negative towards public schools. Shortly after the turn-of-the-century, the state of Michigan contracted with a major accounting firm, Standard and Poor's, to assess how efficiently its public schools were functioning. Since the state was providing a majority of the funds for the schools, it was well within its purview to seek such information. The conclusion of the study was predictable. Test scores in schools located in areas of high socio-economic status were considerably better than those in communities of lower economic status.

Standard and Poor's knows how to count things in the business world. They are good at conducting cost effectiveness studies. They did a good job of applying the industrial model to Michigan's public schools. It is really simple: count up the dollars spent and divide by the school's average test score and one has an efficiency ratio of the instructional program. Schools with a low ratio or cost per score are doing a good job while those with high ratio of cost per score are doing a bad job. It really is a good business technique. Except, the firm's analysts forgot two very important parts of the educational equation.

When it comes to children, teacher effectiveness is only one factor affecting test scores. Children come to school in all sizes and shapes and with a variety of native talents. Some are gifted intellectually while others are not so blessed. Some come with a large body of knowledge and educational skills already acquired from a home environment that is conducive to learning. Others come with severe deficits in acquired knowledge. No valid analysis can be conducted if it excludes data from several sources that affect the learning process. Using the industrial model to determine the efficiency of such social services as teaching and learning is inappropriate and counterproductive. Such misinformation can easily lead to public policy that does nothing to ameliorate the reasons why a school might be ineffective.

### Comparison With Private Schools

The attack against the public schools continues to flourish in a surprising number of formats as indicated in another *Perspective*:

Recently, the largest daily newspaper in our county published an article that designated the public schools as the shame of America. It referred specifically to schools in Washington DC, and contrasted the poor public schools in the District with the upscale private Sidwell Friends School. That is where President Obama has enrolled his daughters.

Sidwell is indeed, an outstanding school. They carefully screen the students who are enrolled to make sure that they have the academic ability to perform at a high level. Working there must be a teacher's dream. Class sizes are no greater than 16. In fact, in the lower grades teachers are expected to instruct no more than 10 students in a class. Remember, these are kids who arrive at school well prepared for learning. One wonders why it costs over $30,000 per student to educate such easy-to-teach children when the public schools here in Michigan have only a fourth that amount. [Note: the tuition for the 2015/16 academic year is $37,500, (Sidwell Friends School.]

Sidwell Friends School does have the right formula for good education: a safe and orderly environment, high expectations for student achievement, strong support from families, and children who arrive at school ready to learn. Now, if the public schools could just replicate that, everything would be wonderful in America, wouldn't it? However, I doubt that we have the political will to spend that kind of money merely to educate a child. I will note that we are willing to spend $30,000 to incarcerate a petty criminal for a year, but that is a different story. (*Perspective*, 2010, October 13)

## IN DEFENSE OF PUBLIC EDUCATION

My *Perspectives* have frequently come to the defense of public schools, especially when an attack is made against them that is not based on rational thinking. An early *Perspective* referred to the criticism against the local public schools regarding low scores in the district on state-mandated tests of academic achievement. The specific complaint by a local critic was that on two of the sections of the test, students in the district scored below the state average, an indication that teachers were not doing their work. He seemed unaware of the fact that half of the classrooms in the state would score below average. That is what average is by definition. The *Perspective* probably went a little overboard in responding with more scorn than necessary. Here is a summation of the *Perspective*:

> If we subjected other occupations to the same emotional scrutiny as teaching, we would have an interesting commentary on American life. Consider that half of the lawyers lose their cases. The same is true with football coaches and tennis players. Certainly, we should have a national commission to investigate this sad state of affairs.
>
> Hospitals give such poor care that people die there and automobiles are so poorly constructed that people are killed when they crash into each other. Chemists make compounds that pollute the environment and engineers design nuclear power plants without a plan for the spent fuel. To make it even worse, the Lions charge outrageous prices for people to watch them play awful football.
>
> Sound absurd? The same logic is used to decry the awful state of our public schools. Is this a defense of poor teaching? Certainly not. Our teachers need to do a much better job than they now do. However, given the nature of American society and the awesome task they have, an objective look at the facts would show that they are the best in the world. (*Perspective*, 1996, October 2)

## *Teacher Qualifications*

Another frequent complaint against the public schools relates to teacher qualifications. Much in the educational literature supports the importance of a highly qualified teacher in every classroom. However, it is well documented that in many schools this is not the case. Teachers with minimal qualifications in the subject matter routinely teach some classes. All too frequently, this situation is found with classes in mathematics and/ or science due to the difficulty in hiring qualified individuals. With all the publicity about the importance of those subjects, one would think that administrators would put the very highest qualified teachers possible in those classrooms. Some years ago, a *Perspective* responded to an article in a national news magazine regarding the situation in public schools today.

> One particular issue in the article that attracted my attention related to the qualifications of the people who teach in our public schools. While we still have much to learn about what makes for good teaching, one of the things we do know is that good teachers must have a deep knowledge of the subject matter they teach. The article cited statistics that "30% of middle and high school classes in math, English, science, and social studies" are taught by people who do not have a college major in the subject they teach. Even worse, non-majors teach 68% of classes in the physical sciences.
>
> I wonder why this is so. It seems so obvious that, at least at the high school level, teachers should have an intensive knowledge of the subject matter, usually achieved by majoring in the subject in college. Why then do school administrators assign unqualified teachers to teach the classes in subjects like science, which should be

at the core of our student's education? Well, this is a question for which I think I have a partial understanding of the answer. It could be that college majors in such subjects as physics, chemistry, and mathematics choose to enter professions other than teaching. Thus, high school principals just plain do not have a cadre of majors in those subjects to employ.

Therefore, they have two choices: do not teach the class or assign a less than highly qualified teacher to teach the subject. It is a hard decision for a school administrator to make. It would be nice if there were a surplus of teachers in the physical sciences from which principals could choose. Unfortunately, school administrators in America do not have that luxury. (*Perspective*, 2008, March 12)

## Sweeping Generalizations

Criticism of the public schools comes from a variety of sources and in a variety of forms. Some of the negative talk is in response to a specific incident at a particular school. In some cases, it might be a single teacher that is the object of public scorn. As long as we deal with people, that is going to happen. Yet, more problematic is when publicly respected individuals broadcast their disapproval over schools in general. They frequently make sweeping accusations against the schools and seldom come with evidence to support their claims. Such was the case some years ago when the largest newspaper in Southwest Michigan published articles by two nationally respected columnists regarding the awful state of America's schools.

One author suggested that it is necessary to have a strong principal to have a good school. He intimated that poor schools are the direct result of a weak principal. The other critic claimed that many of the problems of public education might be eliminated if teachers used phonics as the sole method of teaching reading. In response, several disconnected paragraphs from a *Perspective* suggested that these ideas were overly simplistic and ignored the complexities of the teaching/learning process:

> To start with, it is not very helpful to talk about "the public schools" as if they are all the same. There is wide variation in the effectiveness of America's schools. By any standard, most schools deliver a good product. They take children with a wide variety of abilities, from all kinds of family situations, and from different economic levels, and provide good basic education. . . .
>
> Most schools that fail to provide good basic education are located in either the inner-city or poverty-stricken areas of the country. In such situations, the research does show that a strong building principal can make a difference. However, even a good principal has to have the necessary resources to do his/her job. Rundown buildings, outdated books, overcrowded classrooms, and poorly paid teachers provide overwhelming challenges to even the best principal. Add to that dysfunctional families, a hostile environment, and children who live in poverty and you have an impossible task.

In contrast to the columnist's simplistic view of reforming schools, the Edison Project seems to have some real answers (Marsh, Hamilton, & Gill, 2008). This is a private management project for public schools. It sees public education as a cooperative venture between the school, the student, and the parent. Each is expected to perform at a high level. It does not solve the problem for the teacher to do an excellent job of teaching if the student does not do an excellent job of learning. Parents add to the equation by doing an excellent job of parenting.

It might seem like an impossible task to get teachers, students, and parents working at optimum levels, but the Edison people seem to have had some early success. Such a plan is much more difficult than merely teaching phonics, but it is much more effective. The public should not be fooled by simplistic proposals to improve the schools. It is a much more complex task than most realize. (*Perspective*, 1996, June 12)

I have observed that any institution in the country will have its faults. It is very easy to pick them out and magnify them so it appears that they are characteristics of the entire operation. This is what has happened to public education in America. With many institutions competing for the scarce resources of government, especially state government, the battle lines are often drawn and the schools become the object of a publicity attack. However, Americans do not need to apologize for the overall system of government-sponsored schools that are made available to the children in our country. Many good things happen in public schools. The next section accentuates those positive things.

## A POSITIVE VIEW OF PUBLIC SCHOOLS

In colonial and early America, it was considered the primary responsibility of parents to find a way to educate their children. Instead of relying on state government to provide education, local communities, churches, and parents worked together to give their children the basics of knowledge and skills needed to be a productive member of society. Eventually, though, it was discovered that this program of schooling was not sufficient for a growing democracy. As a result, tax-supported public schools became widespread in America. After the Civil War, schools were more readily available to an expanding population, except, of course, for people of color. African-Americans were routinely under-served by the public schools if they were served at all.

### Disturbing the Social Order

Then came the civil rights movement. With *Brown v. Board of Education* (1954), it became illegal for states to require separate schools for different races. Open-minded people across the political spectrum realized that a good education was essential for a functioning democracy like ours. However, with a segment of the population being denied equal schooling, our republic was not living up to its full potential. A *Perspective* summarized the situation:

America, by almost any measure, is the most productive nation in the world. It owes much of its economic success to the highly educated population that is a direct result of the wide availability of public schools all across the land. I do not deny the benefits provided to society by both private and home schools, but mostly the public benefits from the tax supported public schools. From my perspective, the nation owes a great deal to the schools that are available to all students not just those from families of privilege.

The conservative view is correct in that publically available tax supported schools disturb the social order. They make it possible for children from families of limited means to become equal with those from families of privilege. Liberals view such upward mobility as good. Equality of opportunity provided by universally available schooling is, from the liberal perspective, not something to be feared, but rather a benefit to the advancement of society. (*Perspective*, 2004, September 8)

## America's Best Industry

American public schools, even though challenged in some areas of the country, taken as a whole, do a good job of educating a diverse population of children. Unfortunately, the schools do not get very good press and as a result knowledge of how good they are, is not widespread throughout the country. Most media reports focus on the negative aspects of public education while paying little attention to how good they really are. Statistics published are frequently analyzed in a way that makes them a negative factor in people's understandings of their own schools. While numbers do not lie, they can be interpreted in a way that obscures their real message. This happens all too frequently. On the other side of the coin, author Fareed Zakaria (2011) identifies education as America's best industry. Focusing on higher education, he documents how our colleges and universities are very attractive to students in foreign countries. They flock to America to partake in what they considered to be superior education. Zakaria is only slightly less laudatory when it comes to America's elementary and secondary schools, as noted in a *Perspective*:

Zakaria (2011) is only slightly less laudatory about America's system of elementary and secondary schools. Again, the numbers can be quite confusing. He notes the often-cited statistics of American student's poor showing on international test scores in various subjects. Other systems of education emphasize rote memorization, while in American schools children are challenged to think critically about the subject matter they are studying. While the author decries the lack of discipline in many American schools, he does point out that our schools are much better at helping students develop "the critical faculties of the mind" which are needed for success in this life. "Other educational systems teach you to take tests," he states. "The American system teaches you to think" (p. 210).

This aspect of schooling, critical thinking, creativity, and challenges to conventional wisdom is where American schools excel above the rest of the world. Our biggest problem in our K–12 education system is not so much one of excellence as it is the lack of access by a large number of our population to quality schooling. If we can figure out a solution to that problem, we will continue to dominate the world for a long time to come. (*Perspective*, 2009, September 23)

## A Self-Centered Interest

At a meeting of the Board for the public schools where I reside, a taxpayer questioned the need for a millage request on the ballot for the next election to provide funds to upgrade the physical plant. He wanted to know how many of the voters in our community actually had children who attend the public schools. Further, he wanted to know how many of our citizens had pay increases during the last year. In my view, the larger question could have been phrased more like this: why should people who do not get any direct benefit from the schools, pay for them through their property tax? I viewed this as a good question that deserved an honest answer. My answer was published as part of a *Perspective* on the topic:

> It is not just from a desire to be a good citizen and consider the good of the entire community that I support taxation for public schools. I have a stronger, more self-centered interest in the topic. I have lived in this community for many years and plan to live here until they move my lifeless body to that small plot of real estate I have selected on the hill behind the Union Church. Therefore, what happens in this community in the next several years is very important to me because it will affect my quality of life in my remaining time as a senior citizen.
>
> I know that the quality of a community is dependent in large degree on the quality of the public schools in that community. Anyone who does not believe that fact need only look at places where the schools do not function well and where the physical plant has been allowed to deteriorate. They will find that high quality families are seldom attracted to live in such communities. In fact, solid citizens frequently move away and seek places where the schools are well maintained and the educational program is sound. I do not want to move away, so my next best option is to see that our local public schools are maintained even if I have to pay more taxes to do so. (*Perspective*, 2008, February 27)

## SOME FINAL THOUGHTS

In reading about the seemingly constant daily publicity that weighs heavily on the hearts and minds of those who work hard to make the public schools a good value to our communities, one might become a bit discouraged. What can be done to limit some of the bad publicity that seems to catch on like wildfire as it travels around the country on the Internet as well as by methods that are more traditional?

## Limit Bad Publicity

First, of course, is that the public schools must do a much better job of instruction in the basic branches of knowledge. It should be obvious to parents and others concerned about the children and youth in our society, that there is strong effective academic instruction taking place in the schools at all levels. A *Perspective* provides an alternative explanation:

> It was an interesting week on the Internet. Someone asked the question: "Why does the public view the public schools so negatively?" The answers gave an array of opinions from a group consisting mostly of educators. Some said the public has unreasonably high expectations for the schools. Others said the schools are their own worst enemy. The public schools fail mostly at public relations (Matthews, 2015). Good things never make the news while bad things make the headlines. Still others said the schools really are doing a bad job. They deserve all the negative publicity they get. Finally, some said that parents do not do their job and the schools cannot make up for this deficiency.
>
> These same phenomena hold true in other facets of life. Public perception of Congress is notoriously poor. However, people generally hold their own representative in fairly high regard. It appears then, that as people become more knowledgeable about a topic they have different views than when they just follow the conventional wisdom depicted in the national media. This is scary when one considers how few people take the time to be informed about any issue, whether it is a township rental ordinance or national foreign policy. If our present form of democracy is to survive into the twenty-first century citizens must make the effort to be informed about the issues and not just be followers of the popular press.
>
> This is where public schools can help their own cause. They can teach children how to be good citizens by teaching them how to be informed and thoughtful citizens. They can teach children to be critical thinkers rather than mere reflectors of the thoughts of others. Mostly the schools can teach children that study and careful thought does not end at the schoolhouse door. The learning necessary for effective citizenship is a lifelong process—it can never cease. (*Perspective*, 1995, September 13).

One of the side effects of the continuing bad press that public schools get is that their personnel sometimes develop what is known as a, "bunker mentality." There is a tendency to view any other form of education as "the enemy." Once educators take that attitude it becomes infectious throughout the community and people line up on the side of public schools, private schools, or home schools. In some instances, teachers in the public sector view private education, including home schools, as taking money away from their own educational forum. Having worked in private schools for most of my career, I know all too well the syndrome that develops.

## A Change in My thinking

The *Perspective* presented here reveals a change in my thinking over time regarding the relationship between the various types of schools. After providing a short condensed history of how the tension between public and private schools developed over time, I suggest an alternative approach. My perspective is that if the public schools could join with private and home schools in a common goal to serve the educational needs of their community, the bad publicity might be somewhat overcome.

> From my perspective, there is no need for a war between the two types of schools in our state. They both provide a valuable service to the people of Michigan. They just use a different emphasis in doing so. Both public and private schools have the same goal: to provide a high quality education for the children they serve. There is no benefit to the state for the supporters of public and private schools to be at war with each other. Moreover, there is certainly no benefit to our children for such a political battle to take place.

> Public and private schools have much to gain from supporting each other. Our community has shown the benefit of having two high quality high schools to serve the public. Let the rest of the state take note of what can be accomplished when public and private schools work together in an atmosphere of mutual respect. (*Perspective*, 1999, June 9).

## LIST OF *PERSPECTIVES* REFERENCED

Published in *The Journal Era*, Berrien Springs, Michigan.

1995, February 15. Prayer in the public schools.
1995, September 13. The negative view of schools.
1996, June 12, 1996. Improvement schools need.
1996, October 2. It happens every September.
1997, April 16. Ignoring the facts.
1999, June 9. The tale of two schools.
2004, June 23. A new attack on the public schools.
2004, September 8. A Liberal Defense of Public Schools.
2008, February 27. My selfish reason.
2008, March 12. I wonder why? Part 2.
2009, September 23. America's best industry.
2010, October 13. Tis the season.

## REFERENCES

Berliner, D. C., & Biddle, B. J. (1995). *The manufactured crisis: Myths, fraud, and the attack on America's public schools.* New York: Persuis Books.

*Brown v. Board of Education*, 347 U.S. 483 (U. S. Supreme Court)

Flowers, R. B. (2005). *That godless court? Supreme Court decisions on church-state relationships* (2nd ed.). Louisville, KY: Westminster John Knox Press.

Marsh, J., Hamilton, L., & Gill, B. (2008). Assistance and accountability in externally managed schools: The case of Edison Schools, Inc. *Peabody Journal of Education, 83*(3), 423–458.

Matthews, D. (2015). Putting the public back into public education: An old-fashioned remedy for a troubled relationship. *National Civic Review, 104*(2), 3–10.

Sackler, J. (2013). Save our schools by replacing them. *Vital Speeches of the Day, 79*(5), 154–156.

Sidwell Friends School. (n.d.). *Tuition and Fees*. Retrieved October 15, 2015, from Sidwell Friends School, http://www.sidwell.edu/admissions/tuition-and-fees/index.aspx

Standard & Poor's. (n.d.). *Beyond the averages: Michigan school trends*. Standard & Poor's. Retrieved from http://forumfyi.org/files/MichiganSchoolTrends.pdf

Ullucci, K. (2015). Pathologizing the poor: Implications for preparing teachers to work in high-poverty schools. *Urban Education, 50*(2), 170–193.

# PART II

## SCHOOLS AND THE PEOPLE IN THEM

# CHAPTER 2

## WHY CHILDREN MISBEHAVE

### CHALLENGE IN THE CLASSROOM

Just as soon as the words were out of my mouth, I realized I made a major blunder. I knew that I had better get on top of the situation quickly or I would have a hard time all day long trying to keep control of the classroom. While attending graduate school, I signed up to be a substitute teacher in a school district near where I lived. It was a middle to upper-middle-class population. The kids were smart and did not mind letting you know it. The district had two secondary schools: Millard Fillmore High School housed 9th and 10th graders; the 11th and 12th grade populated Franklin Pierce High school. After having substituted in both high schools, I quickly learned that Franklin Pierce was a much better administered school where the kids were much better behaved.

On my first day of doing substitute work in this school district, as fate would have it, I was asked to cover the classes for a business teacher at Millard Fillmore. The teacher suffered a heart attack the night before and would be out of commission for at least a week. It was the last week of the first marking period. When I reported for duty at the main office, the principal's secretary asked me if I would be the substitute for the entire week, and if I would fill out the grades on student report cards. It was a strange request because I had no idea as to what or how well

*Helping Parents Understand Schools: A Different Perspective on Education and Schooling in America,* pages 25–40.

the students were doing. Nobody found any grade book at this point, so I had no record of student achievement. However, the principal's secretary made such an impassioned plea for me to help them out of the strange situation that I acceded to her request.

## A Foolish Mistake

To complicate matters even further, no one could find any lesson plans or even the teacher's edition of the textbooks. Yet I did not have any time to waste because the warning bell had already rung, and I knew the kids would be in the classroom and aware that no teacher was present. I had enough experience with kids to know that I had better get there and assert my authority as teacher very quickly or it would all fall apart. I arrived at the classroom just as the final bell rang. The kids were milling around the room, making disparaging remarks about their missing teacher. I managed to get them all settled down and in their seats. I had found an extra student textbook for the class with the title *Introduction to Business Operations*.

Surprisingly, I had quickly gotten the students seated, settled, and attending to what I was saying as I stood there in front of the room trying to look like a seasoned teacher. However, my smugness soon evaporated when I made the foolish mistake of asking the students what chapter they were studying in the textbook. Before my mouth could close on the final syllable of my ill-advised question, students shouted an immediate response. Some indicated they completed the textbook while others claimed the teacher did not actually use the book. They seemed to take great glee in trying to confuse their hapless substitute. Yet, I was not so easily taken in.

I did some quick mental calculations. It was about one fourth of the way through the school year. I calculated that a fourth of the way through the textbook would take me to page 100. The beginning of Chapter 6 was close to that page so I announced that we would be studying that chapter starting today. Of course, some groaned in anguish because they thought they could bamboozle the sub and escape doing any serious study while he was responsible for the class. I soon disabused them of that happy thought. The textbook was well organized and I was able to make up an academically credible assignment on the spur of the moment. Students continued to protest either that they had not gotten that far or that they had already completed the chapter.

## Balance of Power Shifts

I informed the class that I would be their teacher for the rest of the week and further, I would be filling out their grade reports. Therefore, I suggested that in the interests of their attaining a good academic record, they should give strong consideration to cooperating with me as much as possible. Most of the students seemed to understand that the balance of power had suddenly shifted and they were no longer in full control, that there would be consequences for continued rebellion. It actually turned out to be a positive week for both the students and me. However, I made a mental note not to be so naive when I asked an open-ended question of a room full of high school students. I had already realized that when dealing with classroom control, kids are smarter than teachers. If I wanted to be successful as a substitute teacher, I needed to wise up and refrain from making that kind of a blunder again.

I tried to profit from my experience in that first period class during the rest of the day and throughout the entire week. I had varying degrees of success on that first day with the different classes I was assigned. I was glad when the last hour was upon us and I had only one more class that day. Nobody had told me and I had not read it in any of my textbooks, but the last class period of the day is always the worst as far as discipline is concerned. The kids were all edgy and ready for the school day to end. I was exhausted and not in the best of spirits myself.

By then I was, to some degree, mentally spent by making up assignments at just a few minutes before the tardy bell rang. I tried to have some meaningful activities so that students would actually learn something. I later found out that I was an oddball among substitutes. Most of them just tried to hold the room together and did not bother about any academic accomplishments among the students. But, I come from a different culture and was determined that I would actually teach the students something of academic value regardless of what they wanted.

### Last Class Period

The kids in that last class of the day were very restless and not at all intimidated when they saw a sub at the front of the room. I found a seating chart for this class and, as required by board policy, my first task was to take the attendance to see who was absent. The standard procedure for this was to look and see if the seat a student was assigned to was occupied. If it was empty, I would put the student's name on the attendance slip that a student worker would retrieve a few minutes after the tardy bell rang. I could tell by the snickering among the students that some mischief was afoot and soon I perceived that they were not sitting in their assigned seats.

I announced to the students that I knew it was a possibility that they were playing a trick on me. I told them I completely understood their temptation to do so. I warned them that since I did not know them by name that whatever the person sitting in their assigned seat did would be accounted to them and that if they did not trust the person who was in their seat to behave well, they better take possession of it themselves. It was the right thing to say because immediately there was a general shifting of the students as they claimed their own assigned place in the classroom.

I managed to get the classroom settled quickly when I noticed that one of the students was not sitting down. Instead, he was wandering around, randomly looking at different objects in the classroom. I spoke to him and quietly suggested that he should find his seat. Since his was the only one vacant, I was able to attach a name to him. He just smiled and kept on walking and finally settled in the back of the room standing there with a look of defiance on his face. Again, I called him by name and quietly suggested that he come up and sit down. He smiled and said, "No, I don't think I will." I was a little frustrated with him, but I knew that a public confrontation would not turn out well for me.

With what mental power I still had left after the exhausting day, I quickly calculated my options. So, with only one kid standing quietly at the back of the room not causing any trouble, should I make a big issue about this or should I just let it go? Will his defiance infect the rest of the students in the room? Would that make them perceive that they have a weak teacher at work here? Again, I realized that direct and open confrontation was a risky tactic. I decided to bide my time and get the rest of the students working on a project related to the subject that would get their attention focused on something other than the defiant student.

## Dealing With a BMOC

Once I managed to get the students working, I looked up to see the recalcitrant student standing at the back of the room with a big smirk on his face. He had certainly put this new substitute teacher in his place. I quietly said, "Let's give it one more try. Please go sit in your assigned seat." His response came back quietly but firmly "No, I am not going to do that." I walked slowly toward the back of the room where he was standing. About halfway there one of the girls whispered to me, "He does not have to sit down. To my puzzled look she explained, "He is a running back on the varsity football team. He does not have to sit down if he does not want to."

This bit of information put the situation in a completely new light. I was dealing with what is known as a BMOC, or "big man on campus." They need special care and handling. Therefore, I simply confronted him quietly and almost in a whisper said to him, "I am going to give you one final chance to comply with my request. Please go sit in your assigned seat." As he had done several times already, he quietly responded to me in a pleasant voice, "No, I am not going to."

I pulled out the last hope in my rapidly diminished bag of tricks and simply said to him, "This is my first day as a substitute teacher at this school. As soon as this class is over, I have a list of several things I need to discuss with the vice principal. Right on the top of that list is your name." The look on his face told me I had said the magic words. So I said, "One more time I would like to suggest that you go sit down." His face clouded over and he simply said, "Well, if you are going to be that way about it, I guess I will go sit in the stupid chair." And with that, he shuffled over to his designated seat and sat down as I had requested him to do.

Now, in the spirit of full disclosure, I must confess that not every confrontation with misbehaving students in my career turned out to be as successful as those in this story. Many times I was not so skilled in my response to students who were challenging the limits to appropriate behavior. In my own defense, I have decided to leave the details of those events undisclosed.

## THE ROAD AHEAD

This is the first of the five chapters in Part Two: Schools and the People in Them. It considers why children sometimes misbehave. The chapter emphasizes the role of adults in setting the limits of acceptable behavior for the young people under their care. The chapter started with a personal experience in the classroom and some things I learned from that experience. The rest of the chapter is divided into four major sections dealing with various aspects of the topic.

First, the central question is: Why do children misbehave? The general theme for the chapter arises from an answer to that question. As children grow and mature, they need to test the limits of behavior to determine what is acceptable in the adult society in which they will eventually claim membership. It is the responsibility of the adults to identify clearly and enforce those limits.

Next is a section on Testing the Limits at a Young Age, which tells a story illustrating the challenge young children can present both at home and in school. In partial answer to that challenge, a section titled Teaching Values in Public Schools provides straightforward suggestions for both educational policymakers and parents. The final section covers Discipline in the Classroom.

## WHY CHILDREN MISBEHAVE

The purpose for telling the two vignettes is to lay the groundwork for the larger question: Why are students at times so purposely disruptive of the teaching learning process as to frustrate the honest attempt of educators to provide them the tools they need for success in adult life? Some 20 years ago, I published a *Perspective* on this topic.

> In a recent conversation with a group of educators, the subject of children's behavior came up—Why do children misbehave?—as a question that evoked much discussion. Some of the participants blamed the influence of television and the breakdown of the family. Some stated that we cannot teach moral values in the public schools anymore. Others believed that churches and other civic organizations are not as influential as they used to be, causing a general decline in behavior. Still others were certain that the pervasiveness of drugs in our culture is to blame.
>
> In listening to this conversation, it dawned on me that the group was missing a key point in explaining children's behavior: children misbehave because they are children. That is what children do. It is part of their job description. From the beginning of recorded history, young people have misbehaved. Remember that the first parents had a serious problem with their oldest son, Cain.
> If the job of children is to misbehave, what is the job of the adults? It is simply to show the children the acceptable limits of behavior in our society. It is when adults fail in their job that society breaks down. (*Perspective*, 1995, September 6)

While this was written some 20 years ago, my thinking on the topic has not changed very much. Nothing I have seen in the literature or observed in action since then counters what I observed. Children need to explore the limits of appropriate behavior as they develop their own patterns of responding to the stimulus that confronts them.

## The Adult's Role

It is still true that adults play a major role as they model adult behavior. When the adult world abandons its responsibility to provide that model, the only thing left is teaching through direct instruction. Unfortunately, too many of the institutions in our society that are best suited to provide such instruction have also shrunk back from actively seeking to fulfill their responsibility. If the public schools decline to teach the core values of our liberal democracy, it is unreasonable to expect the students to pick them up on their own. Sunday school (Brown, 2008) and other organizations of the religious community have, in many instances, changed from emphasizing the school aspect of their function, and turned into a glorified babysitting service. This may provide at least a partial explanation for the decline of these valuable institutions in recent years (Hays, 2009).

## Testing the Limits at a Young Age

Young children are thought by many adults to be blank pages with no capacity to think through their actions (Leafgren, 2008). I had subscribed to that theory for much of my life but events that transpired recently in our home have made me question that thesis and reevaluate my thinking on this subject. I propose that children very early in life acquire the equivalent of a PhD in adult psychology.

Family members of mine from the West Coast were visiting us while on summer vacation. Included in that group were our three great-granddaughters, aged four years and sixteen month old twins. Those three little girls were a whirlwind of activity during the entire time they were with us. They had never been in our house before so there was much for them to explore.

The house was in a constant state of chaos for days with the twins right at the center of the maelstrom. The twins had the uncanny ability of communicating without saying a word. They would stand and look at each other for a few seconds and then in unison let out a scream that startled any nearby adult. The four-year-old, having found the controls to my lift chair, kept me in a state of constant motion. The three girls were not bad kids. I viewed them as having a healthy curiosity about their environment, along with plenty of excess energy. Their behavior would probably be classified as mischievous rather than naughty (Wakschlag, Tolan, & Leventhal, 2010). A *Perspective* describes the experience and what was learned from it.

> The job description for little ones requires them to learn as much as possible about the world around them. They do that partly through touch, both with their fingers

and their mouth. I still have their bite marks on my walker, which they viewed as a wonderful playground implement. My wife had worked diligently prior to their visit to childproof the house as much as possible. The girls proved the futility of that effort. With five adults in the house, you would think we could control their wanderlust. We confined them to the living room that was the safest place in the house for little ones. However, they viewed the exploration of those other rooms as something of a necessity. Forbidden territory has a magnetic quality to young and old alike. Little children are masters of adult psychology and the minute they noticed our attention was diverted in the slightest, they made a break for freedom. The four-year-old sometimes assisted in controlling the twins and sometimes aided and abetted their defiance of the adult imposed rules. (*Perspective,* 2012, August 29)

Parents can team up with institutions of society to teach lessons of proper behavior to their offspring (Wiseman, 2009). I am thinking of such organizations as churches, clubs, and social groups that include children, the public library which frequently has a children's room, the public and private schools, the Parks and Recreation Department, which is active in many municipalities and of course support groups of various types (Ishimaru, 2014). These are just a few examples of the many resources that are available to assist parents in this important work.

## TEACHING VALUES IN PUBLIC SCHOOLS

A few years ago, a colleague at work told me of her reaction on moving to a different part of the country. Being originally from New York City, she found her experience in graduate school in Minnesota to be a great contrast. For example, when she rode public transportation in Minneapolis, she noticed that many people would thank the driver when they exited the bus. She remarked that in New York, people would more likely curse the driver. She appreciated her new environment where people still said "thank you" and treated other people, even strangers, with a good deal of respect.

The question of what constitutes civil behavior is an intriguing one (Ozolins, 2010). America's first president, George Washington, published a list of behaviors that were acceptable in society at that time in our nation's history. His Rules of Civility and Decent Behavior contained 110 specific rules on how a cultured person should act in public. Many of the items on Washington's list would seem rather quaint today. But the general principle behind his list is still appropriate. Both parents and educators would be well advised that society would run much better if children were taught the principle s of civil behavior (Kennedy, 2013).

### Norms of Western Culture

It is a widespread misconception that educators in public schools are forbidden from engaging in teaching civic values because of Supreme Court decisions regarding teaching of religion. It is true that public schools may not engage in religious indoctrination or lead out in religious rituals. There is, however, certainly nothing that would keep them from teaching children the norms of behavior in polite society (Metzger & Smetana, 2009). They can also teach the markers of our value laden Western culture.

Americans are often conflicted when it comes to dealing with authority. We tend to be suspicious of anyone who asserts their superiority over others. Our egalitarian obsession comes quite naturally since a large proportion of American citizens have their ancestral roots in northern Europe where the prevailing culture is not enamored with an authoritarian style of management (Hofstede & Hofstede, 2005). However, our Western culture also values respect for people who take a leading role in the institutions of society and encourages a willingness to show some degree of compliance with reasonable requests of those in positions of leadership. Finding the delicate balance between these somewhat disparate cultural markers is an essential part of the adult role in helping children find the limits of proper behavior.

In a conversation with my fellow school board members, we discussed the nature of children in the modern age and how they seem to show less respect for the adult world than they did a generation ago. As a result, the following *Perspective* was published.

> Children learn by observing the models provided by adults. When they see their parents treating each other with respect, when they see adults showing respect to those in authority, when parents treat their own children with respect, children learn to be respectful. They also learn by direct instruction. When parents talk about the importance of respect and gently admonish them for lapses in attention to the mores established in the home, children learn and practice respect.

> When children arrive at school with an established habit pattern of respect for their teachers, and they know their parents will demand a continuation of that pattern, they will spend less time in rebellion against adult authority and more time on the content of the subject matter. It is well established that the more time students spend on the content, the more they learn. Moreover, learning is what should take place in school. (*Perspective*,1997, August 12)

## Respect is Learned not Earned

A *Perspective* the previous year started at the same point, teaching children to be respectful. It was again emphasized that respect is a characteristic that can be taught (Ertesvag & Vaaland, 2007). Children must learn that respect cannot be based on the idea that respect has to be earned. It is most beneficial to the education of children if they arrive at school already having learned to be respectful. A *Perspective* responds to the issue.

> In working with schools over the years, I have frequently heard parents say that teachers had to earn the student's respect. I strongly disagree with this view of teaching children respect for others. Respect, I have discovered, is learned, not earned. People learn rules of behavior as small children. They learn what society considers

being proper conduct by observing how adults act and by what adults directly teach them.

This places a big responsibility on parents and other adults as they teach children about what constitutes appropriate behavior. It means that adults must at all times model good behavior. That is tough to do given the frailties of human nature, but it is essential if we are to transmit the structures of civil society to the younger generation.

Even beyond modeling good behavior, it is important for adults to set the limits for children's conduct and then enforce those limits. That is much easier to say than to do. When it comes to getting their own way, children are much smarter than adults are and are much more resilient. It is much easier to ignore behavior that is only a little beyond the limits than to face the constant stream of whining about how "unfair" you are or how "you always pick on me!"

I was interested to see that the faculties of our local middle school have tackled this task of teaching civil behavior this year. The middle years are a particularly difficult time of life, and rules of any kind are especially bothersome. However, habits learned at that age, generally stick.

Keeping in mind the nature of the child, the faculty formulated only eight rules of behavior. They are quite different from Washington's more comprehensive list. Yet if the children learn to respect those in authority as well as each other, as required in the rules, our community will be a much better place to live. In that respect, the rules of civil behavior are no doubt among the most important things that are taught in our public schools. (*Perspective*, 1996, January 24)

## Learning by Doing

It is one thing to teach the rules of behavior; it is another to get children to function in a way congruent with those rules. It can be a complex process that involves direct instruction, constant reminders, and modeling by the adult community and practice for the students. This latter activity is something that is seldom done in the public schools. I have seen it work through role-playing but that has to be carefully guided by skilled teachers who function more like coaches. Sometimes just having children go through the motions can help them establish a pattern of appropriate behavior.

For a personal example, some years ago I was involved in the administration of a small educational organization that trained young adults in the basics of entry-level healthcare jobs. This school offered a variety of certification programs, lasting anywhere from one month to a year and a half. I oriented all new students to the sexual harassment/misconduct policy. Because of the culture of the surrounding area, we were very concerned about the potential for a problem to develop within the student body.

I explained the policies and procedures we would implement should students feel that they were being harassed. It is up to individual students to inform their antagonists to stop engaging in the offensive behavior. They can do this by simply saying, "Stop that! That is offensive to me!" All the students seemed to understand what I was saying. But I took it one step further. I had each student face a classmate and say the words, "Stop that! That is offensive to me!" I was amazed at how hard it was for some of our students to say those words, even in a role-playing situation. I can only assume that with younger children one would have to practice much more before it became natural in a real situation.

## A Conflict Management Program

A few paragraphs above, I described how the faculty of the middle school, in the small town where I live, had tackled the matter of student behavior. I discovered that the upper elementary school in the district implemented an interesting program regarding student misbehavior. It is a prime example of the school administration and faculty taking a proactive stance as they help students learn to become self-disciplined and display what might be termed appropriate behavior. The "conflict management" program is described in more detail in the following *Perspective.*

> The "conflict management program" at the elementary school (grades 3-5) is aimed at solving petty little problems that plague every place where children congregate. Four children from each classroom are chosen each year to be trained as conflict managers; they are taught a process that enables them to intervene in playground squabbles before they escalate to major dispute or a physical altercation. The conflict managers work in pairs and offer their help to resolve interpersonal confrontation as it develops on the playground. They have a highly scripted plan to follow and are required to fill out a report on every conflict in which they are involved. In cases where the students are not successful in resolving the spat between their classmates, and for more serious problems such as fighting, teachers or the principal take over.

> How well has this worked? The principal reported that the number of children sent to his office for serious disciplinary offenses decreased by 80 per cent in the few years since the student conflict management system was used. That gave him more time to spend on instruction, which should be the main part of a principal's job. More importantly, kids at the school were learning a method to get rid of their petty little animosities before they got out of control. When children have a dispute that must be settled by the conflict manager team, it takes time away from play. They eventually learn to solve their problems on their own without outside intervention. (*Perspective*, 1999, June, 2)

My purpose for presenting the *Perspective* here is to show methods of helping children learn appropriate behavior can actually make it a part of their habit patterns. Both parents and schools need to be proactive in training children for such skills. They do not just float down to children from on high. It is something that must be initiated by the adult world and then made an integral part of both the parenting and teaching/learning process.

## CLASSROOM DISCIPLINE

It was a tense moment for me, as it was one abounding with possibilities of making a major mistake. The children in my classroom were suddenly out of control and I did not know how to get back in front of the situation. Nothing I studied in college or read in books prepared me for the impending student insurrection. It was early in the school year and I knew that my response to this situation would go a long way in setting the tone in the classroom for the rest of this school year.

I was teaching seventh grade in a self-contained classroom in a religious school in a western suburb of Chicago. It was a well-educated community with most of the students living close by the school. In fact, many of them walked home for their noon meal. Most of the mother's did not work outside the home, so they were able to prepare a nutritious lunch for their offspring. Some of the children did eat their lunch at school, and the teachers supervised them during the noon hour. I was a brand-new teacher and the youngest one on the faculty. The rest of my colleagues were seasoned veterans and tried to be helpful in coaching me on how to be successful in the profession I had so recently entered.

Actually, I did have some experience. During my last year of college, I had a part-time job teaching afternoon classes for grade seven in a public school nearby. I did not have a teaching certificate, but there was such a drastic shortage of teachers in those years that, with the number of credits I had by that time amassed toward a college degree, I was given an emergency credential which permitted me to teach up to half time for a year in the public schools. I had no preparation for the job but tried to learn as much as I could during that year. At the end of the year, I graduated with a bachelor's degree in business and a minor in physical education. I was offered a full-time job at the public school but chose instead to work in a parochial school operated by the denomination of which I am a member.

Experience is a good teacher, and during my year in the public school, I made every effort to profit from all the mistakes I made. I determined that in my new assignment, it was a new year and I would start all over again. I would not have to make the mistakes of the past year. Yet I soon discovered many more opportunities to slip up were lurking in the classroom, waiting for me to stumble into them. The events that were now transpiring gave me a chance to commit a major blunder if I wanted to take it.

### A Lively Class

The class I had was small, less than 20 students. But, they were a lively bunch and mostly smart. The students were friendly and easy to get acquainted with and willing to be open with me about what was going on in their minds. They regaled me with stories of their hijinks during the sixth grade. They had little respect for the sixth grade teacher who had been trained as a minister. He was more than a little disappointed that he had not received a call from the denomination and assigned as a pastor of a church. Thus, he was stuck in a profession where he had adequate academic preparation but little motivation. His students were quick to pick up on that attitude and tormented him as much as they could get away with during the year.

The students in my classroom told me how they had pestered their teacher until he would fly into an angry rage. They could tell when his emotions were about to boil over because the bald spot on the back of his head would turn red. I was thankful I had a good head of hair in those days and nothing that would give evidence of my inner turmoil. I did not realize it but the students were just biding their time until the opportunity to test my emotional stability presented itself.

## Testing the Teacher

It all happened rather abruptly one morning. I presented the lesson and assigned the students some seat-work so they would get practice in applying the knowledge they just learned. They were all diligently working on their assignments and I was helping one of the students who needed extra assistance. Suddenly one of the girls seated in the middle of the classroom stood up and said, "Hey gang, guess what time it is. It is 10 o'clock." And with that the entire classroom burst into laughter. I was more than a little agitated, partly because the student I was helping was almost to the point of understanding when the laughter interrupted my attempt to help her.

Mostly, I was upset because I realized that I had lost control of the classroom in an instant. Holding my emotions in check, I walked to one student after another, imploring them to quiet down. They all obediently sat at their assigned desks but continued to laugh uproariously.

I was about to explode when I heard one of the girls in a loud whisper informing her nearby classmates, "Keep it up guys, he is getting mad." In an instant it came to me that I was being subjected to the same behavior the class had used to bedevil their teacher the previous year. I was being tested so they could identify the threshold for losing my temper. I also realized that I was not giving the students assignments of sufficient depth and quantity to keep them busy during class time. I determined that I would not fall into the trap they had so skillfully set for me, nor would I treat them with a full blown mental meltdown just to satisfy their need for entertainment. So, calling on all the internal discipline I could muster I walked to the front of the room, sat on my desk, and began to laugh. At the same time, I was mentally doubling all the assignments in my lesson plans for the rest of the day. The laughter continued for several minutes.

## Punishment

Finally, the students got tired of seeing me just sitting at my desk laughing with them. One by one they began to quiet down and I once again was in control of the situation. I told the students to get back to their assignments. One of the boys raised his hand and I asked him what he wanted. It was a simple request, "What is our punishment going to be?" In an instant, I knew I had an opportunity to get even with them for the torment I had just endured. Maybe I could teach them a lesson on appropriate classroom behavior at the same time.

I pretended that I did not know what he was talking about. "Punishment? What punishment?" I queried him with a puzzled look on my face. "Oh you know," he said. "Well," I responded, "I guess if you think you have done something bad enough to be punished, I better think up something to do about it." During the lunch hour I considered my options. I decided not to do anything in response to the student's misbehavior. After all, I felt I was partly to blame for not keeping them busy enough with substantive assignments. But, mostly, I calculated that not knowing what their punishment might be would inflict the most pain on the students as they anticipated my decision. This might be the best way to teach them the lesson I wanted them to learn.

After lunch it was the tradition in this school for the teacher to read a story from a book of interest to kids in that age group. Following that tradition, I read to my students for five or ten minutes each afternoon. The kids in those days loved to have stories read to them. But this day, they were still in a state of agitation from the morning's events and were restless during story time. Just as soon as I finished reading to them, one of the girls blurted right out, "What is our punishment going to be?" I ignored the question but soon others chimed in wanting to know what was possibly going to happen.

I simply remarked, "Oh, I don't know. I will probably think of something." And, with that I let the matter ride. I never did punish them for their short-term insurrection and eventually the events faded from their minds. However, they discovered that they could not make me lose control of my emotions and that I did have definite expectations for them in the classroom. It was mostly a good year after that.

### Classroom Management

Teachers are much better trained these days than they were when I started in the profession. Today, they learn classroom management systems that treat misbehavior as part of the larger issues of the instructional process (Pas, Cash, O'Brennan, Debnam, & Bradshaw, 2015). When I was taking courses in education so I could get a legitimate credential, no such thing was available to guide classroom instructors. Teachers were given suggestions on how to make rules and how to apply punishments for violating the rules. This was about all the professional help we had to go on. The rest we had to figure it out on our own.

Over the years, I developed my own set of rules for dealing with student punishment. In general, I do not like responses to student misbehavior that tend to be merely punitive. Rather, the adults in control should use their creative energies to think up reactions that will be corrective in nature. We should try to correct the problem that is causing trouble in the classroom. For example, if students come late to class, a corrective action would be to make them be late to leave class. In other words, they should stay after school to put in the extra time on their studies.

## SOME FINAL THOUGHTS

Insofar as I cannot vouch for the authenticity of the following story, I present it as a possible "urban legend." However, it does illustrate a point congruent to a summary view of the chapter. A young single man graduated from a seminary and accepted an assignment as assistant pastor. He worked hard and soon became the senior pastor. Even before being elevated, he expressed concern to the Board of Deacons about the misbehavior by children in the congregation during services who were so unruly that the noise could be heard all the way from the youth room to the sanctuary. It was especially problematic during the homily. The young preacher found it difficult to provide spiritual nurture to the adults while the sounds of chaos wafting down the hall indicated that all was not well among the younger members of the flock.

The deacons demurred when asked to get the situation under control. The parents were willing to step in, but admitted they did not know what to do. The pastor, a resourceful problem solver by nature, undertook a serious study of parenting from the available literature. As part of his seminary training, he had taken a few psychology classes, including one in child psychology. Thus, he was somewhat knowledgeable about the dynamics of the situation in his church. His study completed, he developed a sermon entitled, "The Ten Commandments of Effective Parenting."

The parishioners responded very positively to his sermon. A nearby congregation invited him to preach the same sermon and he received the same feedback. People really liked his approach to parenting. Parents remarked how surprised they were that he, a bachelor with no experience in raising children, would have such good common sense ideas in his Ten Commandments. His fame soon spread across a wide area. Eventually, he accepted a call to pastor a large church on the West Coast. There, he settled down, married and had three children. A *Perspective* tells the rest of the story.

### The One Rule of Parenting

After several years, the now middle-aged pastor returned to his first church while he was on a vacation trip. Several of the old-timers were still around who remembered when he was their pastor. One of them asked him, "Do you still preach that sermon on the 10 Commandments of good parenting?" "Oh yes," he responded, "I still preach the sermon, but I have modified it a bit after having my own children. I shortened it so that I now have only one commandment for parents."

Word spread around the congregation that he had revised his Ten Commandments, and they pressed him to reveal his new insights on effective parenting. "After having raised three children myself," he said, "the one rule I have to pass on to other parents is, do the best you can!"From my perspective, that is a very good rule. I have observed over my lifetime that children come in all sizes and shapes and with a variety of psychological aberrations. No one set of rules will have universal application when dealing with children.

Far too many parents never engage in the work of parenting. Children are a nuisance in their lives, which has a devastating effect on society. They could at least try to be good parents. The survival of our advanced society depends on them doing so. Parents should commit themselves to doing their very best as a parent and trust in a Higher Power to fill in the gaps. (*Perspective,* 2015, January 28)

## Adults Set the Limits

This chapter started with a short vignette about experiences in substitute teaching, and finished with a short story (probably fictional) that illustrates the futility of finding the perfect list of things the parent should do to raise perfect children. In between, I have tried to deal with the question "Why do children misbehave and what can adults do about it?" I never intended to offer a full and complete answer to that question. Rather, I attempt to provide insight into my thinking on how parents and teachers might best fill their role as adults in this important aspect of education for America's children. If we can help children to understand the limits of acceptable behavior and give them opportunity to practice their skills in doing so, the school will probably have provided to both students and parents, as well is the larger community, one of the best things they could accomplish. (Janssen, Dekovic, & Bruinsma, 2014)

Admittedly, this is not an easy task, and requires much stamina on the part of both parents and teachers (Ellingsen, Baker, Blacher, & Crnic, 2014). It also requires the ability to shoulder disappointment because not all children respond to discipline and limits on their behavior as well as they should. That is the nature of the human species. However, this should not be a barrier that keeps the adults from doing their job. Sometimes success comes in small doses. Probably the best advice is to maximize the positive aspects of filling the adult role and minimize the negative.

### LIST OF *PERSPECTIVES* REFERENCED

Published in *The Journal Era*, Berrien Springs, Michigan

1995, September 6. Why children misbehave.
1996, January 24. Learning civil behavior
1997, August 12. A little bit of respect
1999, June 2. What can a school do?
2012, August 29. Chaos!
2015, January 28. The one rule for effective parenting.

# REFERENCES

Brown, C. G. (2008). The Sunday school movement: Studies in the growth and decline of Sunday Schools. *Journal of Ecclsiastical History, 59*(3), 580–581.

Ellingsen, R., Baker, B. L., Blacher, J., & Crnic, K. (2014). Resilient parenting of preschool children at developmental risk. *Journal of Intellectual Disability Research, 58*(7), 664–6.

Ertesvag, S. K., & Vaaland, G. S. (2007). Prevention and reduction of behavioural problems in school: An evaluation of the respect program. *Educational Psychology, 27*(6), 713–736.

Hays, C. (2009, June 26). Why Sunday schools are closing. *Wall Street Journal—Eastern Edition, 253*(148), W11.

Hofstede, G., & Hofstede, G. J. (2005). *Cultures and organizations: Software of the mind* (2nd ed.). New York: McGraw-Hill.

Ishimaru, A. M. (2014). When new relationships meet old narratives: The journey toward improving parent-school relations in a district-community organizing collaboration. *Teachers College Record, 116*(2), 1–49.

Janssen, H. J., Dekovic, M., & Bruinsma, G. J. (2014). Parenting and time adolescents spend in criminogenic settings: A between- and within-person analysis. *British Journal of Criminology, 54*(4), 551–567.

Kennedy, S. S. (2013). Civic literacy and ethical public service. *Public Integrity, 15*(4), 403–414.

Leafgren, S. (2008). Ruebern's fall: Complicating 'goodness' and schoolroom disobedience. *International Journal of Children's Spirituality, 13*(4), 331–344.

Metzger, A., & Smetana, J. G. (2009). Adolescent civic and political engagement associations between domain-specific judgements and behavior. *Child Development, 80*(2), 433–441.

Ozolins, J. (2010). Creating public values: Schools as moral habitats. *Educational Philosophy & Theory, 42*(4), 410–423.

Pas, E. T., Cash, A. H., O'Brennan, L., Debnam, K. J., & Bradshaw, C. P. (2015). Profiles of classroom behavior in high schools: Associations with teacher behavior management strategies and classroom composition. *Journal of School Psychology, 53*(2), 137–148.

Wakschlag, L. S., Tolan, P. H., & Leventhal, B. L. (2010). Research review: 'Ain't misbehavin': Towards a developmentally-specified nosology for preschool disruptive behavior. *Journal of Child Psychology and Psychiatry, 51*(1), 3–22.

Wiseman, A. (2009). Perceptions of community and experiences in school: Understanding the opportunities, resources, and education within one neighborhood. *Early Childhood Education Journal, 36*(4), 333–338.

# CHAPTER 3

# IMPORTANT THINGS CHILDREN LEARN IN SCHOOL

### I HAVE NEVER HAD AN "A"

I was caught by surprise when seeing seventh-grade student, Jeffrey, in a fight with two girls in the classroom. That was not like him at all and I could not determine what the issue was among the three students. I taught 7th and 8th grade, a combined total of less than twenty students, in a small religious school on the West Coast while also carrying the responsibilities of principal.

At the time, I considered myself a traditional teacher insofar as I had reasonably good classroom control and gave the students assignments almost every day in all of my classes. This meant that most of the students did not finish their seatwork during class time and had to complete their assignments at home. In those days, we called such assignments "homework." Even though I was very comfortable with the traditional methods of instruction, in my mind I always tried to experiment with different ways of approaching the teaching-learning process.

In this classroom with twenty students I taught social studies (world geography), using a multi-text approach. In other words, students did not have textbooks for their own use. We did have multiple copies of three or four different pub-

*Helping Parents Understand Schools: A Different Perspective on Education and Schooling in America*, pages 41–55.

lisher's texts on geography to use as resource materials for the students. Instead of having a lesson around the written text from one of the books, I fashioned a series of questions requiring the students to do research in a variety of the books or other available resources. Of course, this was in the "dark ages" before the dawn of the Internet and the many electronic gadgets most now own. So, student research was confined to the written resources we had in our classroom.

## Team Teaching

As I read in the educational literature, I was enamored with the latest fad in teaching known as "team teaching" (Joyce, 2004). Under that innovation, two or more teachers would be in a classroom at the same time working as a team as they instructed the students. In other instances, teachers specialized in one of three approaches: individualized instruction, small group instruction, and large group lecturing. Educational leaders generally concurred that this method would be most prominent in the future.

One of the articles I read on team teaching suggested that team learning is an alternate approach to classroom instruction. In the latter approach, teachers placed students in groups of three or more and gave them a common assignment. Classroom teachers evaluated each student not only by the quality of his/her own individual accomplishments, but also by the adequacy of the group's completed assignment. This fact was the source of the little fracas that was taking place in the corner of my classroom.

## Experiment With Team Learning

I was experimenting with the team learning process and had simply described to the students what we were going to do as part of our learning activity. I then instructed the students to divide into groups of three. I allowed them to make their own decision as to who would be with them in the groups. I had not expected this process to be problematic with such a small number of students in the class, but had not counted on Jeffrey's sudden misbehavior. I quickly moved over to Jeffrey's corner of the room and asked the students whether there was a problem. Immediately the two girls, who were without question the smartest students in the room, protested that Jeffrey was trying to join their group and they did not want him to do so. The students were emphatic that they did not like him and refused to work with Jeffrey.

I was puzzled why Jeffrey would want to be with these girls because he was not friendly with them during the other parts of the school day. Yet, their loud protestations and negative comments regarding him personally seemed to have no effect on Jeffrey. I asked him why he wanted to be in a group that obviously did not want him to be anywhere near them. I must add that I would have been embarrassed by the whole scene when I was that age. Jeffrey did not hesitate to give a clear answer to my question. "I know this group is going to get an A," he responded with a degree of certainty. "I have never had an A before, so this is my first chance to get one."

The students in the group were deeply suspicious of Jeffrey's motivation. They objected to his using their work to get a high grade for himself when he had not made any significant contribution to the assignment. Yet, Jeffrey's reply indicated his willingness to do his share of the work. "I do not know how to do this assignment," he declared. "You girls just tell me what I am supposed to do and I will do my best at it." I watched their group during the next half hour as they, along with the other students, worked on the assigned project. The girls made Jeffrey do most of the work hunting up the answers in the available resources, seeming to enjoy their new role as Jeffrey's boss. However, I noticed they soon joined in helping Jeffrey and contributed their own wisdom to completing the assignment.

## Work as Part of a Team

Because of this little episode, Jeffrey learned far more about geography than he would have if he had not been with the smart girls. In addition, he learned to work as part of a team of people with a common problem to solve. In turn, the two smart girls learned how to work with people with lesser ability than they had and how to integrate the other person's work with their own. I hope the girls also learned a little bit about tolerance for people of lesser cognitive ability.

This little vignette illustrates the theme of this chapter: children learn many very important things in school beyond the academic subjects that prepares them for life in today's complex society. Of course, school people should focus on the academics. Children should complete the basic education required by the state with a good handle on the fundamental components of our accumulated store of knowledge. Admittedly, children can only learn a portion of that knowledge and additionally, some of it will be redundant by the time they are adults. However, having that resource to fall back on is essential for success in today's world although even that alone may not be enough to have a complete education

It would be almost impossible to list every skill or attitude that children should accumulate during their years of schooling. Still, educators must be perceptive of some of those interpersonal abilities that come almost by serendipity during the school day. This is especially true when classroom instructors vary their instructional techniques (Balfanz, Legters, & Jordan, 2004). In our Nation's more effective schools, this is an unnoticeable aspect of the teaching-learning process (Frey, Lee, Nona, Pass, & Massengill, 2005).

## THE ROAD AHEAD

The story that introduced this chapter, regarding the student who had never earned an "A" grade, provides only a simple example of important things children learn in school that are not part of the goals for the formal curriculum. Perceptive teachers sometimes fashion their instructional techniques to achieve results beyond mere academic achievement. This chapter, while not providing a comprehensive list, provides examples of how this happens in our American public schools.

The first part of this chapter dealt with people working together as a team. It provides a setting for other instances when students learn how to get along with each other in a variety of classroom settings. Team learning is an effective teaching technique that prepares students for the world they will face after their formal schooling is completed.

Social scientists have expressed concern about the decline of the work ethic in our country (Pyszkowski, 1992). Many of the habits that have a positive effect in the workplace have their origins in classrooms. As noted in the section on work habits, school policy has an effect beyond keeping order in the public school.

Turning to more intellectual matters, the next section explains the importance of teaching higher-level thinking. Classrooms can be conducive to the development of sound reasoning processes and critical thinking for students. The next major section relates to formal curricula with a special emphasis on curricular bias. The final thoughts section provides a short summary of the important work that taxpayers expect from public school teachers and administrators.

## WHEN YOU WORK TOGETHER

I was having a great weekend with my two granddaughters who were visiting. The oldest one had just started her education in the public school miles from their rural home; she was a very smart girl and I was amazed at all the things she learned so early in her schooling. It is always a challenge for senior citizens to think up ideas to keep the younger set entertained. One morning I suggested that we put a puzzle together. She thought that was a good idea but it soon became apparent that the puzzle was a bit too hard for her. I tried to explain a strategy of picking out all the border pieces first and then getting those with similar colors together. It was not long before I realized that she was far ahead of me in puzzle solving skills.

My trifocals just did not help at all and she was able to notice the tiny details of the little pieces of the puzzle. Eventually the picture was complete. Later, I used this story as an illustration in a one of the *Perspectives*. As I remarked on how nice the puzzle looked when put all together, my energetic five-year-old with the sharp eyes summed up our effort with a profound statement: "It is much easier when you work together, Grandpa," she said. Therefore, the two of us accomplished much more together then if we had worked separately. I provided the strategy and she took care of the details. A *Perspective* tells the rest of the story.

> My granddaughter learned this lesson well for she repeated it several times during her brief stay. She insisted on helping make lunch because "it is much easier when you work together." Even when it came time to do the dishes, she wanted to help because working together makes that unpleasant task much easier.

Learning how to work together is probably the most important lesson a child will learn in school today. The major problems of American society are not because people cannot diagram a complex sentence or solve the quadratic equation. Much of our trouble is because so many people lack interpersonal skills that are necessary for complex interactions in our advanced society (*Perspective*, 1995, November 29).

## The New Basics

Not only in America, but also throughout the world, business and industry depend on employees who are capable of working together as teams with others (Downing, 2001). This means that different levels of skill are frequently on a single team. The ability to work with variations in skill levels is essential to the success of the organization.

Educators can do much in preparing their students for such a world of work. It is one of the most important things they teach students, even though it is not listed as an academic subject. However, the development of interpersonal skills in preparation for life at work might be considered as what I have identified as one of the "new basics." A *Perspective* illustrates the point:

## Negotiate

Months ago, I witnessed a first grade class learning the *new basics* in a local public school. The lesson was measurement and the children were organized in groups of four to do the assignment. The task was to estimate the weight of several common objects and then actually weigh them using a simple scale. Each group had a work sheet to record both the estimates and the actual weight. A straightforward process it seemed to me.

The teacher placed all the materials needed for the lesson on a table at the front of the room and instructed the class to have one person get the materials for each group. All the groups quickly accomplished this task, except the one nearest to me. Johnny announced that he would get the materials to which Mary replied, "That is not fair. You always get the things up front. It is my turn." Betty complained about how bossy Mary was being and soon a full-scale argument raged. Bill sat passively ignoring the whole scene.

The teacher soon noticed the ruckus and came to help the group. "What is the problem?" she asked. They all exclaimed loudly how the other members of the group were not cooperating. The teacher just smiled and said, "All the other groups have already started on their assignment. You had better hurry if you are going to get your work done. If you cannot decide who is to get the materials, negotiate!" With that instruction, she walked away.

I watched in amazement as these six-year-old children negotiated a settlement to their dispute. Johnny agreed to let someone else get the materials if he could do the first measurement. Mary agreed to refrain from bossing the other children if she could get the materials from the table. Betty was happy when the others agreed that she could write the answers on the worksheet. Bill agreed to help with the work if the others would stop arguing. Soon the group was working on their assignment. They struggled with the concept of estimating and really did not do well on the measurement problems. However, I observed that they had demonstrated a degree of skill in working together, which may be more important than the original assignment (Johnson & Johnson, 1992), I wish adult society could do as well. *(Perspective,* 1995, September 13)

## WORK HABITS

Working in the congenial atmosphere with fellow employees who come from a variety of backgrounds, possessing a variety of skills and aptitudes, is one of the important things educators can teach their students. They also teach other work-related habits that should make them competitive in the labor market, among which is the importance of faithful attendance at the workplace.

Absenteeism is a growing problem that many American workers picked up as a bad habit while in the elementary school. In the small rural district where I live, just a surface study indicated that in the lower elementary school, 124 children had missed at least 10 days of school during one year. This irregular attendance wreaks havoc with teachers who are trying to provide a compact integrated curriculum (Wilson, Malcolm, Edwards, & Davidson, 2008). Here is what a *Perspective* had to say about such a situation.

> We have wonderful schools in our little village, both public and private. These schools can only be successful if they engage in this important educational venture in cooperation with parents. Parents are the most important teachers of children. The schools can only supplement what parents teach at home. If parents teach their children that school is relatively unimportant and that attendance is optional, children will not only be robbed of important cognitive development but they will also acquire negative attitudes towards an ethic of responsibility in the workplace when they become adults.
>
> From my perspective, one of the most important things that parents and schools can teach children is responsibility towards the duties of life (Cam, 2014). That lesson is best learned early in life. I hope that parents in our community can find it within their hearts to do the best for their children by seeing that they get to school on time and on a regular basis. That does not cost much money and is certainly worth the effort. (*Perspective,* 2009, June 24)

### Attitude Toward Work

Some time ago, I had an interesting conversation with a human resource (HR) person from a midsized employer in our part of the state. She expressed concern that it was a difficult task to find enough personnel to fill their vacant positions. This was for not only the technically skilled people but also entry-level jobs. I asked what kind of screening they did for low-level employees. The HR person told me that her company merely tested potential employees for physical strength and basic employment attitudes as measured by an attitude survey.

I am interested in testing because all parts of society use tests for a variety of purposes. So, I asked the HR person what kinds of questions were included. Her answer surprised me. The survey asked job applicants such things as "How important is it to come to work on time?" and, "Is it necessary to come to work every day?" Certainly, no one is stupid enough to answer these questions in the negative, I thought to myself. The HR person must have read my thoughts for she responded, "You would be surprised at how difficult it is to find people who can pass this test."

## Zero Tolerance

As I pondered this situation, I remembered an incident at a meeting of the Board of our local public schools that might give some insight into how our culture has declined in its work ethic. A parent was on the agenda to make a plea for a change in policy at one of the schools. At the upper elementary school, the teachers had a rule that students who missed three assignments in a six-week time had to attend after-school detention. The parent thought this was an unreasonable policy and that it placed too much pressure on a nine-year-old child as it was enforced.

This experience made such an impression on me that it became the basis for a *Perspective*.

> I believe that lenient policies in our schools can be linked to a serious decline in the work ethic in America. Children who are allowed to miss three assignments before a penalty is given, develop poor work habits which have a negative effect on their worth to an employer. From my perspective, schools should not tolerate any missed assignment. If they want to do good service to the public, all schools should have a zero tolerance policy for missed homework. When a child does not get the assignment done, he should stay after school until it is completed. For parents who complain about this policy, I would send them to detention hall and require them to write a 500 word essay on the topic of Good Work Habits.
>
> Society has assigned many tasks to the schools. Most important of these is teaching the basic skills of reading, communication, and mathematics. American schools do a good job of this task. These skills, however, are of little value if students do not learn good personal habits with which they can apply their knowledge. No matter how smart a person is, they must show up on time to work and do so every day of the week. A good place to start acquiring such habits is in elementary school. I strongly urge school boards to consider a zero tolerance policy for homework. (*Perspective*, 1997, October 29)

The rest of the story is instructive. At the next meeting of the School Board, one of my colleagues told me with a grin that "my daughter does not like you!" I was taken back because I did not even know his daughter and asked the cause of her dislike. He informed me that her classroom teacher had read my *Perspective* in which I called for a zero tolerance policy regarding homework. It seems that all of the teachers in that school followed suit, and I was very unpopular on campus. I decided I could live with that reputation.

## HIGHER-LEVEL THINKING

Articles on critical thinking prevail in the educational literature in recent years. This is not the same as thinking "outside the box," which refers to ignoring the "conventional wisdom" about the way things have always been done and try something new or innovative. Such thinking requires managers to ignore the obvious answer to questions and implement counterintuitive policies. This approach pays off sometimes, when really outrageous ideas turn out to be very productive. Some people seem to have a natural ability to sort out productive ideas from nonproductive ones when they are thinking outside the box. By contrast, critical thinking might be considered inside the box thinking, which I view as more practical for every-day use. A *Perspective* written just a few years ago gives one view on this topic.

### Emphasizing Critical Thinking

I do not worry so much about thinking outside the box as I do about the lack of thinking inside the box in so many aspects of American life. Thinking seems to be a lost art in today's modern world. Inside-the-box thinking is sometimes known as critical thinking in which we question the assumptions upon which our understanding of every aspect of life is based.

The word "critical" used in this context is not necessarily negative. It can lead to positive results. It requires analysis of the conventional wisdom that has been passed down to us from previous generations, to determine the validity of that knowledge. Such a thought process seeks out the unstated assumptions and values that we hold, interprets the data we collect, appraises the evidence, and evaluates the arguments that are used to advance our current understanding of the world around us. It frequently requires us to reconstruct our pattern of beliefs based on wider experience and broader information, which we have been able to assemble (Kahneman, 2011).

Skills needed for critical thinking can be taught in school and in fact form an important part of the curriculum in American education. This is what differentiates our approach to educating children and youth from that in many other parts the world that depend heavily on rote memorization. Children there score very high on standardized tests that require students merely to recall facts that they have memorized.

In contrast, students coming out of the American schools frequently are not good memorizers. However, they can think critically about the problems set before them and as a result, they become excellent problem solvers and creative thinkers as well. Educational leaders in a number of other countries have become fascinated with the

American approach to teaching critical thinking. Some of them seek to include it in their own curriculum. *(Perspective,* 2012, August 1)

## Intellectual Rebellion

While critical thinking is generally encouraged, it does have its challenges. It can make persons look argumentative or even in rebellion against the established order. As a school principal, I have dealt with students who were disciplined by their classroom teacher for being disruptive and disrespectful when they challenged some minor point about a topic of study. On some of these occasions, parents supported their offspring and admitted having instructed them to stand up for what they believe.

My response has been that classroom instructors, of necessity, must have near dictatorial powers when it comes to classroom control. The general rule that seems logical to me is, *comply now and argue after the class is over.* It is impractical to have children disputing every minor point on either the rules of behavior or the subject matter of the class. Critical thinking cannot flourish an environment where chaos reigns. Yet, there must be room for honest debate as suggested in a *Perspective.*

> However, an appropriate time and place for rebellion exists. That is rebellion of the mind. Youth are well served when they learn to be critical thinkers without becoming critical people. For example, when the science teacher requires the study of Darwin's theory of natural selection as the explanation for the origin of species, a student may not agree. Yet, the student has no need to engage in heated disruptive argumentation during class time. However, after class the student might want to investigate an alternative explanation for the rise of new species such as symbiosis, (Margulis & Sagan, 2002) which is posited by a few renegade scientists (Gilbert, 2014).
>
> In such an event, it is entirely appropriate for a student to be a rebel in thought without being a rebel in action. While the theory of symbiosis has not gained support among mainstream scientists, no harm is done to the educational process when a rebellious student decides to investigate or even affirm this offshoot theory. As long as he does not become disruptive in the classroom, that is.
>
> The point of all this is that schools teach important things besides knowledge of the subjects in the formal curriculum. Two that I have previously listed are showing up on time every day and following the instructions given by those in authority. I would add to those, learning how to be an independent analytical thinker in the context of behavioral compliance. These are valuable skills for both the workplace and for life in general. (*Perspective,* 2005, April 6)

## THE FORMAL CURRICULUM

Without question, the primary function of the public schools is to achieve academic goals. Along with these goals, other important things become part of students' accumulated knowledge. In one of the *Perspectives*, I recounted my experience in visiting classrooms in the public schools where I live. I was surprised by the complexity of tasks that even first-graders were assigned. It was a humbling experience indeed. Then I briefly visited a kindergarten class, which is considered almost prerequisite to entry into formal schooling. They were studying the culture of the state of Texas at the time, and rather than watching a video or having a book read to them, the children were engaged in a video conference with peers in a Texas public school (Van Horn, 1999).

After the teachers from the two schools exchanged pleasantries, they had the students tell a bit about the culture of their area. Then they opened it up for questions. The Texans wanted to know if it snowed in Michigan. Of course it does, was the quick reply. The Michigan children wanted to know if they had horses they could ride in Texas. Answer: of course they did; after all this is Texas! A short paragraph from a *Perspective* provides my summation of the event.

> From my perspective, the students were learning something of much more value than just the culture of another state. (Vasileva-Stojanovska, Malinovski, Vasileva, Jovevski, & Trajkovik, 2015) Videoconferencing is the way work is being conducted in business today and will become even more prevalent in the future. The kids in our public schools are learning a valuable skill that will be very useful to them in the world of work (Roszkiewicz, 2007). They are getting a head start right here in kindergarten. (*Perspective*, 2009, April 1)

### Identifying Bias in the Curriculum

It should be apparent that, as teachers present the traditional formal curriculum, students have many unexpected opportunities to learn skills and attitudes that may not have easily been identified as part of a formal statement of educational goals. The study of history, for example, has periodically become a lightning rod for conservative critics of the public schools. Some thought leaders are not hesitant to express concern that American history is presented with liberal bias. It generated a good bit of publicity when a conservative critic, speaking not only in her own behalf, but also for her entire board, stated during a media interview that she wanted history taught without bias.

In my view, these critics are asking educators to do the impossible. History is the interpretation of the accumulated documents and artifacts that form the body of information available about a certain topic. Somebody has to determine the meaning of the individual bits of data within the accumulation. Thus, personal bias, liberal or conservative, influences the story that emerges.

In a *Perspective* on this topic, I gave the example of the French invasion of Russia under the leadership of Napoleon. The history of that epic has been written many times, but usually from the perspective of the French. The emphasis on Napoleon is obvious, with the spotlight kept tightly focused on his successes and failures.

Historically, Napoleon was a great military strategist, who just forgot to check the weather reports before he launched his formidable war machine on the hapless Russians living in the borderlands. However, with all the additional documentation available, historians might conclude that the Russian Czar employed a superior strategy in avoiding a big decisive military confrontation and deploying his highly mobile forces in a long, debilitating series of small skirmishes (Lieven, 2010). The conclusion will no doubt be influenced by the historian's bias as implied in a *Perspective.*

> My purpose in reciting all this is not to debate the relative merits of the Emperor's military skill, but to show that it is difficult, indeed, to have a completely balanced presentation of history. From my perspective, the best response for the conservative board members is not to dictate a certain approach to the development of curriculum. However, the Board is certainly within its rights, as well as its responsibilities, by insisting that the curriculum recognizes the nature of historical bias that exists within the subject, as it is taught in the school district. Teachers and others should be more than happy to comply with such a mandate from the board. (*Perspective,* 2014, October 8).

## Students Confront Bias

While the media had its attention focused on the controversy regarding bias in the teaching of history, educators should have put their creative energy into providing an opportunity for students to explore the wider issue of bias in many other aspects of daily life. Unfortunately, I am afraid this was lost in the emotions that raged on both sides of the issue. A week later, another *Perspective* offered an analysis of a different aspect of the topic.

Of particular concern by the conservative school board was that liberal curriculum tended to emphasize negative aspects of America's past. We cannot be proud of many parts of our history. The reaction by the Board to teaching the dark side of America's past is what caught the attention of the media. The Board tried to mandate a curriculum that emphasized the positive aspects of America's story without referring to the dark side of our history. I presented my analysis of the controversy in a *Perspective* from which I extracted three paragraphs.

> In one respect, I do agree with the conservative board as they attempted to restructure the curriculum for the teaching of America's history. That is, I strongly reject a one-sided approach that emphasizes only the negative aspects of our history or that attempts to judge our past leaders by the standards of the 21st century. In many events, America was acting consistent with the standards of that day. While that does not justify some of the terrible things that were done, it is a more productive view of the past.

An additional consideration is the maturity of the student involved in the study of this important subject. I have no objection to providing younger children a sanitized view of our past. Thus, I am willing to have the school engage in the indoctrination of very young children to a love of their country. However, when our youth reach middle school, it is time to begin opening up the full story, including the things that make America look not so good..

From my perspective, a willingness to confront the negative events of the past does not show weakness on the part of our nation or its leaders. Rather, I view that as strength. If we cannot admit to the truth about our nation's history, how will we ever confront our enemies and those who would do us ill? Thus, we can be loyal patriotic Americans and still present the dark side of our nation's history as long as we do not make that the central focus of our discourse. (*Perspective*, 2014, October 15)

## What Should Schools Teach?

The issue of what should be taught in school predates the formation of our Republic. It is an age-old question. In the distant past, education consisted primarily of training young people, usually boys, for specific skills tied to crafts of some sort. Once young men completed their apprenticeships, they were turned loose to ply their trade in the public marketplace. Education was very job specific and might be more descriptively labeled as "training."

This plan worked very well prior to the industrial revolution, but eventually the liberal (or liberating) arts became an important part of the academic world. Some observers had questioned the narrow spectrum of knowledge included in the job-training model. They suggested that students need a much broader education to prepare them for life in an advancing society. When schools include the arts as well as the sciences, they provide better service to their students.

The following *Perspective* was generated in response to news that the Texas legislature was considering an enactment requiring schools to concentrate on just a few subjects such as mathematics, science, and technology. Other subjects within the liberal arts framework might still have been taught, but they would have had a diminished importance in Texas' school curricula.

## Seven Cardinal Principles

Every few years a new wave of "school reform" appears in America.

Of specific interest to me is the Commission on the Reorganization of Secondary Education, which was formed in 1915 and delivered its final report three years later (Wiggens, 2011). The report included the famous *Seven Cardinal Principles of Secondary Education* that provided guidance for American high schools for many years. One of the principles was "command of the fundamental processes" such as reading, writing, and mathematics. If this were the only goal of public education, it would be consistent with the thinking of the Texas legislature.

However, six other principles indicate the necessity for a broad education that would prepare Americans for maintaining good health, fulfilling their position within home and society, and understanding of America's liberal democracy, as well as the development of an ethical character. Since that time, the global economy has placed additional demands on schools as they attempt to provide an adequate education for our youth. As a context to understanding the work of the Commission, one must remember that at the time less than 20% of children and youth completed high school. However, that was rapidly changing and our public schools had to change to provide for the growing educational needs of the nation.

From my perspective, the Seven Cardinal Principles still apply to today's world. We cannot have our high school graduates prepared for one specific job only. Rather, they need a broad education that will prepare them for a variety of potential future jobs as well as being a useful member of society. I hope that wisdom will prevail and the Texas legislature will discard the notion of a return to a narrow education. They would do the citizens of their state a real favor by providing a good solid liberal education. (*Perspective*, 2013, March 20)

## SOME FINAL THOUGHTS

This chapter emphasized a few of the things that are taught in school in addition to the established formal curricula. In many instances, the activities they involve are just as important as traditional studies. I make no claim as to the comprehensive nature of the narrative because that task might be impossible.

Nevertheless, things such as learning to work in groups and the ability to discern the dark side of our history without magnifying it beyond its relative importance in the American history are just two examples of the extra benefits accruing to students during the time spent in formal schooling. The following short excerpt from a *Perspective* provides a small glimpse of the wide variety of responsibilities teachers assume when they enter the classroom. Each of these duties results in identifying important things children learn in school.

Over the years, I have noticed that teachers play a variety of roles especially at the elementary and high school levels. Educators must teach our children the rules of good behavior in polite society, instill in them the love of our country, keep them entertained, provide good day care, and provide a psychologically safe environment.

We call on teachers to teach sex education, character education, appreciation for diversity, health education, and a variety of other things that are important in civil society. Then of course, we expect them to teach the content of the various subjects that we deem important for people to know in modern society. (*Perspective*, 2009, May 6)

It behooves every teacher in our nation's schools to be ever mindful of the "informal curriculum" and take opportunities to meet the unpublished goals that are connected to it. Many teachers find it difficult to suspend their carefully prepared lesson plans to take advantage of an unscheduled "teachable moment." Classroom, instructors who are perceptive enough and flexible enough, will provide an outstanding service to the children and youth entrusted to their care. In addition to the published academic goals, children learn many other important things in school

## LIST OF *PERSPECTIVES* REFERENCED

Published in *The Journal Era*, Berrien Springs, Michigan

1995, September 13. Back to the basics.
1995, November 29. Back to school.
1997, October 29. Zero tolerance in school.
2005, April 6. Important things schools teach—Part 2.
2009, April 1. Smart as a fifth grader
2009, May 6. A day to celebrate.
2009, June 24. What parents can do to help their children learn.
2012, August 1. Thinking, in and outside the box
2013, March 20. What should kids learn in school?
2014, October 8. Some thoughts on the teaching of history.
2014, October 15. More thoughts on the teaching of history.

## REFERENCES

Balfanz, R., Legters, N., & Jordan, W. (2004). Catching up: Effects of the talent development ninth-grade instructional interventions in reading and mathematics in high-poverty high schools. *NSSP Bulletin, 88*(641), 3–30.

Cam, P. (2014). Philosophy for children, values education and the inquiring society. *Educational Philosophy & Theory, 46*(11), 1203–1211.

Downing, C. G. (2001). Essential non-technical skills for teaming. *Journal of Engineering Education, 90*(1), 113–117.

Frey, B. B., Lee, S. W., Nona, T., Pass, L., & Massengill, D. (2005). Balanced literacy in an urban school district. *Journal of Educational Research, 98*(5), 272–280.

Gilbert, S. (2014). Symbiosis as the way of eukaryotic life: The dependent coordination of the body. *Journal of Biosciences, 39*(2), 201–209.

Johnson, D. W., & Johnson, R. T. (1992). Teaching students to be peer mediators. *Educational Leadership, 50*(1), 10–14.

Joyce, B. (2004). How are professional learning communities created? *Phi Delta Kappan, 86*(1), 78–83.

Kahneman, D. (2011). *Thinking, fast and slow.* New York: Farrar, Straus and Giroux.

Lieven, D. (2010). *Russia against Napoleon: The true story of the campaigns of War and Peace.* New York: Viking Penguin.

Margulis, L., & Sagan, D. (2002). *Acquiring genomes: A theory of the origins of species.* New York: Basic Books.

Pyszkowski, I. S. (1992). Restoring the work ethic in America. *Education, 113*(1), 127–132.

Roszkiewicz, R. (2007). GDSS: The future of online meetings and true digital collaboration? *Seybold Report: Analyzing Publishing Technologies, 7*(1), 13–17.

Van Horn, R. (1999). The electronic classroom and video conferencing. *Phi Delta Kappan, 80*(5), 411–414.

Vasileva-Stojanovska, T., Malinovski, T., Vasileva, M., Jovevski, D., & Trajkovik, V. (2015). Impact of satisfaction, personality and learning style on educational outcomes in a blended learning environment. *Learning & Individual Differences, 38*, 127–135.

Wiggens, G. (2011). A diploma worth having. *Educational Leadership, 68*(6), 28–33.

Wilson, V., Malcolm, H., Edwards, S., & Davidson, J. (2008). Bunking off: The impact of truancy on pupils and teachers. *British Educational Research Journal, 34*(1), 1–17.

CHAPTER 4

# TESTING AND OTHER SUCH FOOLISHNESS

## LABELING CHILDREN

People, including educators, place labels on children based on the results of their test scores, or their grades in school. For example, such statements as "she is an A student" or "He is only average in musical skill," are examples of ways we identify people. In more formal settings, students at all levels are subjected to various kinds of standardized tests that provide numeric scores intended to represent their accumulated cognitive skills (Plake, Huff, & Reshetar, 2010). We say such things as "He scored at the 40th percentile on the achievement test."

Reducing a person's identity to a single number or letter simplifies the process of sorting people into categories. It is very useful in transferring information regarding a person to another entity such as a school or a potential employer. Unfortunately, simply quoting a person's grade point average (GPA) gives only one piece of information about a person, while ignoring other very important characteristics that persons bring with themselves to whatever venues they choose. Such things as work ethic, attention to detail, and compatibility in working with a diverse group of people are not captured in single test scores.

*Helping Parents Understand Schools: A Different Perspective on Education and Schooling in America,* pages 57–70.

To complicate matters even more, the question arises, just what does a score on a test represent? What factors influence particular scores?

## THE ROAD AHEAD

This chapter deals with testing which is a large part of the political agenda for public schools in America. A widely held belief is that "If it cannot be measured, it does not exist." Thus, tests of all kinds have come almost to overwhelm some American schools.

The chapter is divided into three major sections. The first of these, Test Scores and Their Interpretation, provides a look at the theoretical foundation for tests as they are typically used in schools. The second major section, Utilizing Valid Tests, looks at selected aspects of evaluating the efficacy of tests students confront in schools. The final section, Testing Use and Misuse, deals with how educators use test scores. The closing section, Some Final Thoughts, provides a summative statement regarding testing.

## TEST SCORES AND THEIR INTERPRETATION

Test scores and grades can be useful tools in understanding the educational attainment of individuals, but they can also be improperly used in determining their value as persons (Taylor, Hume, & Welsh, 2010). Unfortunately, scores are frequently aggregated to make value judgments about groups of people or the schools they attended. It is the purpose of this section to describe in simple terms what test scores and grades mean and how they can best be used in making judgments about students and schools.

Three paragraphs from an early *Perspective* provide an introduction to the topic:

> First, let us look at the meaning of test scores and grades in general. What does it really mean when you say "Mary got a B- on her math test" or "Bill scored at the 3rd grade level on the achievement test?" Ideally, a B- would mean that Mary knew quite bit about math but somewhat less than what the teacher wanted her to know. She knows enough to pass to the next grade, but she is not a top student. However, before that judgment can be made about Mary's knowledge of math, a number of other factors must be considered.

> Many things influence a student's score on a test (Sani & Grilli, 2011), including: motivation to learn, teaching skill of the teacher, student ability, environmental factors such as how quiet the classroom was during the test, the emotional state of the student, and validity of the test, as well as how much the student learned about the subject. People typically believe that test scores are affected most by the teacher's skill in instruction and how hard the student works in school. While these are very important, the other things listed above are equally important. In addition, the influence of the home is probably the single most important factor besides the student's basic intelligence. Students who come from homes that provide a mentally stimulating environ-

ment tend to score higher on all kinds of tests than students who come from homes without such stimulation. Such things as parents talking to children, reading to them, providing books, magazines, and newspapers, taking trips to the zoo, museums, and art galleries, and providing a quiet time and place for them to read, write and study all provide the kind of stimulating home environment that results in higher test scores in school. (*Perspective*, 1995, March 8)

In view of these factors, which make up single grades assigned to students, care must be given as to how that one-bit of information is used. Unfortunately, it is not uncommon that single test scores, or averages of test scores in classrooms or schools, are utilized to rate schools or school systems. However, increasingly test scores are used to evaluate the effectiveness of individual teachers. Unfortunately, this is not an appropriate use of the test and may result in invalid value judgments based on a single test scores.

One should not assume that teachers are incompetent if student scores on standardized tests are low. Too many other explanations must be considered when making such interpretations. The better judgment is for those who want to evaluate the effectiveness of schools or individual teachers, is to use a variety of measures. Just one number will not do.

*Interpreting Test Results*

Some years ago, I was assigned to teach the beginning course in the school administration program at a small Midwestern university. It was a first level graduate course and administration students, as well as those from other departments such as curriculum and instruction had enrolled. Most of the students were experienced educators and were working on a Masters' degree to enhance their instructional skills, move up the pay scales, and/or transition from teaching to administration. Not being novices, the students were knowledgeable about the best practices of their chosen profession.

After teaching the course multiple times, I began to get bored with my lectures. Therefore, I decided to embark on an experiment with group problem solving as my primary teaching technique. Insofar as I had some degree of success using this method at other levels of schooling, I thought I could modify it for use in this graduate class. I divided the students into groups of three or four, assigning them problems related to the topics under study. Each semester at the opening class, I had a special problem designed to set the pace for the remainder of the semester.

In this class, I presented a short lecture on the decline of the public schools. To clinch the argument, I made the following statement, "It is a known fact that half the students in the public schools in America are reading below grade level." Then I divided the students into small groups to discuss the question, "What is the cause of this failure on the part of our educational system?"

Most of the time, a lively discussion ensued in each of the groups. After a few minutes, I brought the class back to order and asked the group leaders to give reports on what they saw as the best answer to my question. They usually had good ideas such as the lack of parental support for the schools, the pervasiveness of TV programs aimed at children, and insufficient funding for the public schools. Over the years, one of the most frequent answers was that the public schools just are not working anymore.

## Defining Grade Level

Now it was time to clear up the confusion and reveal my answer. I asked the class a simple question: What does grade level mean? Seldom would anyone in the class know the technical definition of grade level. I explained to them that grade level, by definition, is the point at which half of the scores are below and half the scores are above. Thus, in a large population, grade level is the same as the average score (Jehlen, 2007). For the psychometricians and other experts on tests and measurements, I realize that there is a more complex definition. The point of my question in the class activity was that it is very easy to misinterpret test scores and make ineffective management decisions as a result of this misinterpretation. One of the early unpublished *Perspectives* provided a short summary.

> Most public schools in America give their students standardized achievement tests on a regular basis. The most popular of these, the Iowa Test of Basic Skills (ITBS) and the California Achievement Test (CAT) are examples of what we call norm-referenced tests. This type of test compares an individual student's score with a large number of other students who take the same test. The average score is called grade level.

> Usually a student's score on the achievement test is identified by its relationship to the average or grade level. If the student gets the exact average of the norm group, his score is grade level, if he gets less than that, he is below grade level, and if he gets more than average, he is above grade level. Half of the students in the country score below grade level because that is the definition of the term (Carwile, 1990). Only in the mythical Lake Wobegon are all of the students above grade level.

> Actually, a better way of recording achievement test scores is the percentile, which simply tells where a student places compared to the norming group. If the score is at grade level, it is the fiftieth percentile.

> That means that fifty percent of the students who took the test scored lower. The student who scores at the sixty-fifth percentile got a higher score than sixty-five percent of the students who took the test.

> Both grade level and percentile are mathematically calculated scores. Just because a student scores below grade level does not mean his education is defective. It just means that his score is below average. Remember that half of the students will always score below average and therefore below grade level. (*Perspective*, 1995, unpublished)

## An Unfortunate Response

It is very easy to misinterpret the meanings of test scores. It is even more perilous when one tries to attach meaning to the average of a group of scores such as all students in classes or school buildings. What exacerbates the problem is that public policy is frequently bases on such erroneous interpretations. One small section of a *Perspective* gives an example of this situation. Reaction to an education plan proposed by George W. Bush as a part of his campaign for the year 2000 presidential election, provided motivation for this *Perspective*.

> Further, Bush makes an error when he assumes that children score low on standardized tests because the teachers do a poor job of teaching. While in some instances that may be, partly true, poor teaching is not the major reason why schools fail to get all their students to score above average on tests of achievement.
>
> A recent story from Chicago illustrates this point. In one school, over a third of the students who had failed academically, also failed a vision test.
>
> The Bush plan would penalize the school by removing all federal funds. From my perspective, it would make more sense to buy glasses for the kids so they could see the words they were supposed to be reading.
>
> The idea of punishing schools that are not successful by removing government funds has been around a long time and it has never made much sense. It is like punishing a hospital by removing its funding because the people there are sick. Some actually die and we certainly should not provide government funds to such an institution. Poor schools enroll poor kids that have severe learning deficits. Effective instruction of such children is much more expensive. Why does Bush think they will learn better if there are fewer resources available for their education? (*Perspective*, 1999, September 13).

## The Ranking Error

A year after that *Perspective* was written, my home state of Michigan embarked on a new procedure for evaluating school effectiveness. In this attempt at utilizing hard data to hold the schools accountable, the state ranked all schools according to their average achievement test score. Then state officials tried to interpret the ranked data, a move always fraught with potential for misinterpretation.

That year (2012), the State introduced a new mechanism for evaluating schools that provides three new categories for reporting purposes. Schools showing high achievement or that made significant progress since the last report are listed as *reward* schools, while those continuing to struggle are labeled as *priority* schools. The third category of institutions, *focus* schools, are those with a wide achievement gap among their students. While I have serious doubts about the value of this type of reporting in general, it is this third category that I find most problematic as explained in two paragraphs from a *Perspective*.

Instead of having valid measures of student achievement as a basis for reporting to the public on the effectiveness of the schools, the state simply ranks them according to achievement test results. It places the school scores on the normal curve and lists each school's place as percentile ranking. Thus, there will always be 10% of the schools in the bottom 10% of the ranking. If every school in Michigan were a high-performing school, there would still be 10% of them listed as failures. Or, conversely, if every school were a failure you would have 10% of them listed as reward schools.

In light of the above-described procedure, the state report card does not indicate how well a school is doing, only its relative place among all other schools in the state. According to state educational leaders, the purpose of this report is to provide transparency and hold schools accountable to the public. From my perspective, such a reporting plan is just a bunch of foolishness and has limited value to the public. (*Perspective*, 2012, August 8).

## Mind the Gap

Of particular interest to me in this example of interpreting data based on test scores is the identification of a gap between different categories of students. In the Michigan example, a gap is the distance between the average of the highest 30% of the student scores and the average of the lowest 30% of the scores in a school. This difference in averages is identified as a gap in learning. These gaps are ranked for every school in the state. The schools in the top 10% of the rankings are labeled as focus schools. This is not a designation of honor because those who control education in Michigan consider gaps in learning as a negative characteristic of schools.

Some years ago, I visited London for the first time. As I rode the Tube (subway), I soon became aware of a recorded female voice repeating "Mind the Gap." It was almost like a mantra chanted by a recent convert to new age mysticism. At first I was puzzled by the meaning of the message. Eventually, I discovered that "The Gap" is the short distance between the transit car and the platform. The chant is a warning to passengers to watch where they step. Those who try to interpret test scores might also consider themselves warned.

The underlying philosophy is that *all students learn at about the same rate,* and therefore there should be little variation in the test scores within each school. This flies in the face the things we know about people, that students arrive at school with a variety of skills, and abilities. Thus, the fact that gaps in their test scores occur should not be surprising (Miranda, Kim, Reiter, Overstreet, & Maxson, 2009). Unfortunately, the misunderstanding on the nature of children will not soon go away. Four paragraphs from a *Perspective* provide more detail.

The State of Michigan recently announced its newest plan to force accountability on the public schools. Our governor, John Engler, has threatened such a program for several years. It is His desire to give a report card on every public school so the public will know if they are doing a good job or not. The report will give a letter grade on the A, B, and C scale to indicate the level of accomplishment of the school. That way, the public will know if the school is doing a good job or is failing in its work of educating the children of the district.

Accountability is a good thing. The public needs to know if its taxpayer supported institutions are doing the job assigned to them. All institutions, public and private, should be held accountable by their stakeholders. When this does not happen, disasters such as Enron are bound to ensue eventually. With schools, it is even more important because the future of our children is at stake. If the children are not well educated, the future of the nation is in jeopardy. In this respect, it is doubly important to do the job of grading schools right so the public has an accurate picture of their success or failure. Unfortunately, the current plan fails to provide an effective method of accountability.

The Governor's plan fails because it relies heavily on the criterion-referenced test known as MEAP. This test is not only flawed in design but also is improperly used in many cases. From the small amount of data about the test that leaks from Lansing, it appears that the test is neither valid nor reliable. The scores coming from the MEAP do not give an adequate indication of how much the kids in school have learned (*Perspective*, 2002, March 20)

## UTILIZING VALID TESTS

The construction of paper and pencil tests is a complex activity requiring some degree of scientific expertise. Any test used to make major policy decisions should be assessed for its validity. A valid test is one that measures what it claims to measure. A colleague of mine discovered that a student who was failing her history class was quite knowledgeable about the subject. She found that his poor reading skills impeded his ability to answer the questions on the course examinations. Instead of measuring knowledge of the course content, the test she utilized merely measured his poor reading ability. The teacher discovered that an oral exam was a more valid indicator of his knowledge of history.

Failure to validate tests renders their results useless. However, in education, it sometimes seems that test validity is a lost concept. Constructing tests that have some degree of validity is a complex and time-consuming process. It is beyond the scope of this book to describe the technical steps to determine test validity. I mention the topic here only to alert parents to the issue.

One good example of questionable test validity is found in my home state where each year public school students must take the Michigan Educational Assessment Program (MEAP) examination. The test itself has developed some degree of notoriety through its years of use in Michigan. I decided to attend a question-and-answer session sponsored by the Intermediate School District [Now called Regional Educational Service Agency (RESA)] to learn more about this test that so terrorizes the children in Michigan's public schools. A *Perspective* summarized my experience.

My short experience with the sample test led me to question its validity. On more than one item, the teacher admitted that those who corrected the tests disagreed on what possible answers would be accepted. My answer to the triangle question would be accepted by some and not by others. Thus the reliability of the MEAP, which is a major component of validity, is suspect.

On the social studies section, 8th grade students are given a bar graph dealing with opinions on a "No Pass, No Play" policy for a school and a line graph with data related to the same subject. Then they were asked a question testing their ability to interpret the graphs. Following that, students were instructed to write an essay in the form of a letter taking a stand on the no pass, no play policy. The letter must include 1) a clear statement of your position, 2) supporting information using core democratic values, 3) supporting knowledge from history, geography, civics, or economics that you already know, and 4) supporting information from the graphs. For all this, reading the instructions, reading and interpreting the graphs, answering the questions about the graphs, and writing the letter on the public policy issue, students are given twenty minutes.

Is this a valid test of an 8th grader's knowledge of social studies? When I was in that wonderful age I was interested in lots of things but public policy was not one of them. I saved that topic for my more advanced years. A mature thirteen-year old might be able to accomplish all the above tasks in twenty minutes, but for most students of that age it will be a real challenge. Could the adult readers of this column pass that part of the MEAP? Remember, if the kids don't get the right answer in the time allotted the news media will announce that the school is a failure. (*Perspective,* 2002, December 4)

## Challenges to Test Validity

Other challenges to the validity of standardized tests have been noted (Cook, Brydges, Ginsburg, & Hatala, 2015). Such tests are given to children with the stated purpose of determining how much they learned over a period of time. One issue is the matter *content* validity. This type of validity is established when a test relates to the same subject matter content as what has been taught. If the test contains material that was not included in the curriculum the students had studied, the test would not be a valid measure of their achievement and the results would have limited value. Two paragraphs from a *Perspective* dealt with this aspect of testing.

The use of invalid tests is of great concern. To be valid a test should indicate with a high degree of accuracy what it claims to assess. A student's score on a reading test should indicate how well he could read. His score on the social studies test should indicate his knowledge of that subject. There are scientific techniques that can be used to make sure a test is valid. Unfortunately, these methods seem lacking in the tests I have seen that are used for Michigan students.

On one social studies multiple choice question from the Michigan test, I observed that three of the four possible answers might be considered correct depending on how you would interpret the question. When I questioned the official from the State, she admitted that the experts who graded the test disagreed among themselves as to which was the correct answer. Such lack of reliability renders the test invalid, yet under the merit pay plan it would be used to determine a teacher's salary. (*Perspective*, 2004, February 18)

In the *Perspective* above, the issue was evaluating how much teachers should be compensated under merit pay plans. The lack of a valid testing measure to evaluate the efficacy of teachers makes the plan not plausible. Another factor making test validation problematic is that the public has broad expectations of what services the public schools should provide for their children. It is not just teaching the content alone that brings satisfaction to parents and community members. Finding a valid test that takes into consideration the comprehensive nature of public school is a difficult, if not impossible, process. Three paragraphs from a document I had written several years ago, but not published, provide a summary of my thinking on this issue.

## Accountability

I have been asked on occasion if I support attempts to bring more accountability to public schools. The answer, of course, is yes, I strongly support accountability. However, I do not support the high stakes testing movement, especially the plan fostered by the federal government, because I believe it to be a fraud on the public in the name of accountability. Test scores are one valid indicator of what is happening in the schools but, when used alone or especially when averages are reported, they do not reveal the level of productivity in a school (Gunzenhauser & Hyde, 2007). Lest I be misunderstood, let me say it again: test scores are one, but only one, valid indicator of what is happening in schools. I am not opposed to testing but I am not in favor of the misuse of test scores as a means of appearing to hold schools accountable (Garcia, 2011).

I was reminded of the multiple expectations of the public while attending a meeting of the school board where I reside. A short report by the transportation director included a video of some school bus drivers taking a re-certification test. The drivers had to guide the big yellow vehicle through a specially marked course without knocking over the orange cones strategically placed on the road. This is no big deal to a truck driver or others experienced with big equipment. However, put 40 screaming meemies behind truck drivers on a rainy day and they would find that the added distraction makes the task much more difficult.

In addition to good teaching, the public demands safe and on-time transportation for their children. A school's record on this important responsibility is not part of the public report card. Why is it not it a part of the national accountability movement? Compared to the airlines on-time record, I would guess that public schools do well. Maybe this is why some politicians are not anxious to have transportation as part of the scorecard on the schools. Or, maybe I am just being cynical.

## TESTING USE AND MISUSE

Two major types of tests are frequently used in schools to measure student achievement: criterion-referenced and norm-referenced tests (Chen, Chen, & Kim, 2015). Norm-referenced tests are standardized on large populations and various points on the normal curve are identified such as the 50th percentile or the median. That is the point at which half of the scores are above and half below. It is also known as the mean or average of the scores.

Criterion-referenced tests are not made to compare children to others in a group. Rather, they measure students' knowledge compared to a set standard. Such tests are best used to diagnose students' learning needs and to report the success of individual students in various subjects.

In Michigan, the statewide assessment program was developed many years ago. Experts on curriculum and schooling decided what students needed to know when they graduated from high school. Then they developed test questions to determine if students were learning the information they considered necessary. They also set the standard for how many questions a student must answer correctly to be satisfactory in each subject area. Reports for each school simply tell how many students achieved satisfactory scores.

There are some real advantages to using criterion-referenced tests (Popham, 2014) because they reveal student knowledge in specific subject areas. The disadvantage of these tests is that there is no comparison with other students throughout the country. It may be a very good thing that a student knows 70 percent of the history facts on the test, but is this average, above average or below average, compared to that of other students?

The second problem with this kind of test is that the report tells only how many students achieved passing scores. It does not tell how high the students scored. If the report indicates that 65% of students achieved satisfactory scores, it does not reveal whether they achieved perfect scores or just barely passed. What about those who did not earn satisfactory scores? How many missed passing by only one point? On the MEAP test, it is possible that the difference between students who pass and those who do not is just one question.

While criterion tests are useful at the classroom level, their application is limited at the district and state levels. MEAP scores give some information but meaningful comparisons with other districts are usually not possible. Further, the way test results are reported makes it impossible to know the full extent of students' knowledge of subject matter.

### The Political Component

It seems that in the past 30 or 40 years, all presidential candidates think they need to propose educational policy changes as part of their political platform. Sometimes it is openly political, but usually it is couched in terms of school accountability. Never mind that education has no federal mandate in the Constitution. Rather, federal involvement comes through financial aid the government makes available to the schools. However, this money comes with strings attached. For example, President Bill Clinton had a federal initiative during his administration that required a considerable amount of testing with a wide variety of tests. It seemed almost that his approach to public education was that America could test itself to superior learning. A short section of a *Perspective,* written at the time, provides a quick look at the issue.

> President Bill Clinton, who looks like a liberal and acts like a conservative, has recently made voluntary national testing of school children a major part of his political agenda. While testing and strictly-enforced high academic standards are all the rage these days, the President's proposal makes no sense at all. It is just a naked attempt to intrude the federal government into the public schools where it does not belong. That schooling is a matter for the states has been well settled in the law. Clinton and his federal followers should stay out of it.

> We do not need a federal initiative for testing. Schools already have that option and for many years have been testing their students with both standardized achievement tests and a wide variety of criterion-referenced tests (Hursh, 2013). Testing improves the schools only as the teachers use the results to modify their instruction to meet any knowledge deficit that may be identified. Publishing the results as a means of embarrassing the teachers in schools where there is a large deficiency in learning serves no useful purpose. (*Perspective,* 1997, June 18)

## Why Run This Race?

As with his predecessors, President Obama also has become entangled in the testing game. His "Race to the Top" initiative was similar to other federal programs in that it required much testing of students. Just a short comment from a *Perspective* at the time shows one viewpoint.

> Not to be outdone, the Obama administration has its own world of fantasy as evidenced by its education policy. His Race to the Top program is designed to solve all the problems of public education by raising standards in public schools. Arnie Duncan, Obama's Secretary of Education, in a recent interview stated as much, bragging that 40 states have raised their standards because of this federal program. Michigan, for example, raised its standards this year by simply increasing the score students must achieve to pass the statewide assessment test. The major result of such a move would be that fewer students would achieve a passing score. Moving the passing score benefits education only in a world of fantasy

> While assessing student learning is important at the classroom level, as a nationally imposed policy it does not work so effectively. You cannot test your way to a literate society or an educated population. (*Perspective*, 2012, February 29)

Subjecting children to a large number of tests in schools just for the sake of having an appearance of accountability is not wise educational policy (Petress,

2006). Children become test weary and their studies began to suffer. While politicians at the state and national levels may feel significant public pressure to "fix" the public schools, improper use of standardized tests does not advance the acquisition of knowledge. In some instances, over-testing may even cripple efforts to meet quality school district goals.

A good example of that situation is the effort in Michigan, and other states, to eliminate the gap in learning between and among the various subgroups of the school population. Measured by criterion-referenced test a gap is considered a specified mathematical distance between average highest score and the average of the lowest scores.

## When Exercise Is Not Healthy

Trying to solve the perceived learning gap is an exercise in futility. To begin with, a sample not randomly drawn from the population of students is bound to have differences between it and any other sample not randomly drawn. If the test scores turn out to be the same, it would be a matter of mere chance. Additionally, efforts to eliminate the achievement gap among students rest upon the assumption that all students are the same when it comes to intellectual capacity. It can be argued that condition does not exist among the population of planet Earth.

For whatever reason, by grand design or random chance, individual students are not created equal when it comes to their intellectual capacity or their natural ability. Even more, children do not have the same environmental experience growing up. Some have families that nurture them and provide a rich intellectual environment, while others have a poverty of stimulating experiences that do not prepare them for school.

On arriving at school, children already have learning gaps that are difficult to overcome by utilizing the tools available to school personnel (Quinn, 2015). Thus, from my perspective, using standardized tests to sort out the learning gaps in school populations is not a useful tool to assist teachers in providing appropriate learning experiences for the vastly different students in their classes. A short commentary on this issue was provided by a *Perspective* a few years ago.

> Given that a major gap in preparedness for schooling exists when children arrive for their first years of formal education, it is not surprising that the gap is still in existence when achievement tests are given in later years. Those who have grown up in an educationally advantaged environment, no matter what their racial or ethnic group is, will always score higher than those children who had no such advantage in their early years. Thus, it is primarily out of school factors that are responsible for the so-called achievement gap.

> From my perspective, educators should not spend so much time minding the achievement gap between various subgroups of the school population. Rather, their energies should be focused on helping parents provide the educational experiences in the preschool years so their children are ready to benefit from the best efforts of

formal instruction. That is the gap that Americans should mind. (*Perspective*, 2010, July 21)

## SOME FINAL THOUGHTS

Americans are obsessed with measuring things and sorting them into categories. Children learn that skill very early in life. It should not be surprising, then, that as adults people expect to see information about their own children reported in simple categorical or numerical forms. Unfortunately, it is not an easy task. It is difficult to summarize adequately the measurement of complex thought processes with one number or letter grade. Knowing this, parents and teachers should both be aware of the pitfalls of oversimplifying the results of testing. This is especially true if test results are used to inform important life decisions that should not be made based on one test score.

## LIST OF *PERSPECTIVES* REFERENCED

Published in *The Journal Era*, Berrien Springs, Michigan.

1995, unpublished.  Another Look at Achievement Tests
1995, March 8. What's in a Test Score.
1997, June 18. Our Intrusive Government.
1999, September, 13. Bush Talks Specifics.
2002, March 20. Grading the Public Schools.
2002, December 4. I Took the Test.
2004, February 18. More Thoughts on Merit Pay.
2010, July 21. Mind the Gap.
2012, February 29. Living in a World of Fantasy.
2012, August 8. The Gap and Other Such Foolishness.

## REFERENCES

Carwile, N. R. (1990). Punching wholes into parts, or beating the percentile averages. *Educational Leadership, 47*(5), 79.

Chen, P.-H., Chen, T.-C., & Kim, S.-K. (2015). Comparison of three different linking procedures between norm-referenced test and criterion-referenced test. *International Journal of Intelligent Technologies & Applied Statistics, 8*(1), 71–76.

Cook, D. A., Brydges, R., Ginsburg, S., & Hatala, R. (2015). A contemporary approach to validity arguments: A practical guide to Kane's framework. *Medical Education, 49*(6), 560–575.

Garcia, D. (2011). The Achilles' heel of school choice policies: The obstacles to reporting the school accountability results to parents. *Journal of School Choice, 5*(1), 66–84.

Gunzenhauser, M., & Hyde, A. M. (2007). What is the value of public school accountability? *Educational Theory, 57*(4), 489–507.

Hursh, D. (2013). Raising the stakes: High-stakes testing and the attack on public education in New York. *Journal of Education Policy, 28*(5), 574–588.

Jehlen, A. (2007). Testing how the sausage is made. *NEA Today, 25*(7), 29–34.

Miranda, M. L., Kim, D., Reiter, J., Overstreet, G., & Maxson, P. (2009). Environmental contributors to the achievement gap. *Neuro Toxicology, 30*(6), 1019–1024.

Petress, K. (2006). Perils of current testing mandates. *Journal of Instructional Psychology, 33*(1), 80–82.

Plake, B. S., Huff, K., & Reshetar, R. (2010). Evidence-centered assessment design as a foundation for achievement-level descriptor development and for standard. *Applied Measurement in Education, 23*(4), 342–357.

Popham, J. W. (2014). Criterion-referenced management: Half a century wasted? *Educational Leadership, 71*(6), 62–68.

Quinn, D. M. (2015). Kindergarten black-white test score gaps: Re-examining the roles of socioeconomic status and school quality with new data. *Sociology of Education, 88*(2), 120–139.

Sani, C., & Grilli, L. (2011). Differential variability of test scores among schools: A multilevel analysis of the fifth grade Invalsi test using heteroscedastic random effects. *Journal of Applied Quantitative Methods, 6*(4), 88–99.

Taylor, L. M., Hume, I. R., & Welsh, N. (2010). Labeling and self-esteem: The impact of using specific vs. generic labels. *Educational Psychology, 30*(2), 191–202.

# CHAPTER 5

# PARENT INVOLVEMENT

## TAKE HIM TO THE BARBER

I have experienced numerous disagreements with parents during the active years of my educational career, but this one was a bit unusual. I was principal of a small religiously affiliated elementary school on the West Coast. Protests over the Vietnam War raged unabated while sweeping change confronted traditional American culture from every direction. It had even begun to affect our isolated rural community, populated mostly by adherents to one conservative religious denomination. The predominant mood among my faith community rejected the outward display of the symbols of change.

For those of us dealing with children and youth, short skirts on girls and long hair on boys comprised the two major "hot button" issues. As school principal, I was expected to enforce the standards, which were heavily influenced by an informal consensus of the older members of our faith. Intellectually, I rebelled. Behaviorally, I tested the limits a bit. I did not grow long hair, but I did grow long sideburns and for a while even sported a mustache.

Meanwhile, I suggested to the school board that I was not comfortable measuring the length of female students' clothing to determine how far out of compliance they were. The women faculty did me a favor by taking the measurements and

*Helping Parents Understand Schools: A Different Perspective on Education*
*and Schooling in America,* pages 71–84.
Copyright © 2017 by Information Age Publishing

gave me a simple report that I then presented to the board members. It was up to them to determine how I should proceed in enforcing the rule. With regard to the length of boy's hair, I resisted making a rule. I saw nothing in the Scriptures that would forbid boys from wearing long hair. When one of the seventh grade boys let his hair grow long, some faculty members protested against my failure to hold up the standards.

The long haired boy gave every evidence that he was testing the limits of faculty patience. He had a beautiful head of hair that he shampooed and brushed every day. I suspected that, as he walked through the halls with those golden blond locks falling just below his shoulders, our female faculty was secretly jealous of his beautiful naturally wavy hair.

Then, one day at the post office, the boy's father confronted me on the matter. "When are you going to make my son cut his hair? Doesn't the school have a rule on that?" I just laughed and said, "I am not going to make him cut his hair. If you want his hair cut, take him to the barber." With just a bit of embarrassment, the father agreed with me that such things are the responsibility of parents, not school authorities. A few days later, I noticed the boy came to school with considerably shorter hair.

The place of parents in the educational process, particularly at level of formal schooling, has been much discussed over the years. James Coleman, a noted sociologist of the late 20th century conducted massive studies on schools from a sociological point of view. He, along with a colleague, Thomas Hoffer, reported the results of a comparative study of public and Catholic high schools to determine a causative agent in the differences in achievement between these two types of schools.

Coleman and Hoffer found that the schools did not make the major impact on student learning. Rather, they suggested that the sense of community that developed among the parents in Catholic parishes was a major factor in the relatively high achievement of their students. The interlocking communication and social connections provided the kind of support that educators engaged in the processes of formal schooling need to be most successful (Coleman & Hoffer, 1987).

## THE ROAD AHEAD

Far more research is available on the part parents play in the formal education of their children but some of it is conflicting. It is not the purpose of this chapter to plumb the depths of the accumulated research findings regarding parents and the schools. However, observations made over a lifetime of involvement in formal schooling at several levels, culminated in a number of published *Perspectives.* Those interested in the topic might find some of them informative. The *Perspectives* form the evidence supporting the recommendations, rather than the findings from carefully conducted empirical research.

This chapter comprises four major sections, each dealing with a different aspect of the cooperative venture between home and school. The section immediately followings this introduction advances the premise that those who are actively engaged in their parenting role are most effective. The author does not shrink from offering parents specific suggestions for things the average person can do.

The next section focuses on how parents can establish an environment in their homes, as well as among the extended family, to provide solid support for the formal schooling experience. The third and longest section of the chapter suggests that parents might team up with educators and other available resources to initiate a culture of learning throughout the community. A final section considers how parents can relate to school officials on the matter of discipline.

## ACTIVELY ENGAGED PARENTS

Many factors affect how much students learns in school. Some observers believe the quality of the classroom teacher is most crucial while others point to characteristics inherent within students. Personal qualities might include such things as basic intelligence, motivation, past learning experience, and genetic disposition. Some research has shown a direct correlation between the socioeconomic status of the parents and student achievement in formal schooling (Lam, 2014).

Now, just a word about correlations and how they can be safely interpreted when looking at social science research. Just because two factors are highly correlated does not indicate that one causes the other. It merely indicates the two factors are somehow associated with one another.

If, in fact, parental wealth is a causative agent in students' test score outcomes, public schools could do a number of things to increase the average achievement level of their district without a large financial investment. District-wide averages of student scores on standardized tests are frequently published in the media with the public considering them a valid measure of educational quality. School administrators could improve the district's average, and thereby enhance its public image, by simply enrolling more students from wealthy families in their schools. They could encourage local realtors to cooperate with them by selling homes only to those people with high incomes. Zoning ordinances could restrict low-cost housing from being built within the geographical limits of districts.

### Acting Rich

What has just been described may sound facetious but it is a description of reality in many parts of the country. Some communities adopt just such restrictions. The school districts in such areas have definite advantages when it comes to statewide testing. Their average published scores will mark them as providing a high quality education. However, what of districts populated by families not so blessed with wealth? What can parents do with their limited economic resources? One of the early *Perspectives* dealt with this issue.

> In reality, it is not the wealth of parents that results in high test scores. It is simply that parents with higher income levels tend to have a higher level of involvement

in the education of their children. If parents with lower incomes had the same type of involvement, their children also would score higher on the states standardized achievement test, and the school would look good on the governor's report. Middle and low-income parents then, should learn to act as if they are rich as far as the education of their children is concerned.

Rich people tend to buy more books, magazines, and newspapers. Their children grow up with reading as a common experience at home and find reading at school a natural extension of what they already know (Mol & Neuman, 2014). By utilizing our excellent public library, less wealthy parents can provide their children more books, magazines, and newspapers then the wealthiest citizen of our community could ever hope to purchase. Poorer children could arrive at school with the same background of reading experiences as their wealthier classmates.

Wealthy people tend to travel, visit museums, and attend concerts and other cultural events more than their lower income neighbors. Such activities give their children a broader background for the complex learning tasks that are required of students in a modern school. Less wealthy parents could never afford such enriching experiences but they can partially make up for this by taking advantage of the opportunities that are available. Our local historical society offers a wealth of information at little cost. Many inexpensive cultural events are available, even in our small community. Public television provides excellent vicarious travel around the world.

I gave just a few examples of how parents can provide for their children to have an extra advantage in school. It does take a good bit of effort on the part of parents though, if they are going to *act rich*. It is certainly easier at the end of a hard day's work to sit in the easy chair and watch TV than to take the kids to the library. It is also much easier to watch a mind numbing comedy than a documentary on some faraway place.

Serious thought takes more effort than casual mental drift, but for the developing minds of children, stimulating experiences at home are essential to high quality learning at school. If Michigan's taxpayers want a significant improvement in the public schools without increased taxes, they can start by convincing parents to act as if they are rich. (*Perspective*, 1995, September 20)

## It Takes the Whole Village

Some years ago, I attended the first staff meeting of the school year at our local public schools. All employees of the school meet together at the beginning of the school year. The agenda included a variety of items such as greetings from the superintendent, introduction of all new employees, and in-service on blood-borne pathogens. Of special interest to me was a short presentation by the Board President.

In his very first statement, the President acknowledged that it took more than classroom instructors to provide a proper education to the district's children. He identified classroom aides, custodians, maintenance and grounds workers, bus

drivers, cooks, coaches, counselors, the school nurse, secretaries and office workers, administrators, and board members. That is quite a list, I thought, of essential
people to support instruction that takes place in the classroom in our school system.

The Board President continued by acknowledging that schooling today is different from what it was half a century ago when he was a student. In his childhood,
he noted that schooling primarily concentrated on the 3Rs, reading, writing, and
arithmetic. Of course, students were taught the other common subjects, but not
much of, what is called today the "frills" of education was available to students.
Nor did schools have all of the nonteaching support staff that are usually available
now. As in the past, our district employees today give the same compassionate
personal attention and care to our children. The two paragraphs that follow are
taken from the *Perspective* written in response to my observations that day.

> From my perspective, the Board President is correct in his analysis of the work
> carried on in our local public schools and the accolades he gives to the people who
> serve us there. The public schools in Berrien Springs provide a good place for kids.
> It is a safe environment supportive of high academic standards. They have become
> the schools of choice in this part of the state. Well over 200 kids from other districts
> have applied to attend the Berrien Springs schools this year. People around us know
> what a good thing we have here in our town.
>
> However, good schools do not just happen by accident. It does indeed take the whole
> village to do the job (Van Hoose & Legrand, 2000). It takes good leadership at the
> schools and it takes dedicated teachers and other workers to provide the setting for
> good schooling. It takes strong families and supportive parents who take the job of
> parenting seriously. In addition, it takes a good interface between home and school.
> It also takes the rest of us to provide a community that is a good place for children
> to grow up and learn. (*Perspective*, 2003, August 27)

## THE HOME ENVIRONMENT

Language is the medium through which much learning takes place (Goldin-Meadow, 2014). A child who has a good mastery of the mother tongue is at a distinct
advantage when s/he arrives at school and is placed in a learning situation with
formal instruction. Parents are the first teachers of their children and how they
verbally interact with them has a big impact on their future educational accomplishments (Hindman, Skibbe, & Foster, 2014). Thus, it is suggested that parents
talk to the children from the moment of birth using Standard English. They should
not use "baby talk," which inhibits the child's language acquisition.

Parents would do well to include listening as an important communication
device. That enables them to engage in real dialogue with their young children.
When children arrive at school with five years of experience in adult language,
they are certainly ready to learn at an optimal pace.

Next is the matter of the written word. A good strategy is for parents to read to their children at an early age. Some homes with preschool children have a regularly scheduled reading time. This family tradition might be maintained even after the children are enrolled in formal schooling and are reading on their own. The whole family becomes bookworms in the process. It might sound like parenting is a full-time occupation. That certainly could be true. A *Perspective* provides some strategies for parents.

> When kids go off to school, a parent's life sometimes gets more complicated. It is a challenge to keep up with a child's schedule with a full range of school activities. As kids advance in the grades, the matter of homework becomes an additional challenge. A good strategy for parents is to find some means of communication with their child's teachers regarding what the expectations are for schoolwork that is sent home. Teachers can give good counsel on how parents can be most helpful with homework. There should be a quiet place where kids can do their schoolwork without interruption. It is usually not a good strategy for parents to do the assigned activity themselves. Their best involvement is to see that the assignment is completed. They can also see that the work gets to school so the child gets credit for its completion.

> This business of communication between home and school is very important to the educational process (Adams, Forsyth, & Mitchell, 2009). Schooling (and life in general) is a confusing matter for many children and dealing with teachers and large numbers of other children is sometimes bewildering to them. Little problems frequently seem earth shattering and they tend to magnify in the telling. Parents need to support their children and they need good strategies to do so. One is to reserve judgment on school matters until they have heard all sides of a situation. Usually little problems at school can be solved with good communication although sometimes there needs to be direct adult intervention. In that case, the best strategy is for the home and school to work together in a cooperative manner.

> The final strategy I have to suggest is more global in nature. Create a culture of learning and achievement within the home. Make educational achievement an integral part of family life. Encourage the kids to do their best work in school and do not let them turn in sloppy homework assignments. (*Perspective*, 2007, April 25)

In the small rural district where I live, it is traditional that near the end of the school year the 10 top students of the graduating class are given a special honor. Recognizing the importance of parents to the educational process, the high school principal invites parents to join their offspring for the short ceremony. As a board member, I always enjoyed attending these events and hearing what students had to say about their parents. Not all parents in our community take their educational responsibility so seriously, but enough do to make an impact on the quality of learning in the school district. A *Perspective* provides some additional focus on parents' responsibility in preparing their children to succeed in school

Fortunately, many parents in our community do take seriously their responsibility for the education of their children. They introduce them to books and learning at an early age. They limit the amount of television they watch and monitor carefully the type of programs they see. They provide stimulus for their child's intellectual curiosity and are not annoyed when they are bombarded by endless questions. Such parents are a joy to school people and in return find their child's school experiences a joy.

What concerns me is the increasing number of children who have never seen a book until they start formal schooling. Their parents do not read to them and the world of books is quite a foreign experience. They never hear adults using grammatically correct complete sentences. Thus, their language development is stunted and it is no surprise that they have difficulty learning to read. Children from such homes seldom end up in the top ten students in high school for even if the school does its very best; the parents have not done their job.

Therefore, here is an appeal to parents: if you want your children to be among those with high academic success when they complete high school, take note of the role parents of such children play in their success. It is not enough just to choose a high quality school for your offspring. (Reece, Staudt, & Ogle, 2013), you must also be a high quality parent. The time to start on that important project is right now. (*Perspective*, 2005, May 25)

## A CULTURE OF LEARNING

Some time ago, I noted that the public school boards spent a good sum of money on professional development for their teachers. Reading instruction was the focus of the expenditures for which boards voted. It may seem somewhat strange that qualified teachers need to go back to school and learn how to teach. I defended the administration's action in recognizing that our knowledge base about how children learn and under what conditions they learn the best is still primitive. We must always be ready to learn more about the teaching-learning process.

One of the greatest challenges, both to parents and teachers is that a wide variety of learning abilities are found among the school population. This is especially apparent when it comes to the ability of children to read. What is needed to make reading instruction in the public schools successful is a partnership between the schools and parents, because parents are the first instructors of children. This is especially true when it comes to language formation. Parents, and/or other frequent caregivers, are the ones who teach children the rudiments of the English language.

I make no claim to expertise in human development, but it seems that parents can do a few simple things to help provide their children with the tools needed to succeed in school. For example, parents can model the proper use of language generally by speaking in complete sentences to their children and using adult vocabulary. Baby talk is cute, but it does not help children develop good language skills. As students grow and develop, parents ought to carry on regular conversations with them about all aspects of life so that, when children arrive at school, they are not only well developed in the language, but are also knowledgeable about life in general. With the all pervasiveness of learning experiences, children develop a culture of learning.

A number of years ago, I attended a presentation on social issues that perplex our political leaders. One of the experts in healthcare startled the audience when he indicated that no healthcare solution exists to the health problem in America. He explained his statement by reminding the audience that science has well defined what we must do to be healthy. Good health involves various aspects of diet and exercise. If people do not live the way they know they should, there will not be any improvement in the overall health of our nation until the American people follow the rules of good health.

As I pondered that statement, it occurred me that the same advice might apply to education. We know children's environment during the preschool years, heavily impacts their learning in school. The challenge now is for parents to make learning an integral part of family life. A *Perspective* speaks to that issue:

> Children whose parents provide purposeful learning experiences for them have a much better opportunity to learn in the formal environment of the school. Unfortunately, too few children come developmentally prepared for school. Teachers make a heroic effort to help kids catch up, but from my perspective that is almost a lost cause. When a student arrives at school never having heard an adult speak a grammatically correct sentence, he is at a distinct disadvantage. The classroom teacher is hard pressed to make up for the time the child should have been learning from the adult world outside of school.

> Contrast this with the advantaged child who has not only experienced adult conversation but has been exposed to the larger world of ideas. At a research conference I recently attended, a Rabbi told of his experience growing up in a Jewish family. Each evening at the dinner table, his father would lead in a discussion of theology, politics, philosophy, or some other stimulating topic. Even as a young child, he was expected to dispute his father's statements. There ensued a real family fight, an intellectual one of course. This child arrived at school far more ready to learn than one raised on Roseanne's guttural pronouncements. *(Perspective,* 1997, November 19)

It is the creation of just such a culture of learning in homes and communities throughout the nation that would most positively influence American students who are academically behind their classmates. Some evidence of this is found in the study of children who are homeschooled. While the research is not entirely conclusive, most of the findings point to the efficacy of homeschooling (Cogan, 2010). This is not because parents are better instructors than highly educated teachers are, but primarily because the all-encompassing atmosphere of the home school gives strong support to continuous learning. Homeschoolers, especially those who participate in an organized circuit of like-minded parents, develop cultures where learning is a normal part of everyday home life. This is a worthy goal for all families who want the best education for their children.

## Leveling the Playing Field

The introductory section to this chapter cited the work of James Coleman regarding a comparison of public and private schools. (Coleman & Hoffer, 1987)

Some public school apologists have suggested that there should be a leveling of the playing field when comparing the two kinds of schools. In response, the following *Perspective* suggested an alternative approach:

> From my perspective, the best way to level the playing field between the two types of schools is to develop a culture of learning in the public schools rather than to impose new regulations on private schools. In this, the public must give massive support. Such a culture starts not with the school but with the home. Parents must develop a culture of learning for their children. This is not as difficult as it may seem.
>
> One researcher, who is an expert in language development, told me that if a parent would just talk to their child every day in complete sentences (not baby talk) from the moment of birth it would do a great deal to develop not only language ability but also basic learning capacity. Beyond that, a parent should read to their children at least a half hour each day, she suggested. Parents can do many other things to ensure that their children arrive at school ready to learn, but these are basic to the effort. (*Perspective*, 2004, April 21)

## Form a Tactical Partnership

A few years back, I discussed public education and how it is organized in America today with a non-educator business friend of mine. Yet, he had a distinct interest in how the schools function and read a good bit of the current literature on the subject, especially those authors finding fault with the public schools. At issue was the instructional technique utilized by most teachers. I was somewhat familiar with that literature, much of which originated with the cultural revolution of the late 1960s. I do have some thoughts on the other side of the issue. However, not much of an argument existed between us even when he asserted that the public expects too much from their schools. He was well aware that heredity and parental nurturing are major factors in student learning.

Days later as I was reminiscing about our conversation, I was reminded of a then recent meeting of the public school board. It was held in a large auditorium, which was packed with parents and other relatives who came to witness the main event on the agenda. The students who passed all sections of the state assessment test at the proficient level were individually honored as part of the ceremony and were given certificates by a member of the board and personal congratulations from the Superintendent. It was really an exciting experience for young students to be awarded and recognized. Two paragraphs from a *Perspective* provide a follow-up experience:

A few days later, I discussed this event with a young friend of mine in grade three. "Oh, I did not get a certificate," she said. "My father just brought me there to see the other kids get their awards." That, from my perspective, is an example of a father who has his priorities straight. He evidently sees the importance of school achievement and desires his own child to be influenced by other children who do achieve. This father's action in support of the school helps build a foundation upon which teachers can do their best work in the process of formal education.

What seems to work best in the business of schooling is when parents and children team up with the school to form a tactical partnership in the process of formal learning (Coulombe, 1995). What does not work is when either parents or children fight the system. There has been a long-standing argument as to who, parents or teachers, plays the pre-eminent role in helping children learn. To me it does not matter. What does matter is that teachers and parents work collaboratively in helping children learn. It appears that in our local community such collaboration is happening at a significant level. I give my congratulations to both the schools and the parents for their success in this important endeavor. (*Perspective*, 2007, February 28)

## Supporting Academic Rigor

A few years ago, I finally decided to unpack many of my professional files, accumulated through 40 years of teaching and administration. This activity brought back many memories as I perused the contents of each file folder. In one file, I found only two pieces of paper that had significant meaning in my professional life. They contained the first part of the first draft of the research proposal for my doctoral dissertation. It was what I had actually presented to my professor along with the comments he had written directly on my paper in response to the proposal. The professor had been a high school English teacher early in his career, and he knew how to mark-up student papers. He wielded his instrument of correction with great vigor on my two hapless pages.

That research proposal took multiple drafts before it was acceptable. Yet, this was only one in a long line of confrontations I have had with the forces of academic rigor. Some years later, I was responsible for a system of church related schools in two Midwestern states. In talking with the mother of one of the students she remarked, "My daughter is so happy here and she is doing so well in school compared to the previous school she attended," she said. "She is getting all As and Bs this year where last year at the other school she got mostly Cs and Ds on her report card."

I was immediately suspicious that the suddenly improved grades might not be indicative of an increase in learning at the new school. My concerns were proven correct when the school's standardized test scores were released. While students at the school consistently earned high grades, the test scores were considerably lower. A serious disconnect existed between academic expectations of the school and what it takes to develop serious intellectual output. A *Perspective* naturally followed:

Schools do their students no favor by giving them easy tasks in their classwork. Classroom teachers who do not confront their students with an atmosphere of academic rigor are not worthy of their calling. The earlier in their school experience that they have this confrontation; the better it is for children. High learning output takes a high-level of input, both on the part of the teacher and the student. Kids in school will not normally submit themselves to intense mental discipline without prodding from the professional educators.

Many teachers in both public and private schools shrink back from confronting their young learners with the demands of serious intellectual discipline because they know the kids will complain to their parents and parents in turn will complain to the school administration. No parent likes having an unhappy child at home and no school administrator likes dealing with unhappy parents and kids.

From my perspective, the answer to all this is not to provide an artificially easy and pleasant atmosphere in which learning is to take place. Instead, parents and educators might team up together to determine the proper level of pressure that should be placed on students so they have maximum output as far as intellectual development is concerned (George, 1977). When kids complain to their parents about how "mean" the teachers are with all that homework, parents can fill their proper role by lovingly consoling their disconsolate offspring, and then providing the time, place, and atmosphere that is conducive for them to get on with the task of completing their homework.

I cannot emphasize enough this business of home/school partnership in confronting students with academic rigor. It is essential that parents and educators be united in seeing that their children get a quality education. Quality will not happen unless a sufficient level of rigor is included in the educational process. (*Perspective*, 2011, September 21)

## IN MATTERS OF DISCIPLINE

The county-wide daily newspaper printed where I live, in the southwest corner of Michigan, published a letter from a complaining parent who criticized the school board for being overly harsh in matters of discipline. The mother noted the large number of children in the district who were labeled as having "behavioral problems." The responding *Perspective* included the following two paragraphs:

From my perspective, a parent whose child is labeled by the school district as having behavioral problems, should view this situation with alarm. Instead of complaining about the school district, s/he should join forces with the schools to help correct the child's problem. While the parent should continue to love the boy unconditionally, s/he should demonstrate that love by insisting that he correct his behavior problem. That is more important than any academic learning that could take place at the school.

When he sees that the parents and the school form a united front, he will more easily develop the habit patterns that are necessary for acceptable behavior in today's society. He will also benefit more directly from the instruction he receives at school. Children who are causing disruptions cannot be doing their best learning of the academic content. (*Perspective*, 2007, December 5)

In considering parental relationships to schools over matters of discipline, I learned most of this topic from personal experience. My parents allowed me to attend a private boarding school at some distance from home. Although my parents were strict in their rules of the house, I found the boarding school somewhat more unreasonable in officials' control of student behavior. The prescriptive rules of the school severely impinged on my desired lifestyle. The tyrant who was head of the place was not impressed by my proclamation of a constitutional right to "freedom of speech."

We had other disagreements such as the exact legal description of the boundaries of campus. I took a much more liberal view than he did. Because of one such dispute, the dictator called the entire faculty together, and they took official action that the school would be a better place if I were not among its student body. What a shock that was to me. I admitted to myself that I liked the school and that I really did want to stay there. I decided to appeal my case to the Supreme Court, which in this event had only one justice, my father.

In a phone call to Dad, I complained bitterly about the unfair discipline I had received at the hands of the school dictator. Dad was angry about the shabby treatment meted out to his firstborn son and called the chair of the board of trustees. He demanded that I be reinstated to the school and given a due process hearing so my rights could be protected.

> The answer was "Absolutely not!" What he told me made a lasting impression and proved to be a valuable lesson in life. My remembrance of his exact words fifty years after the event is somewhat blurred but the message is just as clear as if he had delivered it today "Son" he said. "You need to learn to comply with the reasonable requests of school authority. Now, if you really want to stay at that school, I suggest that you get down on your hands and knees and crawl down the hall to the principal's office and beg forgiveness for your bad behavior. You kiss his feet, cry and blubber, and promise on six stacks of Bibles that you will happily obey the rules of the school. If he is foolish enough to reinstate you to the school, I will let you stay. Otherwise, pack your things and get home where I can keep an eye on you. (*Perspective*, 2005, March 30)

The rest of the story is instructive. The faculty heard my pleas for mercy and agreed to reinstate me as a student. However, they put severe restrictions on my activities and what few freedoms students normally had were not available to me. I made it through the academic year without further drama.

From my perspective, schoolchildren should obey the reasonable requests of their teachers. In return, teachers should treat the students with respect. Teachers should also be willing to have a dialogue with students about the reasonableness of their classroom behavior rules. However, the classroom is not the place for extended arguments on student behavior to take place. Students should cooperate with teachers as they present lessons and reserve arguments about the rules for after the school day is completed. In addition to gaining knowledge of the subject matter, students are well served if they develop an internal comfort with compliance to simple requests of those in authority.

## SOME FINAL THOUGHTS

This chapter presented a series of *Perspectives* regarding parents and how they can best work with school officials in the educational process. Education is more than passing on to the next generation, the accumulated store of humankind's knowledge. Even this mundane task is more effectively accomplished when parents and educators are joined together in a partnership. Public school teachers are formally educated in the techniques of instruction. Even so, parents are actually the first teachers of their children. Moments after babies are born, they can feel the influence of their parents.

The process of educating children is a long-term project. Some parents get heavily involved in the school activities of their children while others merely watch from afar. Unfortunately, too many parents appear to be unaware of the needs of their offspring when it comes to support at school. From my perspective, the best thing our political leaders could do would be to develop public policy in a way that encourages parents to have more involvement in the education of their children. If such a policy was put in place and managed well, public schools in America would indeed be transformed.

## LIST OF *PERSPECTIVES* REFERENCED

Published in *The Journal Era,* Berrien Springs, Michigan

1995, September 20. Act like you are rich
1997, November 19. A solution to the educational problem
2003, August 27. At the beginning of the new school year
2004, April 21. A culture of learning
2005, March 30. The most important things schools teach
2005, May 25. Ten in a row
2007, April 25. Some strategies for parents
2007, December 5. To a complaining parent
2007, February 28. A tactical partnership for schools
2011, September 21. Confronting academic rigor

## REFERENCES

Adams, C. M., Forsyth, P. B., & Mitchell, R. M. (2009, February). The formation of parent-school trust: A multilevel analysis. *Educational Administration Quarterly, 45*(1), 4–33.

Cogan, M. F. (2010, Summer). Exploring academic outcomes of homeschooled students. *Journal of College Admission,* (208), 18–25.

Coleman, J. S., & Hoffer, T. (1987). *Public and private high schools: The impact of communities.* New York: Basic Book.

Coulombe, G. (1995, January). Parental involvement: A key to successful schools. *NASSP Bulletin, 79,* 71–75.

George, W. C. (1977). Parental support—Time and energy. *The Gifted Child Quarterly, XXI*(4), 555–558.

Goldin-Meadow, S. (2014, July supplement). In search of resilient and fragile properties of language. *Journal of Child Language, 41,* 64–77.

Hindman, A., Skibbe, L., & Foster, T. (2014, February). Exploring the variety of parental talk during shared book reading and its contributions to preschool language and literacy: Evidence from the Early Childhood Longitudinal Study: Birth cohort. *Reading & Writing, 27*(2), 287–313.

Lam, G. (2014). A theoretical framework of the relation between socioeconomic status and academic achievement of students. *Education, 134*(3), 326–331.

Mol, S. E., & Neuman, S. B. (2014). Sharing information books with kindergartners: The role of parents extra-textual talk and socioeconomic status. *Early Childhood Research Quarterly, 29*(4), 390–400.

Reece, C. A., Staudt, M., & Ogle, A. (2013). Lessons learned from a neighborhood-based collaboration to increase parent engagement. *School Community Journal, 23*(2), 207–225.

Van Hoose, J., & Legrand, P. (2000). It takes parents, the whole village, and school to raise the children. *Middle School Journal, 31*(3), 32–37.

# CHAPTER 6

# LIFE IN THE CLASSROOM

## VISITING SCHOOL

Early in my teaching career, the principal of our small religiously-affiliated school scheduled a day each year for faculty to visit some other school either public or private. Sometimes we went as a group. The faculty numbered only 10 or 12, so we did not overwhelm any of the schools we visited. One year, the principal allowed the faculty to make individual choices regarding in which school they would observe.

I wanted to go to a school where I would be the only one from our school visiting there that day. For that reason, I chose an elementary school quit similar to my own, but with a larger enrollment than where I was currently teaching. It was about 100 miles distant from my place of employment.

I knew just a little bit about the school and had established a friendship with one of the teachers. In discussing with him what I might observe, he suggested that I visit both of the seventh grade classrooms. The middle school concept was not widespread in those days; many schools, particularly the smaller ones, had self-contained classrooms with one person responsible for teaching all the subjects. On my friend's advice, I scheduled a half-day visit in each of the grade 7 classrooms.

*Helping Parents Understand Schools: A Different Perspective on Education and Schooling in America,* pages 85–104.

That choice was most beneficial for me because that is the grade I was teaching.

## A Tale of Two Classrooms

In the first classroom that I observed, the teacher was a middle-aged gentleman, nicely dressed in a well-worn business suit. It was very quiet in the classroom. This was evidently the standard because as the children came into the room, they immediately got quiet. By the time the tardy bell rang, all students were in their assigned seats, and ready to go to work. I recoiled at the dictatorial demeanor of the teacher who was almost military in his control of the classroom. "These are seventh grade students, not little children," was the thought that ran through my mind as the teacher reprimanded a student who had opened his desktop to get a pencil without permission.

Initially, I had very negative thoughts about the teacher and questioned his effectiveness as an instructor. However, I decided to reserve judgment until I had spent more time in observation. Not long after the incident I just described, I noticed that a quiet respect existed between the teacher and his students. While he seemed very rigid, he also seemed to have a good personal relationship with each of the students. I had learned, by that time in my career, that personal contact in building positive relations with students was an important ingredient in effective teaching (Ellerbrock et al., 2015).

It seemed to me, as I continued my observation throughout the morning, that what appeared to be an overly rigid teacher had found the secret to good interpersonal relationships with young people who are just entering their teenage years. This perception was corroborated during the short recess in the morning when the students gathered around the teacher and engaged in informal discussion as they walked to the playground. It was an eye-opening experience for me, although I never tried to be as rigid and strict as he was.

My visit for the afternoon was in the classroom right beside the first one. It was the polar opposite of what I had observed in the morning. The teacher was a vivacious young woman who was fashionably dressed and seemed to be no more than 25 or 26 years old, although she was probably a few years older than that. Her classroom seemed to be in a state of constantly fluctuating chaos, and her role appeared to be stimulator of all that commotion. My first thought was, "How can any learning take place in such a noisy room with everybody seeming to be on the move? The teacher glided from student group to student group as they were working on a project they had been assigned prior to my arrival. They engaged in good-natured banter and joking as they did their class work. I later discovered some scholarly support for a casual atmosphere in the classroom (York, 2012). After my visitation, I spent some time reflecting on what I just observed in the two rooms. They each had vastly different expectations for student behavior within the classroom. Yet, as I observed closely, it seemed a good learning experience was available for students in either of the classrooms. Evidently the teachers had communicated their expectation quite well (Lane, Pierson, Stang, & Carter, 2010) and managed in a way that was neither oppressive nor permissive. Thus, both teachers were able to achieve their educational goals, regardless of the method used in doing so.

## A Quick Look at a Modern Classroom

Some things never change in schools, but other things are always subject to change. The combination of these two factors often confuses parents and others who have fond memories of "the way it used to be." Few schoolrooms today have rigid seating arrangements as in "the good old days." The modern classroom is noted for its bustling activity. Observers note a much greater emphasis on student-centered learning as opposed to teacher-centered or textbook-centered learning (Deakin, 2012). In such classrooms, the teacher's role is more of a guide on the side, rather than a sage on the stage.

Students in today's schools are more frequently involved in collaborative learning where they work together as a group, rather than individually on their assignments. Technology, of course, pervades the learning atmosphere and is frequently used to connect students with the world outside the confines of the classroom (Scogin & Stuessy, 2015).

While some schools using student-centered techniques have found a decrease in discipline problems since the students are more engaged than in traditional classrooms, others find that no matter what they do, their classrooms are somewhat like a war zone. Teachers are overwhelmed with trying to keep order while at the same time engaging the students in real learning.

Many teachers and administrators have had success with classroom management systems that consider the whole learning experience and environment of the classroom rather than just dealing with a naughty child's misbehavior. The most successful of these systems seem to be those that involve the students taking responsibility for their own actions. Student centered learning and student centered behavior seem to go hand in hand (Parish & Mahoney, 2006).

## THE ROAD AHEAD

This introductory section merely touched the surface regarding what life is like in the typical American classroom. More detail is presented in the remainder of the chapter. It is divided into four additional main sections that provide a comprehensive look at American education in the twenty-first century.

First, schools utilize a much more challenging curriculum than was the case just a few years ago. That topic is followed by a section on higher-order thinking. Sometimes referred to as critical thinking, this is a skill that requires deeper thought processes, which are necessary, today and in the future, for success in the American workplace.

A major section focuses on the culture of the classroom rather than the individual students. Several Perspectives identify a variety of approaches to instructional technique. Different children learn differently. When teachers rely on only one teaching method, it is more likely that some of the students will not be able to grasp either the content or concepts as well as if a variety of approaches to presenting the lesson had been used.

The final section explores the comprehensive nature of the teaching profession. Teachers do much more than just give assignments and grade papers. They have responsibility for many other aspects of student life. One major factor that affects the work of a teacher is the high level of diversity found in many American public schools. Two Perspectives provide some focused thinking on this situation.

## A CHALLENGING CURRICULUM

Several years ago, a friend of mine convinced me to take the American Civic Literacy test that was popular among some circles of politically conservative citizens. That crowd is vocal about the importance of preserving knowledge of the past. The examination was available on the World Wide Web. As my friend explained, this assessment of historical knowledge was administered to thousands of recent college graduates who did very poorly on it. The low scores of those who took the test indicated that American college graduates do not *know* much about the history and culture of their native land.

I took the test and found it quite difficult. It included a broad range of questions about America's history, the Constitution, and philosophical foundation, such as those found in economics and political science courses. It was hard stuff! A few questions required only a recall of basic facts. However, several of the questions required a synthesis of information one should know about our country. It assumed that the test-taker had at least a surface knowledge of the writings of major economic theorists.

To be successful, one had to not only know a lot about America's past, but also be able to synthesize the information and assign meaning to it regarding the broader issues of the American experiment with democracy. I passed the test but I have an advantage over the average person. I read a lot, including many of the topics on the test. Just as important, I am a good guesser, which was very useful in getting me through graduate school. Unfortunately, the media has been quite willing to make judgments about America's public schools based on student scores on such tests.

### Hard Stuff

As a follow-up to my confrontation with the Civic Literacy test, a *Perspective* was published on the topic that included the following two paragraphs:

Speaking of hard stuff, last week I spent several hours visiting seventh-grade at the Middle School in our little village. In math, the students were studying the intricacies of the quadratic equation. Yes, seventh graders wrestle with the big Q these days. Through the fog of more than five decades, some of it came back to me. The next class was science where Newton's third law was the subject of interest. The young gentleman who was my guide for the day was called upon to give an explanation. He did so with considerable ease. However, to one of my generation it was hard stuff. I am glad I got out of school when I did.

From my perspective, the curriculum that students are expected to master today is much more challenging than that of earlier generations. It is all the fashionable thing to criticize our educational institutions, be they the middle schools or the halls of ivy. Educators have a challenge of covering a wide spectrum of knowledge that is deemed necessary for successful people in modern society and at the same time meet the needs of a diverse population. While the poor scores on the Civic Literacy Test may call into question the effectiveness of schooling in America, one must remember that formal schooling is just the beginning of learning. It prepares us for what should be a lifelong experience of learning. Most of the stuff, I know that was covered on the exam, I have learned since getting out of school. (*Perspective,* 2008, May 7)

During my several years of visiting classrooms in the public schools, I noticed a subtle change in topics of interest among students. Imagine my surprise while visiting a middle school, to find that more than half of the girls identified math as their favorite subject. Part of it may have been charisma of one of the math teachers, but that cannot account for all of the girls that were interested in the subject of math and/or science. Such a change in the way students view subject matter is quite unusual. It seems that when students are confronted with more challenging work, they are more motivated than if they are tasked with what they consider simplistic assignments (Motivate students with challenging work, 2000). A *Perspective* describes my observation in a classroom.

On another day, I visited a fifth grade classroom where I got an interesting look at mathematics instruction in the middle grades. The class I visited was studying algebra. Yes, algebra in the fifth grade. They were learning to solve some complex equations. After the teacher had gone over the lesson, one of the students handed out a worksheet for them to do. He gave it to me also and with the look in his eye, I knew I was expected to do the work. It has been more than half a century since I took a class in algebra, so I found it a bit challenging. I really struggled on a couple of the problems and was tempted to peek at a student's paper who was sitting next to me.

However, I resisted the temptation and completed the work myself. When the kids had finished their worksheets, they took them to the teacher to be graded. Several of them got perfect scores. I was not about to walk up in front of that whole class of kids and have my paper graded, so I just sat quietly in my seat observing what was going on. Then the teacher glanced over at me and smiled. "Are you all done she asked?" I grimaced and nodded. Then she called on one of the students who had a perfect grade. "Why don't you go over and correct his paper and see how well he did." I panicked. With a whole classroom of fifth graders staring at me, I sat there while one of their number graded my work. How pleased I was when he wrote 100% on the top of the paper. So, now I can hold my head up high in our little village. I am as smart as a fifth grader. However, I will save the story of my attempts to do high school work for a later column. Believe me it is nothing to brag about. (*Perspective*, 2009, April 1)

## Removing Artificial Barriers

During my career as an educator, I have worked in a number of different places. In one situation, I was responsible for the operation of a system of parochial schools in a two-state region of the Midwest. Along with an assistant, I visited schools and observed teachers and classrooms all over the two states. One experience I had in a small high school was quite instructive to the concept of quality education in the modern classroom.

The algebra teacher, in whose classroom I was observing, also served as vice principal. He was late to class because he was dealing with an administrative problem. As soon as the tardy bell rang Roscoe, the class clown, stood up in front of the class and announced that, since the teacher was going to be late, he would teach the lesson. I was fascinated as I observed all the students opening up their textbooks as their young teacher requested. He proceeded to introduce the topic for the day and worked some examples of problems they might have in their assignment. He displayed these on the chalkboard, showing each step in the process. Then, after answering some questions students had, he said, "Your assignment is to do the problems on page 95, even-numbered rows."

About that time, the teacher entered the room, and seeing Roscoe up front admonished him for his foolishness. He then told him to go to his assigned seat. I watched in amazement as the teacher presented the lesson almost word for word as Roscoe had done. Meanwhile, the precocious student had finished the assignment and caused one disruption after another during the remainder of the class period. Later in the day, I met with the teacher to discuss my observation of his instructional technique. I informed him of what had transpired prior to his arrival in class.

The teacher was well aware of how bright Roscoe was, especially in mathematics. However, he was much more concerned about his pattern of poor behavior than his academic potential. I made a suggestion regarding the curriculum in the school. It seemed to me, that if Roscoe could teach the lesson, he should not be held back going at the same speed as the other students. "Why not let Roscoe work at his own pace and go through the algebra book as fast as he can?" The teacher was puzzled by my suggestion. "But, he will finish the book by

Christmas time and then what will we do with him?" I paused for a moment, hoping he would be able to answer his own question before I replied. "Why not let him do Algebra II?" I suggested. "But what will he study next year?" was the quick response of the teacher. My summation to this experience is found in a *Perspective* I wrote several years after the event.

I have faced this situation many times in my career as an educator, where structural barriers tend to block good educational procedures. Over the years, our educational system has constructed a number of artificial barriers, which restrict the learning opportunities of many of our young people. Confining students rigidly to grade levels based on their age cohort is one of them. I do not know what happened to Roscoe, but I have long been concerned that he, and many other bright students, has had such barriers restrict his opportunity to learn at the pace suited to his ability. (*Perspective* 2009, September 9)

## HIGHER ORDER THINKING

Several years ago, I discovered a new game show called "Are You Smarter Than a Fifth Grader?" While I do not watch much television, I was drawn to this program because I had, at one point in my career, taught grade 5. I enjoyed watching the program and seeing adults squirm when they were asked questions related to the fifth grade level curriculum. The adults who put themselves forward as contestants frequently had to rely upon a real student who was currently in the fifth grade.

I was able to get most of the questions answered, but I must confess that some of the facts called for had left the recesses of my memory. Most observers from the public were more than a little surprised at the high level of learning that is required of our students. This is especially interesting in view of the critics of American education, who claim that students in our country are shortchanged by the public schools. Two paragraphs from a *Perspective* published at the time expand on this point.

The point of all this is that kids in school today are required to learn at a much higher level than most adults realize (Pinkey & Shaughnessy, 2013). Politicians like to rant and rail against the public schools, but many of them would have to admit that they are *not smarter than a fifth grader* if they were on the game show. From my perspective, kids in America today do in fact get a good education. Unlike many countries in the world, we offer an opportunity to all children to attend a comprehensive school through high school. In many places, fierce competition for scarce seats in the secondary schools results in only the smartest being admitted. Those who do not pass the test are relegated to a trade school where they learn basket weaving or herd goats on the hillside for the rest of their lives.

By contrast, in the United States even marginal students have a chance to get a good academic education, even if they pull the average down when the proficiency tests are graded. They may not learn it all but they are surrounded by a high-level curriculum and teachers who care about their academic future, even if they are slow to catch on. Do you know how many cups in five and a half gallons? If not, do not worry, the fifth grader missed this one by a cup. (*Perspective*, 2007, March 14)

*Making Connections*

One of the benefits of being a member of a public school board is the opportunity to observe the brightest and best of the most creative talent within the district. Wise administrators will frequently arrange for their best teachers to display the most interesting lessons and learning activities for the board to see. One memorable experience during my tenure on the board involved a second grade student who demonstrated a specific technique of teaching reading. The children write their own stories (using a recorder of course) in a multi-step process. They are then typed out and the children use them as their reading textbook.

Effective reading requires a good deal of higher-order thinking, sometimes identified as "critical" thinking (Thompson, 2002). While the presentation involved a simple little essay, the process of reading is more complicated than most people realize. It involves much more than decoding words. As demonstrated by the young boy, reading includes children making connections from the written text to: a) their own experiences, b) to other things they have read, and c) to the world around them. Two paragraphs from a *Perspective* illustrate this in more detail.

> The teachers not only explained the process, but gave an example by having one of their students read his own written work in which he had made connections between a story he had read about a dog and an experience he had with his own dog. It was a simple little connection but it is the start of a long intellectual journey, for this skill will be with him through life. In another little essay he wrote, the student made a connection between two different stories he had read. He found the similarities in certain aspects of the two stories.

> Making connections is a complex mental activity. I imagine most people would be surprised to find this is what second graders are being taught. In fact, one of the adults present remarked that he wished he had such lessons when he was in second grade. Most people in the adult world remember reading as learning how to sound out groupings of letters phonetically on the printed page. While that is the foundation of reading, it certainly is not enough to succeed in today's complicated world. Thankfully, our public schools are giving children the skills they need for life in the 21st century. (*Perspective*, 2007, November 21)

*Visit to a Middle School*

As an older elected member of the public school board in a rural area of Southwest Michigan, I found myself at a distinct disadvantage compared to other board members who had children in attendance at one of the district's schools. I was keenly aware of my lack of inside information on daily life in the schools of our district. I compensated for this inadequacy by visiting each school at least once a year, spending at least half a day observing student life in the classroom.

One memorable visit was to the Middle School. Of the five schools in the district, that was the source of a majority of the discipline problems that were referred to the board. In response to my request, the principal assigned one of the students to be my guide. I followed her through her schedule all morning long. That gave me a distinct picture of what students have to face day after day in school.

It was a most fascinating half day. The first event was hanging out in the gymnasium waiting for the first bell to ring. My guide introduced me to her friends, mostly girls, since the boys were either shooting baskets or huddled in their own corner of the gym. The kids were friendly and willing to dialogue with me about life in the middle school. When I queried them as to their favorite subject, they quickly identified math as the academic study of their choice. This surprised me because in my day, girls were not known to enjoy the study of numbers. Two paragraphs from a *Perspective* give a little more detail to my observations that day.

> I was impressed during the morning with the responsibility placed on students today for their own learning. They have a good deal more independence then in my day. They do much independent research with the teachers helping them to distinguish the difference between valid sources of information and those whose credence is questionable. Further, I found considerable integration of subject matter with assignments crossing the disciplines of math, science, and English. In my day, those were all different subjects taught at different periods during the day.

> The teachers were friendly enough, but had that unmistakable sense of purpose as they guided the young scholars under their care. Crowd control with over three hundred young people, all grappling with the strange new body chemistry that afflicts people of that age group, is a major part of the teacher's assignment. One little lapse of attention and hundreds of chemical reactions reach critical mass and explode down the hallway to interrupt the educational process. (*Perspective*, 2006, April 5)

After my visit to the middle school, I reflected on the challenge that our teachers face every day as they encounter a seething mass of energy. What I observed was a good job of keeping order, and at the same time teaching critical thinking skills. The trick is for teachers to keep an open line of communication with students, while at the same time keeping their energy focused on the process of learning (Godfrey & Grayman, 2014). That is a major challenge in American education

## A VARIETY OF APPROACHES TO CLASSROOM INSTRUCTION

It might seem as if nothing has changed in the last hundred years as far as what goes on in the classroom is concerned. Students still study out of textbooks, and teachers still lecture as their primary teaching method, especially in the secondary schools. Yet, most adults would be in for a big surprise if they were to visit a modern classroom. Educators today use a variety of instructional techniques in addition to lecture and the traditional direct instructional method (Antonacci, 2012).

## The Fuss About Phonics

Several years ago, an editorial in a major national newspaper decried the sad state of American education. Unfortunately, the *Perspective* that followed was written long before I had any thoughts of a book being put together, so I did not save the documentation on any of this. Children, claimed the critic, are not being taught phonics, which is the correct way to teach reading. Children should learn to decode words by learning the bits and pieces of which they are made, said the writer. I wrote the following *Perspective* to show the futility of an instructional focus based solely on phonics.

> The critic's statement echoes the cry of political conservatives for nearly half a century (Flesch, 1955). Since English is a phonetic language, it only makes sense that learning to read it should be done through phonics instruction. Teach kids the sounds of the letters and once they have them memorized, along with the rules of phonics, then every kid will be able to read. Sounds simple, doesn't it? Unfortunately, it is not that simple. While our language is phonetic, the formalities are confusing. It is very difficult for little children to remember all the rules as they try to read a whole sentence.
>
> For example, in the first paragraph of the story The Three Little Pigs, which consists of 54 words, the letter "a" is pronounced six different ways. The different words that contain the letter "a" are as follows: a, had, are, any, take, care. Seven different words with the letter "e" have different sounds: there, little, the, grew, them, here, mother. If we think that is complex wait until you encounter two letter combinations. Words such as their, said, too, build, and does, do not follow the general rule of phonics. Sound confusing? Imagine what a six-year-old encounters on a daily basis when phonics rules are the only way that is allowed for learning to read. What I have given as an illustration are just some of the words found in one paragraph of a simple little story for children. (This illustration came from a source that I have been unable to find.) Our language is filled with such exceptions to the rules. When kids have only one way to learn this language, they are indeed handicapped. The best evidence we have is that when teachers use a variety of teaching strategies, it is more likely that all the children in the class will learn to read than if only one method is used. Not all children are auditory learners. Some children do not distinguish small differences in sound. For them, phonics instruction is a waste. Moreover, for all children, the many exceptions to the rules of phonics make for a confusing situation at reading time. (*Perspective,* 2001 April 25)

For many years (actually decades), critics of the public schools have identified teaching of reading without a strong emphasis on phonics as the root cause of the "failure" of public education. They look, with a great amount of nostalgia, at the time in the 19th and early 20th century when the rules of phonics were predominant in American schools. They seem to ignore the fact that in those days, most of the children in the country never completed high school. In today's world, we would not allow that large a dropout rate to exist.

Language acquisition is a very complex process (Pinker, 2007). Developing the ability to gain meaning from language in its written form shares in that complexity. Success in the formal approach to education is highly dependent on the preparation children have prior to their enrollment in the school system. Parents who talk to their children in grammatically correct complete sentences, read to the children from an early age, and surround them with a wide variety of reading material, give their children a sound preparation that the more formal schooling will build upon. Whatever the situation, the child who has lived in an environment rich in language has a distinct advantage at entrance into formal schooling. It takes more than phonics to have an effective instructional program in reading.

## Controlled Observation

On another occasion, I visited a first grade class during science time. The students were working through a process the teacher had taught them in a previous lesson. It consisted of the various steps in the scientific process, observe, predict, test, and conclude. From an adult standpoint, it was a simplistic little experiment and quite boring to someone in the educated adult world. I had seen that demonstration on other occasions. Then I remembered this was a first grade classroom and these were six-year-olds. Yet, they were dealing with words such as meteorology, precipitation, and condensation. Starting in first grade, they were being trained to make scientific observations. A *Perspective* tells the rest of the story.

> It was this background knowledge of science that helped them make predictions about what would happen if they put ice cubes in a tin can in a warm room. Working in groups of four or five they first observed an empty can, each one in turn feeling how warm and dry it was. They then recorded their observations and made a prediction as to what would happen if they put ice in the cans. As good little scientists, they did not just make a wild guess about what might happen. They based their prediction on what they already knew about the laws of nature—the things other scientists have discovered. They predicted, of course, that the ice cubes would make the tin cans cold and then applying their knowledge of precipitation they predicted that the surface of the cans would become wet. However, as good scientists, they were not satisfied to accept the conventional wisdom on the laws of nature. They had to test it for themselves. They were not disappointed, for when the teacher put ice cubes in the tin cans they became cold and with the warm air of the classroom little drops of water appeared on the surface of the cans. They concluded that when warm air meets a cold surface, precipitation occurs.

> What would have happened, I wondered, if they had predicted that the cans would remain dry? Would they have continued to deny the evidence of the drops of water they observed on the tin cans filled with ice? Probably not, although they would have been justified in conducting more experiments before arriving at a conclusion. However, eventually observation would lead to a correct conclusion. (*Perspective*, 2006, November 22)

## The Self-Directed Learner

As the years accumulate, it is only natural for one to reminisce about the good old days of the past. Schools have been the center of my life, both as a child and, as an adult. I have seen major changes in the way we do school over that period of time. My second grade teacher enforced discipline by spanking our hands with a thick wooden ruler. The desks were nailed to the floor and we were not allowed leave the assigned place without permission. In fourth grade, I had what was considered to be a progressive teacher. She actually differentiated instruction and divided us into three learning groups. I languished in the lowest group for half a year before I caught on to what learning was all about. A *Perspective* expands on the topic.

Things are a bit different now where schools make accommodation to a variety of learning styles (Dieker, 2014). Kids are not rigidly kept on the same pace in every class. Teachers are particularly adept at giving individual help. Moreover, students in modern classrooms have much more flexibility. They are actually allowed to move around the class during study time and get help from the other students. Sometimes they are assigned to work together in groups on special projects.

While there have been many changes in schooling during my lifetime, many more will come. Schools of the future will be quite different. Teachers will not be primarily dispensers of information; rather they will be more like guides as students search for information on their own. Learning will be much more self-directed with students actually prescribing their own curriculum at times. Flexibility in schooling will be taken to an extreme. Self-initiated learning will be very common.

Home schooling, which is looked down upon by many school people today, will in the future be viewed as a normal alternative educational process. In fact, the animosity between home schools, private schools, and public schools will mostly disappear with all three forms of education operating together for the benefit of student learners. Some students will do their studies primarily at home while still enrolled in the public school.

Computerized instruction will make such a thing possible. Students will be allowed to advance in any individual subject as fast as they want; they will not be held back by a rigid graded curriculum. A student in fifth grade might be studying high school algebra even though he is only at the fourth grade level in reading and social studies. That is what education will be in the future. (*Perspective,* 2009, August 5)

Actually, even at the time it was written, that last statement was not correct. The self-directed student learning described is already being used in a number of schools throughout the country. (Ellerbock & Kiefer, 2014) Since then flexibility in schooling has become quite commonplace. It is the method of the present, not something we have to wait for in the future.

*Project-Based Learning*

Educators have for many years attempted to make schooling relevant to the real world of work. It is one thing to have a good grasp of book knowledge but quite another to be able to put that knowledge to good use in a complex situation such as those that most employees find in today's world. It is not just the workplace that has become complex, but everyday life is increasingly complicated. Some years ago, I visited a first grade classroom. What a difference from when I was in first grade. Beginning at that early age, children today learn to work together as a team. They collaborate to complete whole projects, rather than work at an individual level for most of the day.

On a visit to a high school history class, I found the same method being used, only at a much more sophisticated level. Much to my surprise the instructor took her students from the classroom to the cafeteria where they were joined by a junior English class. They worked together on a project centered on the topic of terrorism. I later discovered that project-based learning was of growing interest in American schools (Gonzales, 2015). In this situation, the two teachers worked together as a team, guiding the students in their study of the subject. The reason for meeting in the cafeteria was that no classroom in the building was big enough to hold nearly 50 students. A *Perspective* written soon after my visit gives more details.

I was very interested in observing how the teachers would function with 48 students in the school cafeteria without a public address system. I was also interested to see how the students would respond to the tasks assigned to them by the teachers. This was the first session of a new unit so a good bit of organizational work needed to be done. Teenagers frequently do not respond well to attempts at organization and chaos sometimes ensues.

Not in this class. The kids seemed to know how to work well in groups and found no problem with older students from the English class being teamed with younger students from the history class. Then I remembered that they had first learned how to work in groups with other students in first grade. Teenagers have resonant voices and seldom exercise volume control, so I expected some problems with the poor acoustics of the cafeteria. They were able to keep it under control with a minimum of urging from the two faculty members. They had some simple tasks of getting their group organized for work and some complex tasks dealing with the subject matter. The topic of terrorism has some complexities built into it and I was not sure if teenagers could grapple with them. I need not have worried. The work they submitted indicated to me they had comprehended the reading assignment and drawn from it some real meaning in their own lives. (*Perspective* 2011, March 16)

To verify my observations, I talked to several students after class and discovered that they did, indeed, come to grips with the issue they were studying. Most of the students expressed a positive attitude towards the project-based learning and the complex issues they had to deal with. I also talked to the teachers for a short time. I discovered that they had the authority granted by the administration to determine with whom they would work as a team and what subjects they would develop as part of their curriculum. The school district, both administration and faculty, was very supportive of the project-based learning approach to teaching.

## THE COMPREHENSIVE NATURE OF TEACHING

It was never my intention to become a teacher and certainly not to have an entire career in education. It came to me quite unexpectedly, almost as if I had stepped into a trap. I worked at a number of jobs trying to pay my tuition to get through college. My parents helped me as much as they could, but the rest was on my shoulders. I worked in the furniture factory, and housekeeping unit at the University, at road construction during summers, and in an automotive factory as a welder. I had to drop out of school for a semester for that last job. I was very concerned that I would not be able to retain the job when the summer layoffs for model change occurred.

I happened to be in the administration building at the college I attended one day in early summer, and saw a notice on the bulletin board that quickly captured my attention. It was a help wanted advertisement for a part-time teacher in a public school near where I lived. Michigan faced a shortage of teachers at that time and I was able to qualify for an emergency credential because of the credits I had accumulated in college.

I answered the ad and went for an interview with the principal of the small public school. Since it was such a small school, he was allotted only half days for his principal's work. The other half days he taught the eighth grade class. He needed someone to fill in for that half day. In a strange rotation, the seventh grade teacher switched to the eighth grade in the afternoon, and thus I was hired to teach grade 7 in a rural public school in Southwest Michigan.

I was very aware of my lack of training and preparation for teaching. However, I was in need of a job that would pay more than student wages for on-campus work. I did not intend to become a teacher, and thus I had avoided what was reputed to be those "insipid education classes." I thought in my mind, how hard could it be? Just write the assignments on the black board, watch over the students as they do their work, and then grade the papers. What a surprise I got! The intensity of demands placed upon a classroom instructor is far more than meets the eye (Jones, 2012). It is difficult to make an accurate list of all the things to which classroom instructors must attend. Some of the duties are essential to achievement of curricular goals, while other duties merely impinge upon the teacher's time and energy. I completed the year as a halftime teacher with some degree of success as evidenced by the offer of a full-time contract for the following year. I must say that I gained more information and knowledge about teaching from that experience than in the teacher training courses I eventually had to take.

It became very apparent to me that the formal teacher preparation program did not adequately prepare one for the intense demands of the job. The next three sections provide a glimpse of the comprehensive nature of classroom teaching.

## Classroom Control

Discipline in the classroom is frequently a major problem for teachers, especially those new to the profession. The rather loosely held controls in America's urban schools give the whole profession a bad name and tend to provide critics of public education an opportunity to paint the whole system of public schools with the same negative brush.

For so many years, teacher-training programs put the emphasis on student discipline, mostly on appropriate punishments for misbehavior. That has all been changed. Teacher preparation programs typically teach methods of controlling the whole classroom rather than one individual student at a time. My observation has been, when a system of classroom management is quite rigidly adhered to by the teacher, a minimum of discipline problems will interfere with the teaching/learning process (Parish & Mahoney, 2006). However, when the teacher's guard is down and s/he starts making exceptions to the rules, classroom control quickly flies out the window.

Years ago, my young grandson, who was quite precocious and had an almost adult vocabulary by the time he entered school, discussed the relative merits of being under the care of older people. They are fun to be around, he confided, because "they let you do stuff." I was aware that my own grandson was quite active in school and was in many situations overly impulsive. I thought about my offspring and his analysis of things when I visited a first-grade classroom in our public schools. A *Perspective* resulted from that visit.

I was impressed by the instructional technique I observed. All those restless bodies were in constant movement with lungs ready to spring into action on the slightest impulse. Yet with all the wiggles and squirms, real learning was going on in the classroom. Moreover, it was not just the facts of arithmetic that were on display. The kids were learning the applications of their factual learning as well as the beginnings of algebra. Yes, today kids are being grounded in more advanced mathematics even in first grade. However, it was not only the academic stuff the teacher presented. The children practiced teamwork, cooperation, and control of those ubiquitous impulses.

From my perspective, teachers today have a formidable task with all the demands that are placed upon them. With the compressed content and large class size, it is a challenge to get it all done. In some cases, classroom control takes as much time and energy as teaching the content of the subject. Channeling the vigor of those restless impulsive bodies in a direction that allows for learning, takes real talent. Being with one grandson at a time is a true joy, but I am not sure I would make it with 26 of him all in the same room! (*Perspective,* 2006, February 15)

*Community Expectations*

In many locations throughout America, a public school serves as much more than a place for instruction of children and youth. The schoolhouse essentially becomes a community center, around which much of the life of local citizens revolves. At the same time, teachers are expected to do much more for the community than teach the assigned subject matter to the children under their care. This fact complicates the life of the teacher. Those who are new to the profession find this an unexpected part of their chosen profession. It seems, at times, that every broken part of our society is placed on the public schools for repair (Labaree, 2011). A *Perspective* published at the turn of the 21st century posed as a message to teachers at the beginning of the new school year.

> Thank you for teaching kids to read. That is mainly what we want you to do this school year—teach the kids to read. And write and do some math. And maybe a little history and geography. And give them an appreciation for music and art and literature. And be sure to make them computer literate, and prepared for the work place and for higher education. And teach them to be good citizens. Oh, and by the way, teach them some science. But be very careful how you teach about origins of life. And if possible teach the kids some manners, and how to behave in public and the basic values of our culture, and how to drive a car.

> And provide our kids with health education, and special education, and sex education, and career education and physical education and character education and substance abuse education and while you are doing this please, please do not offend anyone in our diverse community. And whatever you do make sure all the kids pass the MEAP test and please give us another winning football team. That is about all we ask of you teachers. Thank you for doing all this and much more for our children. If I have missed anything, I am sure you will hear about it from parents, taxpayers, or media critics. So try to think of what it might be and add it to the few things I have listed for you before they do. (*Perspective*, 2000, August 30)

While this was written somewhat tongue-in-cheek, it does show in a very stark manner the comprehensive expectations of Americans for their public schools. The teaching profession now has a job description that has been significantly expanded from what it was years ago. That situation probably will not go away; so, educators at all levels might just as well get used to the fact that guiding their students through the intricacies of the subject matter is only a small part of their responsibility (Cooper, 2007).

*Dealing With Diversity*

During my time as a member of the public school board, I made it a practice to visit at least a few classrooms every year. My favorite place to visit was one of the first grade classrooms. The teacher was a master instructor, from my point of view. She was also the president of the teacher's union and a very tough bargainer.

She would not let me merely observe the classroom, but put me to work helping with the activities of the day. The result was I got a good look, from the level of a first grade student, at what life was all about at the beginning of the young person's educational journey.

Unlike my own experiences in first grade, students have much more freedom to move about the classroom. Today, some class assignments actually require the kids to work together and converse with each other. In my day, that would have been considered possible cheating. One time when I visited that first grade classroom, the teacher was helping a small group of children. She asked me to be the resource person for the rest of the class as they worked on their assignment. I thought I could handle first grade work, so I readily accepted the job.

I noticed that the colored pencils available for the children to use were quite blunt, so I volunteered to sharpen them. I did quite well at that task. Then, the moment I dreaded arrived. One of the girls was working on the computer nearby and asked me for help. I tried my best to conquer the mysteries of that unfamiliar software. I gave up when my first grade companion said, "Maybe I should just try a different program." A paragraph from the *Perspective* that followed identified a major change in the way classrooms are run today.

> Some things are still the same after 60 years. The kids in first grade today get a strong dose of phonics in their reading program as they did in my day, although the curriculum now integrates other approaches to instruction in reading. In addition, a strong emphasis on personal values is apparent. Doing one's best, treating others well, making good choices, and taking responsibility for one's own behavior is reflected in the school pledge. Yet, some values are much different (Dack & Tomlinson, 2015). Today, our schools are racially integrated and special needs children are provided an appropriate education. That is a major improvement over schooling in past years. (*Perspective,* 2004, November 10)

Diversity in education has become almost an overworked term. When used with a negative connotation, it usually refers to racial diversity. In further reflection on what I had observed, I noted that a great deal of diversity existed in first grade in regards to many other factors. However, the schools I visited are not representative of public schools across the country. They have a large number of children from other countries where English is not the first language. The reason for this diversity is a nearby University with an international student body. The challenge for classroom teachers is to be aware of the diversity of *culture* as well as *race*.

The school district has embraced the variety of students who come to them, and places a positive value in having them in the classroom (Gottfried, 2014). This attitude makes what could be seen as a serious problem for the faculty, staff and administration, a positive factor for the school district. A *Perspective* written shortly after my visit identifies some of the details in dealing with diversity.

In addition to physical diversity, much variation was apparent in other factors that are more important to the educational process. I noted a large range of skill and ability in the classroom. Some had good verbal abilities with a well-developed vocabulary while others could barely express themselves in the English language. However, I did note a couple of boys who never ceased to express themselves. It is a challenge to teach children to read when they have such a limited vocabulary. It is a much easier job when children arrive at school with a knowledge and understanding of a large number of words used in normal conversation. Some children start school never having heard adults use grammatically correct complete sentences. Books at school are their first experience with such use of the English language.

I also noted a wide variety of prior knowledge that children bring to the classroom. Some of them are very aware of the world around them. They know about other places, other cities, other states, and even other countries. A couple of the children did not even know which street they live on in our own little village. What a challenge the teacher faced with them as she introduced them to the world of social studies including the geography of our own community!

I observed a diversity of behavior patterns within the classroom. Some had well-developed self-control while others needed a good bit of external control by the teacher. A couple of the students seemed to be oblivious even of that authority. They were not belligerent about it; they just did not seem to be able to restrain themselves. They tended to be victims of their own sudden impulses. I thought the teacher exercised amazing patience as she gently encouraged good behavior while keeping focused on the academic lesson at hand. (*Perspective*, 2008, April 30)

## SOME FINAL THOUGHTS

This chapter is the longest and most complex in the book. It was placed in the center of the book because, from my perspective, it is the center of education. When the term classroom is used, it does not necessarily refer to a specific room in a building. The way it is used in this chapter, the term "classroom" has a much broader conceptual base. Any time the mind of the teacher confronts the mind of the student, a classroom is created.

Education is the work of a lifetime and cannot be confined to just the years of formal schooling. That statement, however, should not be interpreted as dismissive of the work of the classroom instructor or the value of associating with other students in an organized learning community. For some students a relationship is the best way for them to be launched on their life of learning. Others do not fit into the regimentation of the traditional school, and sometimes alternative methods serve that student best.

This chapter presented several different ways of looking at classroom instruction. The basic premise is that no one best method fits all of humankind when it comes to the matter of learning. Effective teachers, be they formally trained to the profession or an ordinary person who has intellectual contact with the student, will ever be aware that human beings are unique individuals. Sometimes it takes a great deal of creativity to find that special combination of experiences to unlock the resources for gaining knowledge that reside within the human mind, which is what life in the classroom should provide for every student who attends school, formally or otherwise.

## LIST OF *PERSPECTIVES* REFERENCED

Published in *The Journal Era*, Berrien Springs, Michigan

2000, August 30. A Message to Teachers
2001, April 25. The Bits and Pieces of Words
2004, November 10. On Returning to First Grade
2006, February 15. Wiggle and Squirm into Learning
2006, April 5. Seething Mass of Energy
2006, November 22, Lessons From First Grade Science
2007, March 14. Just How Smart Are You?
2007, November 21. Make the Connection
2008, April 30. Diversity in First Grade
2008, May 7. Hard Stuff
2009, April 1. Smart as a Fifth Grader
2009, August 5, The Future of School
2009, September 9. Removing Artificial Barriers
2011, March 16. Not all Wisdom Emanates From Washington

## REFERENCES

Antonacci, P. (2012). *Promoting literacy development: 50 researched-based strategies for K–8 learners.* Thousand Oaks, CA: Sage Publications.

Cooper, J. E. (2007). Strengthening the case for community-based learning in teacher education. *Journal of Teacher Education, 58*(3), 245–255.

Dack, H., & Tomlinson, C. A. (2015, March). Inviting all students to learn. *Educational Leadership, 72*(6), 10–15.

Deakin, Q. (2012, June). Teaching by the numbers—Inside the modern classroom. *Contemporary Review, 294*(1705), 192–199.

Dieker, L. (2014). *Strategies for teaching content effectively and the inclusive secondary classroom.* Boston, MA: Pearson.

Ellerbock, C., & Kiefer, S. M. (2014, November). Fostering an adolescent-centered community responsive to student needs: Lessons learned and suggestions for middle level educators. *Clearing House, 87*(6), 229–235.

Ellerbrock, C. R., Abbas, B., Diciccio, M., Denmon, J. M., Sabella, L., & Hart, J. (2015, May). Relationships: The fundamental R in education. *Phi Delta Kappan, 96*(8), 48–51.

Flesch, R. F. (1955). *Why Johnny can't read—And what you can do about it.* New York: Harper.

Godfrey, E., & Grayman, J. (2014). Teaching citizens: The role of open classroom climate in fostering critical consciousness among youth. *Journal of Youth & Adolescence, 43*(11), 1801–1817.

Gonzales, L. (2015, May). The project-based learning movement. *District Administration, 51*(5), 88.

Gottfried, M. A. (2014, September). The positive peer effects of classroom diversity. *Elementary School Journal, 115*(1), 22–48.

Jones, B. K. (2012, May.). A new teacher's plea. *Educational Leadership, 69*(8), 74–77.

Labaree, D. F. (2011). Targeting teachers. *Dissent, 58*(3), 9–14.

Lane, K. L., Pierson, M. R., Stang, K., & Carter, E. W. (2010, May/June). Teacher expectations of student's classroom behavior. *Remedial & Special Education, 31*(3), 163–174.

Motivate students with challenging work. (2000). *Curriculum Review, 40*(4), 6.

Parish, T. S., & Mahoney, S. (2006). Classrooms: How to turn them from battlegrounds to connecting places. *Education, 126*(3), 437–440.

Pinker, S. (2007). *The stuff of thought: Language as a window into human nature.* New York: Viking Penguin.

Pinkey, J., & Shaughnessy, M. F. (2013, May). Teaching critical thinking skills: A modern mandate. *International Journal of Academic Research, 5*(3), 346–357.

Scogin, S. C., & Stuessy, C. L. (2015, March). Encouraging greater student inquiry engagement in science through motivational support by online scientists-mentors. *Science Education, 99*(2), 312–349.

Thompson, M. C. (2002). Vocabulary and grammar: Critical content for critical thinking. *Journal of Secondary Gifted Education, 13*(2), 60–67.

York, J. G. (2012). Democratizing laughter. *Philosophical Studies in Education, 43*, 73–83.

# PART III

## MATTERS OF PUBLIC POLICY

# CHAPTER 7

# SCHOOL REFORM

## I BECOME AN EXPERT

I thought it was a rather strange request the principal was making of me. Yet, as a young inexperienced teacher, I realized it might be wise for me to give a positive answer to this veteran administrator. After all, he was my boss. I was teaching in a small religious school in the Midwest at the time. My assignment was to teach all subjects in grades 7 and physical education classes for both boys and girls in grades seven through 10. While I had a college degree, I did not have a teacher's credential. In fact, I had completed only a few of the education courses required for certification.

The principal requested that I enroll in an evening class at a nearby college. The course dealt with teaching the "new math." The Soviet Union had taken a sudden lead in the space race when in October 1957 they launched the first artificial satellite in space known as Sputnik. Americans were shocked. They soon discovered that America did not produce enough engineers, and part of the reason was that the schools did not emphasize mathematics sufficiently. The curriculum was woefully out of date.

Calls for reform resulted in the "new mathematics" curriculum. The principal confided in me that some members of the board were getting a bit restive that our

*Helping Parents Understand Schools: A Different Perspective on Education and Schooling in America,* pages 107–125.

school had not even investigated the new math curriculum. He did not know anything about changes in the subject matter or instructional technique. He asked me to attend the class so somebody on the faculty would know as much about New Math as the board members did. With the desire to please the principal as motivation, I enrolled in the course.

I soon became recognized in our small school as the resident expert on the "New Math." I was not impressed with my rise in status, but I did enjoy the class and the opportunity to learn a new way of teaching. I do not remember much about the shift to the new math, but a few parts of the reformed curriculum did stick with me. A change in approach in the lower grades from arithmetic to mathematics provided for a smoother transition for students as they progressed through the grades. This involved simply arranging problems in a horizontal position rather than vertical as in the arithmetic style. This seemed to prepare the children for algebra much better than the old method.

The reform mathematics curriculum introduced two new topics into the junior high grades: Number bases other than 10, as well as "set theory" challenged students to think at an abstract level. The students had very little reaction to the new curriculum. However, parents experienced a major trauma when they tried to help their children with homework. When they complained to me, my best defense was that parents had just as big a challenge trying to help their children with the old math as they did with new math. Since that time, mathematics instruction has undergone several waves of reform, and no doubt will continue to do so in the future.

## THE ROAD AHEAD

American educational thought leaders continuously impose change on the public schools under the general title of "school reform." Other names used to denote the same concept include, educational reform, innovation, change, educational restructuring, and paradigm change. I am certain even more ways of referring to the phenomena of school reform exist. This chapter contains four major sections as it presents *Perspectives* from the past 20 years on various aspects of school reform.

The first section, Setting the Stage for School Reform, provides the philosophical underpinnings for the concept of school reform. Next comes the section on some general issues that impact schools as they attempt to implement change. This is followed by a section entitled, Tinkering Around the Edges of Reform. In the fourth section, some specific reforms that have been imposed on the public schools are discussed and evaluated. Some Final Thoughts completes the chapter.

## SETTING THE STAGE FOR SCHOOL REFORM

The public schools in our country have an interesting history. For many years, only those who lived in urban areas with sufficient population support for schools had them available for their children. In the less settled areas of the country, parents were responsible for the education of their own children. They could either band together and have a community school or they could each employ tutors to instruct the children individually at home.

Early in the 19th century, all that began to change, especially after Horace Mann obtained an official office. He projected considerable influence regarding schools and schooling, even beyond the boundaries of his home state of Massachusetts. Mann might be considered the first American educational reformer. Much time passed before the formal reform movement coalesced around different ideas. Some new ideas were complementary to those already in force. Some political leaders were bitterly opposed to the changes he recommended. Frequently those ideas, or reforms, that prevailed did so because of the strength of commitment by the first wave of reform. As Peterson (2010) so succinctly stated it, "Effective ideas and ideals acquire a force and energy that overwhelm the opposition" (p. 15).

*Two Old Books*

Not long ago, under severe pressure from my oldest daughter, along with several not so subtle hints from my wife, I agreed to clean out some of the hoard of books I have deposited in the basement for many years. I am really more of an accumulator than a collector, but it pains me to get rid of a book. In respect for these two important women in my life, I ventured into the basement and began eliminating many of the books for which I could not find a compelling reason to keep. In the process I discovered two old classics that I had forgotten. *Why Johnny Can't Read* by Rudolf Flesch (1955) caused a real stir when first published in the mid-20th century. The author proposed a simplistic view of the process of reading instruction that emphasized phonics as the only way to teach the subject.

The other book is entitled, *The Saber Tooth Curriculum* (Peddiwell, 1939), was published just prior to World War II. Written in satirical form, it carried a clear message that America's schools must be open to changing their curriculum to keep up with the times rather than remaining faithful to traditional ways of doing things. That got my mind to thinking about this whole matter of school reform. My observation on the topic is that most of the current school reforms are based, to some degree, on a basic philosophical flaw.

Almost every proposed reform I have seen during this century is based on the unstated assumption that all children can learn. Further, they can learn the same amount of material and learn it at the same rate. The first reform of this century was No Child Left Behind (NCLB). Race to the Top (RTT) followed. Somewhere along the way, Common Core based, in part, on the same defective reasoning quietly entered the educational reform scene. The *Perspective* that naturally followed concluded with this paragraph.

> The idea that all children can learn the same amount at the same time was bolstered by the mantra repeated for many years by educators throughout the nation: all children can learn! While it is true that all children can learn, it is not true that all chil-

dren can learn to solve the quadratic equation. Some can master that concept in the sixth grade while others struggle to memorize the multiplication tables by the end of grade 12. All that the testing mandates do is to sort out children into groups for labeling and identify the so-called "failing schools." From my perspective, the nationwide school reform movements are bound to fail and should be discontinued before huge amounts of money are poured into a futile effort. (*Perspective*, 2014, June 4)

## A Punitive Plan

It is not only a faulty premise that negates the benefits of school reform. In recent years, higher levels of government, both federal and state, have utilized the practice of embedding punitive measures within educational reform acts for lack of full compliance by a school or school district. When government at any level imposes reform on an entity lower on the organizational structure, they usually impose penalties in case of noncompliance. Two paragraphs from a *Perspective* written at the time, relate to the first school reform in the 21$^{st}$ century.

What Bush and many other conservatives fail to understand is that piling new tests on the ones already in existence will not help children learn. While testing is an important part of the teaching/learning process, it does not make children more knowledgeable. In fact, much of the inappropriate testing that already is mandated by government actually interferes with learning. It restricts the curriculum and takes much time that should be spent on instruction. The best use of testing is to give guidance to the classroom teacher in designing the instructional process. Government mandated tests that are primarily for political purposes are not only worthless but also detrimental to the educational effort of schools.

The punitive part of the Bush plan is that schools whose students do not score high enough on the federally required tests would have their federal aid cut off. All this in the name of accountability. If schools do not do well they must be punished. This part of the plan is not only ineffective policy, it is also just plain stupid. It is roughly similar to telling a sick man that since he failed his physical examination we are going to take away his medication. When he learns to be healthy then we will give him his pills back. Many of the schools whose students do not score well on standardized tests are already underfunded. Making their financial situation worse will not help the kids learn. (*Perspective*, 2001, January 31)

## Mandating Intelligence

It is not uncommon for politicians to misjudge the level of power they have over the common citizenry. Too many federal officials take action thinking that they can bring about fundamental change in government institutions. This may explain why a provision that I consider to be foolish was placed in the No Child Left Behind Act. The item in question is a mandate that the achievement gap among various subgroups of students must be narrowed. Chapter 4 examines the futility of such requirements in more detail. A *Perspective* written at the time, reveals my thinking about this provision of the No Child Left Behind Act (NCLB).

The new federal education act contains another noxious aspect that makes it even worse than previous proposals. Now public schools are required to close the achievement gap experienced by poor children and will be punished if they fail to do so. In other words, the law now mandates that all children must be equally intelligent. And if they are not, teachers and administrators will be held accountable. From my perspective, this is the most misguided piece of legislation since prohibition. Even George Bush should know that intelligence cannot be decreed by the government.

All children can learn is the popular mantra that seems to drive the federal education act. What the politicians ignore is that not all children can learn the same amount at the same time. Some children can learn to solve the quadratic equation while others might find it a stretch to learn how to tie their shoes. Learning is a function of a number of factors. One major variable in the learning equation is basic intelligence, which has been unequally distributed through the human family. No federal law can change that fact. (*Perspective*, 2002, January 16)

## School Leaving Age

Many good ideas make the rounds of school reform. Some of them have real merit while others appear to be in the right direction, but have consequences that negate the benefits. Thus, it is essential that schools in America be given a chance to speak to the issues of any reform the legislators impose upon them.

Americans are a restless people. They are never satisfied with the way things are. Constant pressure is ever present to make fundamental change in almost every aspect of life. It should not be surprising that a continual call for school reform exists in today's society. Diane Ravitch, (2000) summed it up quite well when she stated, "It is impossible to find a period in the 20th century in which education reformers, parents, and the citizenry were satisfied with the schools" (p. 13). It is imperative then, that any attempt at school reform is looked at with a certain level of skepticism. A *Perspective* written some years after the Ravitch statement gives a good illustration of this matter.

One of the reforms the Michigan legislature passed is a change in the compulsory school attendance law. They moved the age of compulsion from 16 to 18. That means that a student must attend school until the age of 18. Most people think it is a good idea for everyone to complete a high school education. It is hard to get a decent job without it. So, why do I think it is such a bad idea? It is the compulsory part that bothers me.

Having been a high school principal in a previous life, I know the challenges of keeping a building that is housing a large number of teenagers all together in one piece. With all those chemicals flooding their systems, emotions on the edge every moment, and the constant challenge of determining their individual identities, a building full of adolescents presents a real challenge to educators.

So, why add a cohort of kids who just plain do not want to be there. They will attend school only because state law compels them to present their bodies within the building. But, they cannot be compelled to learn. Will they be eager to cooperate with the educational process or will they be a challenge to it? I predict that the result will be a disruption to the delivery of high quality education in many classrooms. I see no advantage for the state of Michigan in having this additional problem in schools. (*Perspective*, 2010, February 3)

It is not only the problem of students who do not want to be in school that is problematic with the suggested reform. School districts must prepare adequate classroom space for the additional students in attendance, who otherwise would have left school at age 16. At the time, the state had already been skimping on its financial support for the public schools. I know that only a small minority of the population agrees with my view. Raising the compulsory school attendance age is not a beneficial reform

A number of factors impact the success of any school reform. A beneficial change must be comprehensive in scope. It must address factors that are not under the direct control of the school. The student's experience in the classroom is only part of the equation. The accumulated knowledge a child brings to school, the stability of the home environment, and his/her native intelligence can line up to block the benefits of any educational reform. The values of the larger society must be considered as change is in the planning stage. Two short paragraphs taken from a *Perspective* entitled "Reforming America's Public Schools" show my thinking on the topic.

> Many parents have not introduced their children to the world of books and learning prior to the entrance into formal schooling. Further, they do not take an active interest in their children's progress in school or the support they need to give them at home. Even parents at the upper levels of the economic scale sometimes tend to value such things as music practice and ballet lessons more than they do basic learning that should be taking place at school.

> From my perspective, no amount of school reform can bring about the changes in our American culture that need to take place if we are to have a fully effective public school system. If we are going to reform the schools, we must also at the same time reform American society. It does indeed take a whole village to educate a child. It takes community resources, parental engagement, and skilled professional educators, all working together in collaboration, to get the best results from formal schooling. (*Perspective*, 2009, October 14)

## SOME ISSUES BASIC TO REFORM

School reform takes on many sizes and shapes. Some years ago, Michigan Governor Engler expressed concern when he discovered that half of the children attending public schools in the state, scored below grade level. It seemed that he saw an opportunity for a politician to do some good for the people they claim to serve. After considerable thought, the good governor suggested that children who were at the low end of scores in reading, be given tutors to help them get up to grade level. Meanwhile, in our nation's capital, the President had another school reform in mind. My reaction is caught in two paragraphs from a *Perspective* in the next section.

## Reform Must Be Practical

Most good ideas have unintended consequences. High cost is one of the unintended consequences of Governor Engler's good idea on tutoring students with reading problems. If all the school districts in Michigan abide by Engler's order, the cost of public education will be greatly increased. Who will pay the additional costs? And where will all the additional teachers needed to implement the program come from? And who will pay the cost for them to be trained in special techniques? Someone should help the governor answer these questions before he rushes out to enforce his good idea.

President Clinton came up with another good idea for education that will have serious unintended consequences. He suggested that lowering class size should be a national goal. To achieve that goal, he proposed that 100,000 new teachers be hired. What the President ignores in his good idea is that no research has shown that small decreases in class size result in better learning on the part of students. It is not until classes get smaller than 16 that the learning curve increases in any significant manner. It will take a lot more than 100,000 new teachers to achieve that goal. (*Perspective* 1998, February 25)

A few years ago, I wrote a column giving my perspective on the attempt by billionaire Bill Gates to find a formula for good teaching so all public schools in America can be effective. I suggested that other factors besides teaching quality determine how well a child learns. One of the readers of my column sent me a private email in part agreeing with me. "The problem with schools is not the teachers," he suggested. "The problem is bad students." He suggested that one of the key ingredients in effective schools is good students. I was curious to see what his definition of a "good student" might be.

First on his list is a desire to learn. Second is stubbornness, the refusal to give up when learning is difficult. Third, a good student arrives at school already having a fundamental grasp of basic skills, reading writing and math. Even in kindergarten, children should come to school with a good basic education they received from their parents. Next, a good student has already developed some degree of skill in critical thinking. Finally, such students are themselves teachers, willing to help others who are struggling to learn.

I also have a list of the characteristics of a good student. First, a good student comes to school ready to learn. He or she has all the materials that are necessary to work in school. They never let the dog eat their homework! Good students also cooperate with the teacher in the learning process. They strive for excellence. Good students are socially adept, they get along well with their class and are comfortable working on projects in the group. The last two paragraphs from a *Perspective* provides my conclusion to the issue.

> Do such students really exist or is this just a pipe dream? In the years I have taught, I have been fortunate to have had many of my students fit that description. Not all of them have been "A" students, in fact some have had limited capacity to learn. But, it is not necessary to have a high IQ to be a good student. At whatever level a person functions s/he can meet the criteria for a good student. Of course, if I were a teacher who was being evaluated on the basis of student test scores, I would want the smartest students possible. However, I have known a number of really smart students who were not very good students.
>
> From my perspective, those who are searching for a magic formula to make schools highly successful should consider good students as part of the equation. Public policy should move toward implementing systems aimed at developing good students among the youth who attend our schools. Such an effort might be more cost-effective than many of the current schemes to motivate and develop good teachers. (*Perspective*, 2011, March 23).

## Consider the Culture

Some time ago, I had an interesting conversation with my grandson about one of his classmates who was from a country in Asia. The boy had accompanied his parents when they came to America to work on an advanced degree at a nearby university. My grandson shared with me what he had learned regarding the nature of schooling his friend had experienced in his home country.

Schools are highly competitive in that particular Asian nation. The public schools carefully select the best and brightest children. Many parents enroll their young children in academic preschool so they might be accepted to attend one of the best elementary schools. Elite high schools enroll only the best of these. The prestigious colleges and universities, in turn, accept only applicants with the highest test scores.

The top corporations employ only those who have graduated from the very best colleges. Those who graduate from institutions of lesser repute are tracked for low-level jobs with little chance for advancement. Parents in my grandson's friend's home country start thinking about this at a child's early age. The Asian boy was not looking forward to returning to his home country because he knew he would face a life of intense academic study with a little time left for leisure activities. I felt compelled to write a *Perspective* in response to this discussion with my grandson.

> Sounds like a great life for a child, doesn't it. This may explain why children in some countries score higher on standardized tests than here in the United States. It also may explain the high suicide rate among children in such educationally competitive countries. Not getting high marks in kindergarten may doom a child to lifelong failure. That seems like a heavy burden for a five-year-old to carry. By contrast, here

in America if a child fails a grade it is not the end of his academic career. There is always another chance. A child may not wake up academically until high school or even college. I have known people who finally caught on to the structures of knowledge and learning in graduate school.

From my perspective, I am glad that America is still the land of opportunity when it comes to schooling. While our children could stand a little more personal self-discipline, I think most Americans would not want to have such a highly regimented life for them. Kids benefit from free time just to be children. Free play and unstructured time help mature the soul and lead to the development of well-balanced personalities. Hopefully we can salvage some of that part of American culture in the mad rush to improve test scores in our public schools. (*Perspective*, 2008, October 8)

## Avoid Negative Reforms

The off-year election of 2010 brought major changes to the political landscape in America. Several states elected conservative governors. Faced with tight budgets, several of them cut funding to public schools. In Wisconsin, for example, Governor Walker's attempts to strip public sector workers of their collective bargaining rights angered the state's teachers. Soon the atmosphere descended into near civil war between the governor and the teachers.

Governor Walker is not bashful about expressing his disdain for public school teachers. When it was revealed that the average salary for teachers in his state was $50,000, he proclaimed that it was excessive remuneration for those who taught school. In Michigan, the new Governor Rick Snyder proceeded to raid the state school aid fund to fill in gaps in the state budget. He used the money for other things that were experiencing a shortage of funds. The result was very disconcerting for most of the school districts in the state.

I watched in amazement as teacher contracts were changed in the middle of the year, and the political rhetoric castigated the teaching profession. Under the guise of reforming the system, the governors were able to retain the support of their conservative constituency. My frustration generated a *Perspective* related to the nation's downgrading of the value of public schools. I share the last three paragraphs of that essay. The lesson is obvious: beware of negative policy changes that masquerade as educational reform.

The constant attack by conservative governors on public educators cannot help but have a deleterious effect on the public schools. If $50,000 is too high an average salary the Governor should explain why he found it necessary to offer several times that amount to get one of his cabinet members to work for the State. It takes good money to attract good people, so he claims. How can we attract good teachers when they are constantly under attack and publicly proclaimed as not being worth a salary of $50,000 per year? Why would any highly competent young person coming out of college want to work in a profession that is held in contempt by political leaders and do so for a low salary? The answer is they won't, and Michigan's public schools will suffer as a result.

A further issue is the validity of contracts and the willingness of governors to breach those contracts because of financial necessity. I find it interesting that when Wall Street bankers were awarding themselves million dollar bonuses even after they had given evidence of incompetent behavior, the defense was that they were under contracts which could not be broken. Why is a $1 million person's contract inviolate while a teacher making a mere $50,000 has no similar protection? That is a question that needs to be answered.

From my perspective, Midwestern governors ought to take the target off the backs of public educators. They provide a valuable service to the public and cannot be expected to do their best work in the negative atmosphere that has been created by politicians. Our Governor, as well as those in other states, should cease and desist from his attack on the public schools and those who work in them. (*Perspective*, 2011, March 30).

## TINKERING AROUND THE EDGES OF REFORM

Just a few years ago, a friend of mine sent me an article from a conservative newspaper responding to attempts by the state legislature in Texas to reform public education. The Texans developed their own reform curriculum that concentrated on math, science, and technology. While they would teach the other subjects, it would be only a casual contact with the structure of the subject matter. An article in the paper suggested that Texas should adopt a "classical" curriculum rather than one with such a narrow focus. Such an approach to education will result in a course of studies with a heavy dose of the liberal arts. The issue of what should be taught in our schools has been around for a long time.

### Misusing Reform

In the distant past, education consisted primarily of training for a specific skill; then came the concept of the liberating arts where students got a broad education. Recently it seems that the pendulum of school curriculum is swaying back to a model of training for a job requiring a narrow set of skills. Such a reform would be akin to stepping back into the past. The liberal arts are not held in high regard in much of America. A *Perspective* provides a concluding thought on the issue.

Every few years there is a new wave of "school reform" in America. Of specific interest to me is the Commission On the Reorganization of Secondary Education, which was formed in 1915 and delivered its final report three years later. The report included the famous *Seven Cardinal Principles of Secondary Education*, which provided guidance for American high schools for many years. One of the principles was "command of the fundamental processes" such as reading writing and mathematics. If this were the only goal of public education, it would be consistent with the thinking of the Texas legislature.

However, six other principles are included in the list, which indicates the necessity for a broad education that would prepare Americans for maintaining good health, fulfilling their position within home and society, and understanding of America's liberal democracy, as well as the development of an ethical character. Since that time, the global economy has placed additional demands on schools as they attempt to provide an adequate education for our youth. As a context to understanding the work of the Commission, one must remember that at the time less than 20% of children and youth completed high school. However, that was rapidly changing and our public schools had to change to provide for the growing educational needs of the nation. (*Perspective*, 2013, March 20).

## The Broad Impact of Reform

Sometimes I get quite discouraged about the future of American education and the teaching profession. Not long ago I struggled through a time of low spirits because of what was happening to public schools. In the past few years, the State of Michigan slashed per-pupil financial aid to its school districts several times. When it finally did get around to giving districts a slight increase in funding, it was not nearly enough to make up for previous cuts.

It grieved me all the more because I was chair of the finance committee and Treasurer of the board for most of my 19 years serving as a member of the local school board. I know the agony that school administrators and board members experience when they try to operate within a balanced budget and provide an excellent educational program at the same time.

The biggest blow came when a local district, not far from my domicile, terminated the employment contracts for several teachers. The reason for this action was not incompetence or violation of district policy. Student test scores did not meet the required standard. Federal law requires that punitive action be taken against classroom instructors. The lawmakers who designed this provision thought they were reforming education. From my perspective, this is not the type of reform American schools need. Two paragraphs from a *Perspective* provide the foundation for my thinking on this emotion-laden topic.

For normal people like myself, many challenges arise to stress one's mental health, although I try not to think about them too often. However, events of the past several days have proven to put a real strain on my own stability of mind. To start with, I had a discussion with a young person just on the verge of choosing a lifetime career regarding what his choice might be. I have known this person for quite some time and know he has natural abilities in teaching young children. Some people will never make good teachers, especially of the younger set. Other people can learn the tricks of the trade and do a passable job of it. Others are just naturally born with the instincts that are necessary to be highly effective with youngsters who are just beginning their academic journey. The unfortunate part about this conversation was that I felt it necessary to counsel this bright young person not to go into the field of teaching. From my perspective, there is just no future in it.

This left me in a confused state, as far as my mental health is concerned, because I have spent the better part of my adult life involved in education at one level or another. I have found it a very satisfying career, although not highly remunerative. I spent several years evaluating teachers and I know a good one when I see one. I have observed this kid in action with young children so I know that he has a natural gift to make an outstanding educator. It disturbs me greatly to have to counsel him against joining my own chosen profession. (*Perspective*, 2013, June 12).

## Faulty Assumptions

To be effective, any reform must stand on a solid foundation of sound assumptions. Several years ago, the legislature in my home state of Michigan, proposed a reform that would potentially save the schools considerable amounts of money. The reform made retirement mandatory as soon as an employee is eligible for it. The assumption underlying this idea is that schools would replace teachers at the upper end of the salary schedule with those with the lowest pay rate.

A further assumption is that the new teachers will be as effective in their instructional techniques as the retiring veterans of the teaching force. In a few rare cases that might be true. Getting new blood into the school system is beneficial at times, but from my perspective, not all teachers are of the same quality. In any institution, including schools, having a sizeable corps of experienced employees provides a great deal of strength in achieving organizational goals.

Veteran teachers ply their craft with a storehouse of experience to call on if trouble arises. They provide a necessary level of stability in an ever-changing profession. Those who have been around for a while accumulate institutional memory, a commodity whose value is not always recognized. As a young school administrator, I made it a point to consult frequently with the old-timers on the staff. This misguided legislation is based on the assumption that all teachers are about the same. They are like interchangeable parts on a machine. They are not all the same. This point is emphasized in two paragraphs from a *Perspective* on the topic

> The result of the mandatory retirement for older teachers is that the most experienced educators throughout the state will be eliminated from our public schools. Monetary penalties can be imposed on those who fail to cash in on the incentives for them to retire. The strategy is to replace experienced teachers at the high-end of the salary scale with less experienced teachers at the lowest levels of income. It is true that for a period of time there will be some cost savings to local school districts. However, because most districts have a salary schedule that rewards experience, within a few years these new teachers will be more highly paid and nearly as costly as the ones who retired.

> The assumption behind the mandatory retirement plan is that when it comes to teaching personnel, all parts are interchangeable. A brand-new teacher just out of college is just as effective as one who has been in the profession for a number of years. In the legislative mind, there is no value to experience when it comes to classroom instruction. From my perspective, that is an extremely myopic view of things. Any organization that is highly focused on human resources is most effective when

it has the best people employed. Experience does not always result in the best people but it tends toward that direction. (*Perspective*, 2010, May 26)

Even prior to the state law, the superintendent in the district where I served on the board proposed an early retirement plan for teachers with a certain amount of years of seniority. I opposed this plan because we would be losing our most experienced classroom instructors.

## Organizational Reform

Some years ago the Governor in our state decided to get more involved in the operation of the public schools. He pushed reforms especially aimed at the city of Detroit and its highly troubled public school system. One plan he proposed would separate an individual school from control by the school district's Board of Education, and put a board selected by parents in charge of day-to-day operations. To be eligible for this plan, two thirds of the school's parents must be willing to declare their dissatisfaction with the school's operation. While I am not certain that such a plan would improve test scores, it does have some merit. Two short paragraphs from a *Perspective* provide a simple analysis of this reform.

From my perspective, how schools are organized has only a marginal effect on how much children learn. True, teachers need classrooms that are in good repair and books and supplies provided with a minimum of bother. They need administrative support. But mostly they need to teach. And the primary function of the building principal is to support the teacher's effort in the classroom.

Beyond that, parents need to provide a home environment that is conducive to their children's development. Kids do not do well in school if they have a rotten home life. The Governor seems to have forgotten that parents who can't run their own homes will probably not do well trying to run the school. I doubt that the Freedom Schools will do much better than the public schools are now doing. Yet, I applaud Engler for making the effort to find solutions to the sad state of schools in our largest city. So far, educational leaders have not been very successful. So, we might as well let the politicians have a shot at it. They can't do any worse than what we already have. (*Perspective*, 1998, September 9)

## A QUICK LOOK AT RECENT REFORMS

Up to this point, the chapter has dealt with several aspects of reform that have been put forward over the years in American public education. Now, we turn to some specific reforms with the intent to analyze and possibly offer at least a tentative evaluation.

## A Narrowly Focused Reform

Several years ago, Michigan Department of Education came under intense pressure to develop a coherent plan for the accreditation of public schools. The results of their work produced a narrowly focused standard for schools. This attempt at school reform served as a catalyst for a *Perspective.*

> I recently came across a summary of a presentation made by a Lansing bureaucrat who visited our part of the state to bless us with his insights into the future of public education. It seems that the Michigan Department of Education is under some degree of duress to develop a rational system of accreditation for public schools. If they do not, the elected public servants will do so and leave the appointed servants to implement a plan not of their own making. And that is a fate the educators have grown weary of, not only here but also around the nation. Yet, the plan the professional educators are considering is no better than what the politicians would probably contrive so I guess it does not really make any difference who gets the credit or the blame.
>
> The proposed model for Michigan schools is a focus on elementary reading and mathematics. This is in line with the federal emphasis on those two subjects. President Bush has made reading a special topic of interest in his education plan. In fact, he wants to mandate federal standards for all public schools in the nation. There is no question that reading and math are very important subjects and probably essential to success in the modern world. But it seems that schools are really for children not for reading and math. Not only was the attempt at reform overly narrow, but the measurement of success was based on a flawed concept. Teachers should be directed to focus on the kids more than on the subjects they teach. (*Perspective,* 2001, November 21)

The Lansing bureaucrats approached the problem by utilizing a flawed evaluation technique. They based success on each child achieving one year's academic growth for each year of instruction. This set up an impossible standard in that it would require every child to be above average. At the time this attempt at reform was proposed, I had a deep suspicion that it was motivated more by political posturing than by a sincere desire to serve the children in the public schools. From my perspective, schools should serve the needs of children. Children should not be required to serve a flawed political agenda.

## Merit Pay

Merit pay is an attempt to reform the teaching/learning process through an external motivation technique. Teachers whose students score high on standardized tests of academic achievement are awarded a bonus. One paragraph from a *Perspective* written some years ago indicates my thinking on the merit of merit pay for classroom instructors.

> Proponents of the merit pay plan suggest that it only makes sense to pay a worker on the basis of how well they perform in their job. Bricklayers get paid by how many bricks they lay and barbers by how many heads of hair they cut. So, why not pay teachers by how many facts they teach the children who sit at their feet each day? That might work if all children arrived at school with the same capacity to learn and

if they learned at a constant rate. However, as I have written in the past, the human mind is not quite that well programmed. (*Perspective*, 2004, February 11)

The merit pay scheme as an incentive for teachers to do a better job has been around a long time (Peterson, 2010). It has not succeeded in the accomplishment of any notable educational goal. Far too many factors are involved in determining a student's score on a test to assign all the credit (or blame) to classroom instruction. As I explained in a short statement from another *Perspective,* there is too much room for manipulation in a merit pay scheme.

> Any teacher would love to be part of a merit pay system if they could choose which students would be in their room. Give me all the smart kids and I'll get a nice bonus at the end of the year. Give another teacher all the slow learners and they will never get a bonus. (*Perspective,* 2009, April 15)

A number of problems exist with any merit pay scheme. The most important is the fact that education involves more than just learning the facts of a few subjects. Schools have a variety of goals not all of which are academic. If teachers discover that their pay is based only on testable knowledge, there will be a tendency for them to teach only that particular part of the curriculum. The informal curriculum will be left by the wayside (Ravitch, 2013). A summary paragraph from a Perspective expands on that same concern.

> From my perspective, the craft of teaching, combining the art and science of instruction, is far too complicated to be identified by a child's scores on standardized tests. How much of the children's learning is a result of their native intelligence? How much is because of the home environment? And how much is a result of the teacher's skill? Until we can answer those questions with some degree of mathematical certainty, I suggest that the merit pay plan has no merit. So, let's give it a rest until the next round of bad news hits the media. (*Perspective*, 2004 February 11)

## No Child Left Behind

For some unknown reason, the guardians of public education housed in our nation's capital, assume it is their responsibility to impose every reform worthy of its name upon the public schools in our blessed Republic. Thus, we have seen in the first fifteen years of the new century, three major reforms that have made life very difficult for serious educators. Most reforms have originated in the highest seat of government. I find it strange that the Constitution gives the federal government no role in education or public schooling. Yet, the federal government has consolidated its power over the operation of public schools in a not so subtle manner. The three reforms provide a classic example of how this happens.

First is the No Child Left Behind (NCLB) act, proposed by the supposedly conservative administration of George W. Bush. It was seen by many observers as nothing more than a grab for power by the federal government. The NCLB was primarily a punitive reform in that severe sanctions were brought against any public school that did not make "adequate yearly progress" (AYP) in the improvement of student test scores.

The ultimate goal of NCLB was for every student to be proficient in reading and math by the academic year of 2013–2014. A school that did not make adequate yearly progress toward that lofty goal was subject to severe punitive measures including possible closure. Diane Ravitch (2010), a frequently cited authority on school reform, identified the proficiency mandate as the biggest flaw in the NCLB. Supporters of this enactment assume that the cause of low student achievement is lazy educators who could best be held accountable by a rigorous round of student testing.

Ravitch's summary statement is most instructive for would-be educational reformers. The "assumptions were wrong. Testing is not a substitute for curriculum and instruction. Good education cannot be achieved by a strategy of testing children, shaming teachers, and closing schools" (p. 111). Two paragraphs from a *Perspective* show my early agreement with that summation of NCLB.

> From my perspective, the No Child Left Behind act is fatally flawed from a legal standpoint in that it violates the clear mandates of the Constitution. The Tenth Amendment delegates to the states matters not specifically enumerated as belonging to the federal level of government. Education and schooling are not listed in that hallowed document as being a federal matter. Thus, control of the schools belongs to the states. This along with the mandate to violate legally binding employment contracts makes the educational enactment doubly repugnant.

> Supporters of the law have argued that the sad state of education in America requires federal intervention. The evidence does not support such a conclusion, but even if it did, violating the bedrock of the American way of life as found in the Constitution is hardly justified. Further, there is no evidence that abiding by the hundreds of new federal mandates found in the law will bring any new benefits to the children who are its intended beneficiaries. Just a surface glance at a summary of the law reveals that it will be a record keeping nightmare for even the best of schools. The cost of all the new records and reporting will be added to the local school districts who are already struggling with budget cuts. Very limited educational benefits will accrue as a result of this added cost. (*Perspective*, 2003, April 9)

## Race to the Top

Unfortunately, the Obama administration did not get the message (McGuinn, 2014). It tightened the grip of federal control with a revision of the education act known as "Race to the Top" (RTT). It maintained the testing requirement as well as punitive measures for schools that failed to meet the educational goals prescribed for them. Actually, the burden of accountability was placed on individual teachers under this reform. While the revised law gave states some flexibility, it mandated that student test scores must be included in the formula by which teachers are evaluated. (Leonardatos & Zahedi, 2014)

In my view, this requirement indicated an almost total takeover of the control of the public schools by the federal government. I was unconvinced that any good thing would come to the children in our public schools as a result of RTT. I was not alone in my thinking (Abbott, 2013). A number of researchers raised serious questions about the validity of the teacher evaluation process developed to meet the demands of the reform imposed by Race to the Top (Herlihy et al., 2014). To make matters even more difficult, the Common Core State Standards was imposed on America's already beleaguered corp of classroom instructors (Kitchen & Berk, 2016).

### Common Core

No government agency produced Common Core. The standards came about through the collaboration between The Council of Chief State School Officers and the National Governors Association. While the standards were intended to be voluntary, the federal government soon made them mandatory as part of their implementation of the Race to the Top. Some observers find value in these standards (Graham & Harris, 2015) while others question the value of posting the same standards throughout the entire United States. They further question the validity of using results from test scores tied to the standards to evaluate the effectiveness of individual teachers (Brenneman, 2016). There is no question that the imposition of the Common Core standards has an effect on the public schools where they have been adopted it. It directly impacts both content and the instructional strategies used by classroom teachers (Chandler, Fortune, Lovett, & Scherrer, 2016).

### SOME FINAL THOUGHTS

This chapter has only scratched the surface on the topic of school reform. My purpose was not to be comprehensive, but to identify some underlying principles that parents and other observers of schools can use in evaluating proposals for reform at the local level. Not all suggestions for reform actually result in improvement in the educational process. In fact, some reforms tend to inhibit improvement in classroom instruction and student learning. In general, my observation has been that reforms imposed from a government bureaucracy are least effective, while those reforms that arise close to the classroom are most beneficial.

School reforms that have mandatory requirements, especially those that are punitive in nature are, from my way of thinking, detrimental to the success of public education. If educational leaders at the national level want to make an impact on the effectiveness of schooling in America, they might better make recommendations than impose mandates. This topic will be further explored in chapter nine, which deals with the role of the federal government in public education.

In my lifetime, most reform movements have not lasted long. For example, the short vignette at the beginning of this chapter regarding the new math illustrates the point. All the wonderful things I learned in the class I took on the content and teaching of the new math have long since passed off the instructional scene. Since then several waves of reform have come and just as quickly disappeared. I try not to be cynical about efforts to improve the schools but I have observed many attempts at reform fall flat. In the next chapter, reforms involving school choice will provide a much more positive view of school reform.

## LIST OF *PERSPECTIVES* REFERENCED

Published in *The Journal Era,* Berrien Springs, Michigan

1998, February 25. On the Intended Consequences
1998, September 9. Engler's Takeover Plan
2001, January 31. Bush Flunks the Test you
2001, November 21. Forget about the Children the
2002, January 16. Mandating Intelligence
2003, April 9. Trifling with the Constitution
2004, February 11. No Merit to This Plan
2008, October 8. Who Is to Blame for This Mess
2009, April 15. Another Simple Answer
2009, October 14. Reforming America's Public Schools
2010, February 3. More bad ideas for Michigan Schools
2010, May 26. Strategy and Tactics
2011, March 23. Needed: A Few Good Students
2011, March 30. A Target on Their Backs
2013, June 12. Bad for My Mental Health
2013, March 20. What Should Kids Learn in School?
2014, June 4. School Reform and More

## REFERENCES

Abbott, C. (2013). The "race to the top" and the inevitable fall to the bottom: How the principles of the "campaign for fiscal equity" and economic integration can help close the achievement gap. *Brigham Young University Education & Law Journal,* (1), 93–123.

Brenneman, R. (2016, February 17). Five-state study examines teaching shifts under core. *Education Week, 35*(21).

Chandler, K., Fortune, N., Lovett, J. N., & Scherrer, J. (2016, February). What should, common core assessment measure? *Phi Delta Kappan, 97*(5), 60–63.

Flesch, R. (1955). *Why Johnny can't read: And what you can do about it.* New York: Harper and Row.

Graham, S., & Harris, K. R. (2015, June). Common core state standards and writing. *Elementary School Journal, 115*(4), 457–463.

Herlihy, C., Kargger, E., Pollard, C., Hill, H. K., Williams, M., & Howard, S. (2014). State and local efforts to investigate the validity and reliability of scores from teacher evaluation systems. *Teachers College Record, 116*(1), 1–28.

Kitchen, R., & Berk, S. (2016). Educational technology: An equity challenge to the common core. *Journal for Research in Mathematics Education, 47*(1), 3–16.

Leonardatos, H., & Zahedi, K. (2014). Accountability and "racing to The top" in New York State: A report from the front lines. *Teachers College Record, 116*(9), 1–23.

McGuinn, P. (2014). Presidential policymaking Race to the Top, executive power and the Obama education agenda. *Forum, 12*(1), 61–79.

Peddiwell, J. A. (1939). *Saber-tooth Curriculum.* New York: McGraw-Hill.

Peterson, P. E. (2010). *Saving schools: From Horace Mann to virtual learning.* Cambridge, MA: Belknap Press.

Ravitch, D. (2000). *Left back: A century of failed school reforms.* New York: Simon & Schuster.

Ravitch, D. (2013). *Reign of error: The hoax of the privatization movement and the danger to America's public schools.* New York: Alfred A.Knopf.

Ravitch, D. (2010). *The death and life of the great American school system: How testing and choice are undermining education.* New York: Basic Books.

# CHAPTER 8

# SCHOOL CHOICE

### THE MOTHER SHED TEARS

When people cry in my presence, it makes me very uncomfortable. That happened when I visited with the parents of a first grade student at a small religious school in northern California, where I was a teaching principal. The first grade teacher talked to me several times during the school year regarding her concerns for the boy. He was not making good progress in school. He tried very hard and his parents were cooperative in doing all they could to help. The teacher said she knew the boy was trying hard but he did not have the capacity to learn as fast as the rest of the children in the room. "We just have to face the fact that he is a slow learner," the teacher said.

Having come to that conclusion, we then faced the question of what do we do with him for another year? If he gets a failing grade, he will have to repeat the first grade. In addition to being an embarrassment to the boy for having flunked his first year in school, I was not certain that he would benefit by another year in the first grade. However, if we move him on to the second grade he will be behind the other children right from the start. The teacher and I discussed this several times but could not arrive at a final decision.

*Helping Parents Understand Schools: A Different Perspective on Education and Schooling in America,* pages 127–144.

I puzzled over this matter for some time. The teacher had given up trying to decide her student's future and frankly told me that, since I was the principal of the school, it was my decision, not hers. That is when it finally dawned on me that we were missing an important component in the process of making decisions regarding the educational future of children in the school. After reviewing all the documents and academic records available, I decided to visit the parents and involve them in the decision. Should we retain their son in first grade for another year, or place him in the second grade?

The parents were responsive to my request to visit them at home. After exchanging pleasantries, I explained to them the reason for the visit. I was open about the teacher's evaluation of the situation and that we had looked at two alternatives for their youngest son the following year. I then told the parents that I wanted them to have a major part in deciding the boy's educational future. At that point, the mother began to shed tears.

` I was stunned at the response and apologized for having upset her. "Oh no," she said. "It is just that this is the first time anyone from a school has asked us for our opinion about what to do with our children." She described how they had been treated at other schools their children had attended. Every time a decision was to be made, school administration simply announced it to them without giving the parents any chance to make suggestions. They had to accept what school officials decided without being able to give any input.

I do not remember what we finally decided for the boy's future in our school. I do remember quite well the emotion of both parents when, for the first time, they were given the opportunity to make choices for their children. Since that time, the matter of parental choice has become quite common in American education. As Kahlenberg (2001) noted, "In more recent years, Americans have become increasingly enamored of school choice. Liberty, of course, is a deeply American notion..." (p. 6).

## THE ROAD AHEAD

School choice is a common factor in American education reform. This chapter identifies and analyzes several options available to parents as they make choices regarding the educational journey of their offspring. First, a section on the philosophical basis for school choice provides a broad look at the topic in general. Then, I list several of the most common choice options including, charter schools, vouchers, public school choice, home school, and non-public schools. Some final thoughts will tie it all together.

## SCHOOL CHOICE IN GENERAL

For most of America's history, public schools funded by tax dollars held a virtual monopoly on the business of educating America's children and youth. The only "competition," to use a business term, was from the religiously affiliated schools such as the Catholics, Lutherans, and Seventh-day Adventists. The idea of parents having options available to them did not become widespread until late in the 20th century. The educational reform movement provided the conceptual source of school choice as part of efforts to bring change to the public schools.

## A Community With Many Choices

I must admit to a bias in favor of school choice. I am a strong supporter of the public schools. I think I made that point very clear in Chapter 1. However, my experience in public schools, as well as the atmosphere in the small community where I have established my domicile, has given me a broad perspective on the value of options available to parents as they guide their children to adulthood. My thinking on this topic is captured in a *Perspective* written after attending the graduation ceremonies for the public high school where I served on the Board of Education.

> As the ceremony proceeded I considered the richness of schooling options available in our town. We have high quality public schools that have attracted over 200 children from other districts to enroll here. Evidently, people from outside the school district have discovered we have something of great value in our public schools. In addition, our district is blessed with several very good private schools. Further, we have a vibrant group of home school parents who daily make a personal commitment to preparing their children for the future. On occasion, they team up with either the public or private schools to fill in the gaps they find missing in their own schooling efforts.
>
> It is rare for a community to have the compatibility among the three approaches to schooling that we have. In most places, more than a little rivalry exists among public, private, and home schoolers. Parents and their children are at a disadvantage when such tension exists and frequently face pressure from friends to be loyal to their chosen educational venue. I view such a situation as unfortunate for children as well as the whole community. (*Perspective*, 2005, June 8)

## Voices in Opposition

Not all educational leaders have embraced the concept of choice. Noted educational thought leader, Diane Ravitch, (2010) mounted a stirring defense of the traditional public schools in opposition to school choice:

> In barely 20 years, the idea of school choice rapidly advanced in the public arena and captivated elite opinion. Given the accumulating evidence of its uneven results, this was surprising. Even more surprising was how few voices were raised on behalf of the democratic vision of public education. (p. 147)

Other voices have also been raised against the idea of parents having choice in schooling decisions regarding the education of their children. Several years ago, the largest newspaper in the county where I live in Southwest Michigan, published an article by a guest columnist in opposition to school choice. Unfortunately, that was prior to the time I decided to write this book, so I am, unable to retrieve the documentation. The writer gave as an example of the destructive force of choice, the decline of the Grand Rapids public schools. He estimated that the school district had lost 7,000 students in recent years as parents chose to enroll their children elsewhere. Then he asked what I consider to be the central question on this issue: "What business can thrive when it loses a substantial portion of its revenue each year?" Two paragraphs from a *Perspective* written in response are presented here.

> From my perspective, an even more important question is, "What business would continue to lose a substantial portion of its revenue without taking actions that are necessary to reverse that trend?" The answer is, of course, only a business that is on the fast track to bankruptcy. A business that wants to thrive in a competitive market gets competitive. The result is definitely beneficial to the consumers who will get better service and better products as a result. The same thing can happen in education when school leaders get competitive. Parents and children benefit most when schools work hard to provide a high-quality education.
>
> The columnist was correct in stating that school choice doesn't solve all problems in education. However, school choice does provide a platform for schools to improve. It is up to school leaders, then, to take the opportunity that is provided to them. I don't know much about the Grand Rapids schools but they get the same basic per-pupil allowance from the state as other school districts do, so they should take their money and put it to the best possible use. Why not make their schools so attractive that students from other districts are attracted to them? That's a good way to increase their revenue stream. (*Perspective*, 2008, February 20)

### Parent Voices Must Be Heard

Parents are very aware of the options available for their children's educational needs. That awareness puts their relationship with school officials in an entirely different setting. School leaders must be aware that parents have the power to exit their institution and go elsewhere. Many public school administrators are not comfortable with the fact that parents now have a voice that must be heard and they must respond to it (Smrekar, 1996). Failing to do so may result in serious consequences for the schools under their control. That is the nature of business in America.

In the waning days of the 20th century, a number of school choice plans circulated around the state of Michigan. Included were two that had already been implemented elsewhere: charter schools, known as Public School Academies, and public school choice. These choice plans were put in place just a few years previously and seemed to be off to a good start.

Two other proposals under discussion elicited strong opposition from supporters of public schools. First, a controversial voucher program was openly debated.

Vouchers are discussed in a section to follow. Also, a proposal for tuition tax credit for parents who send their children to non-public schools generated considerable interest, although opposition was quite fierce. The following three paragraphs are from a *Perspective* written in response.

> Opponents of these plans say they would take money away from the public schools and harm systems that are already short on resources. From my perspective, just the opposite would result. If many students take advantage of one of the choice plans, it means less cost for the public schools since they would have less students to educate. Under the tuition tax credit plan, the state school aid fund would be greatly benefitted since the credit is for only half the cost of the state aid payment to a public school district. The more students who attend private schools, the less cost to the state.

> Another concern is that all the good students would enroll in private schools, leaving the public schools with the more difficult to educate students. School administrators should ask themselves why all the good students in their schools want to leave. Why don't the bad students want to leave also? Perhaps they should develop an educational program that will make all students want to stay.

> Most responses in opposition to school choice have assumed that the public schools cannot compete in the free marketplace. From my observation of both public and private schools, this is a faulty assumption. Our public schools here in Southwest Michigan are very effective and can compete with private schools as well as charter schools. The only thing the public schools have to fear is the feeling of self-sufficiency that has developed as a result of the long standing monopoly they have had in education. (*Perspective*, 1998, March 11)

## The Drive to Innovate

I have no doubt that the public schools can compete in the marketplace with all other forms of schooling. I am concerned by the complacency I observe among too many school leaders. I attribute this attitude to the near monopoly they enjoy. When one has the only game in town, little incentive exists to be constantly engaged in the hard work of making educational change. However, when some form of competition is experienced, innovation seems to be more easily accepted. This concern regarding the lack of innovation in existing school systems is echoed by British researchers in their massive study of education in the United Kingdom (Woods, Bagley, & Glatter, 1998).

## ANOTHER LOOK AT CHARTER SCHOOLS

At one time, charter schools were considered to be the most effective school reform measure available to politicians who seek to upgrade public education. These schools are widely misunderstood and thought to be a competitive threat to public schools. However, they are public schools; and although the specifics vary from state to state, charters are under control of a public agency. Each state has its own set of policies and procedures for opening and operating a charter school. In Michigan, they are referred to as Public School Academies. Between the courts and the state legislature, a strange series of events occurred in determining the legal status of the academies. They are, by law, public schools, under the control and supervision of a public agency (Furst, 1996).

## A Change in My Thinking

For several years I observed public school academies develop and grow in Michigan. I admit to a certain level of bias against charter schools. No doubt this bias arose from my work on the local public school board. Even though my professional life had been in private education, I developed a strong loyalty to public education. At first, I was very skeptical and doubted they would be effective. But eventually I took a broader view of charter schools as they functioned within the state's system of publicly supported schools. Slowly I experienced a change in thinking about the efficacy of the Academies. Many people have expressed great concern about the potential negative impact of charter schools on the public schools. In reality, charter schools get the same financial aid payment from the state as the regular public school districts get. Our education laws do not guarantee a monopoly to any form the schools might take. Charter schools are thus public schools.

When the state allocates funds to a charter school, it is not taking money away from public education. Children enrolled in an academy are public school students and have a legal right to public financial support for the school that they have chosen for their education. Once I accepted that concept of charter schools, it became easy to give them support in the *Perspectives* I wrote on the topic. The concluding paragraph of one such *Perspective* gives evidence of my changed thinking on charter schools.

> The crux of the matter, from my perspective, is that parents should be able to make certain choices regarding the education of their children. No parent will choose to send his child to a substandard school. Thus if a corporation does engage in a raid on the state school fund available to charter schools it will not be for long. Parents will not enroll their children in such a school, thus depriving it of state aid payments. I may be a bit naïve on this matter, but I do have great faith in the ability of parents to make intelligent decisions regarding the education of their children. In my view, charter schools are a benefit to the public education system in our state. (*Perspective*, 2012, January 4)

## Strong Opposition

While I have changed my thinking on the efficacy of charter schools, that position is not universally held by America's educational thought leaders. Diane Ravitch, (2013) dedicated an entire chapter for an attack against charter schools. Then, buried deep in the chapter is a grudging admission that, "Some charters are excellent schools by any measure" (p. 174). On the next page the author once again admits that, "To be sure, there are good community-based charter schools that do not skim the easiest-to-educate students and do not "counsel out" the students they do not want" (p. 175).

Several years before that critical analysis appeared, I published a *Perspective* that answered some of the objections to charters that continue to be raised.

> The prime difference between the two types of public schools is that the regular schools are subject to local political forces in governance and accountability. Charter schools operate like private corporations as far as governance is concerned and are held accountable by market forces. If they cannot convince parents that they are doing a good job of educating the students under their care, parents have the option of taking their children elsewhere. And the state aid payment goes with the child. The dollar becomes the motivator. And if the charter school does not live up to its mission, its charter can be revoked and it will be out of business.
>
> Are charter schools the answer to low educational achievement in the state? Certainly not. Test results so far show that on the average children in charter schools score lower than children in regular public schools. Charter school supporters say that it is too early to tell. Give the schools some time and they will surpass the other public schools. Anyway, the tests used are not really an adequate assessment of student learning.
>
> From my perspective, charter school's best contribution to the public is to give parents an additional choice in educating their children. The competition has been healthy for both the regular public schools and also for private schools. It has spurred educators to new efforts in providing the best education possible. The real winners in this competition are the children of the state. (*Perspective*, 1998, June 24)

## SCHOOL VOUCHERS RECONSIDERED

No other proposed school reform has generated as much emotion as the school voucher plan. In this program, the educational funding agency provides parents a voucher that can be cashed in by a school that the parents choose for their children. It covers the child's tuition in a private school that has been approved for the program. The philosophy behind this program is that it gives children from economically deprived situations a chance to attend high quality private schools. In the inner city, this usually means Catholic or other religious schools.

Several years ago, a private consulting firm suggested that the best solution for the problem of low academic achievement in the state's public schools in Michigan was to discontinue them entirely. In their place, parents would be given a voucher to cover the cost of tuition at any private school. Any person or organization had the opportunity to start a school and compete for available students. The free market, it was predicted would result in greatly improved schools.

## Economic Considerations

Some evidence exists that indicates the possibility of economic benefits from a school choice plan such as vouchers (Merrifield & Gray, 2013). However, even though I am a strong supporter of the free market, I remain skeptical. A *Perspective* written several years ago indicates my equivocation on the topic.

> Public and private schools have been in competition for about 150 years and the marketplace theory has been proven true. Administrators from both sectors have worked hard to be competitive. Except in the inner city, that is. People there just do not have enough discretionary income to make the private school decision. No real educational choice is available for those living on the edge of poverty. The lack of competition has resulted in a serious educational crisis in the nation's urban centers.
>
> Vouchers would change that. Public school administrators would have to get competitive or face a decline of enrollment which might eventually close their schools. Such a possibility would bring about a surge of creative energy with a resulting improvement in education. Children would be the main beneficiaries.
>
> The most recent suggestion is at the far extreme of the various voucher plans that have been proposed. And it makes very little sense at all. To close all public schools and turn the entire educational process over to private vendors is like swatting a mosquito with a sledge hammer. Public schools provide valuable competition to the private sector. They must submit to public scrutiny in a manner that private schools would find offensive.
>
> In a totally free market system of education there would be no elected school boards. The public would have no recourse if they were cheated by the private vendor. There would be no due process for either student or employee. Fly-by-night operators would flourish and serious educational innovation would quickly decline. Hard to educate students would be left at the schoolhouse door.
>
> From my perspective, a mixed economy provides the best of both worlds. Public schools are needed to serve the public need. Private schools are needed to serve special market niches. Both are needed to provide competition for the other. When both public and private schools flourish, the public interest is best served. (*Perspective*, 1996, November, 20)

## Dispelling the Myths

The idea of school vouchers is firmly grounded in political ideology (Chubb & Moe, 2001). Another author provided a description of the political support for school vouchers in Washington D.C. even though the educational programs in some of them have disappointing results (Boston, 2015). A *Perspective* in which I identify some common myths about vouchers as proposed in Michigan indicates my early support for them as a legitimate school reform.

*Myth:* The voucher proposal in Michigan will divert scarce resources from public schools. This myth is based on the assumption that thousands of students would leave the public schools for the private schools. What it ignores is that the state pays an average of $6,000 to public schools for each child in attendance while under the voucher plan it would pay a private school only $3,000 for students in attendance. This provides a savings of $3,000 for each student that transfers. If large numbers of students are already enrolled in private schools, the state would also have to provide them with a voucher. However, no evidence exists that this would be a greater number than the transfers.

Further, parents who feel the public school is doing a good job would not be likely to transfer their children. It seems that the anti-voucher forces are not very confident about the quality of public education. In this, they sell the public schools short. I believe the public schools in Michigan are well able to compete in the open market. Good public schools have nothing to fear from the voucher plan. Those that are not so good can use the incentive to get better.

*Myth:* The voucher plan subsidizes private and religious schools which are not subject to any oversight from any elected officials. The voucher plan does not provide a subsidy to schools. Rather it reimburses parents for the cost of tuition. And this reimbursement is only half what is provided to a public school. Further, private and religious schools are subject to considerable regulation by the state and federal government to ensure that they operate in the public interest and do not violate public policy.

*Myth:* The voucher program would likely increase discrimination and segregation. However, no definitive evidence is found in the literature that private schools discriminate any more than public schools. Private and religious schools are subject to the civil rights laws. While they may have religious requirements for attendance, they may not practice racial or other kinds of discrimination. Some evidence does exist that private schools are more open to diversity than many public schools.

*Myth:* The voucher program would narrowly assist wealthy families by using tax dollars to subsidize students from affluent homes who are already enrolled in private and religious schools while excluding low income students who cannot afford to pay the remaining cost of private school tuition. While it is true that a voucher program would assist all students in the districts that qualify, no evidence has been found that children from low-income families would be excluded from private or religious schools. In fact, many religious schools have tuition lower than the $3,000 voucher. Religious schools throughout the country have an admirable record of assisting low-income children in their educational journey. Churches provide large subsidies to their schools so they are affordable to middle-income parents. Further, many have needy student scholarship programs for low income-students. (*Perspective*, 2000, October 11)

## Another Shift in Thinking

Meanwhile, in Michigan a proposal was put on the ballot in 2000 to change the state Constitution to remove any restrictions on a school voucher program. My support for vouchers as an effective mechanism for school reform soon wavered. One week after the *Perspective* above, another one indicated a slight shift in my thinking.

> The specific proposal on the Michigan ballot has two additional problems. First, educational vouchers would be available only to children in qualified school districts. Qualification is based on graduation rates. Currently only seven districts in the state would be qualified. The graduation rate is probably the poorest basis upon which qualification should be decided. Schools have no control over graduation. Students in Michigan are required to attend school only until age 16, which is well before they could be expected to graduate.

> An additional problem with the Michigan voucher proposal is that it provides for local initiative for districts that are not qualified. That is, people in a school district could call for a vote on vouchers for their district. This would result in a contentious election process with communities divided largely along religious lines. We have enough wars of religion in the world right now without adding Michigan to the battle scene.

> From my perspective, the voucher proposal on the ballot for the November election is seriously flawed. It is neither educationally nor politically sound. While I am philosophically supportive of vouchers, I plan to vote no on this one. I hope a majority of other voters do the same. (*Perspective*, 2000, October 18)

## Consider Negative Effects

Fear about the potential negative effects of a voucher program exist on both sides of the issue. After studying the voucher program in Milwaukee, Wisconsin, one author found decreased community support for the public schools (Fleming, 2014). On the other side, another researcher found that the availability of school vouchers had an effect on the academic program as well as the religious composition of the student body (Austin, 2015). A *Perspective* explained my concerns regarding the potential negative effect a voucher program might have on private and religious schools.

> A second concern I have for the voucher program is the divisive nature that is inherent in such provisions as the patriotic school item. Would a school sponsored by the Jehovah Witnesses be considered patriotic? They decline to pledge allegiance to the flag, which is considered by many Americans to be an act of patriotism. What about schools supported by religious organizations that oppose war? Would they be considered not patriotic because they do not support America's ongoing wars in other parts the world?

Sorting out the answers to these questions and others like them would not be beneficial to the educational process nor to the schools who supposedly benefit from a voucher program. I'm afraid there will be a number of unintended consequences when this program is enacted into law in our neighbor to the south. Thankfully, we have been spared such things here in Michigan. (*Perspective*, 2011, April, 27)

I generally favor competition in and among schools within a school system. When schools compete, the result is the delivery of an improved education. Michigan provides for both public school choice and charter schools, known as Public School Academies. These different types of schools provide a good bit of competition between and among them. However, it must be recognized that they are all public schools. Vouchers are based on the concept that schools outside those publically supported by tax dollars, may receive payment from the state for the vouchers they have collected.

This section has just scratched the surface on the topic of school vouchers. Readers must be aware that the topic is much larger and more complex than what has been presented here.

## PUBLIC SCHOOL CHOICE

When I first got involved with the public schools in the small town where I reside, all of our students lived within the geographic boundaries of the district. Only under special circumstances could students from outside the district be allowed to transfer in. All that changed when the school finance formula was changed. The State Legislature, at the prodding of the governor, made provision for schools of choice in the public sector.

Public school choice, sometimes referred to as "open enrollment," is also identified by one author as "inter-district choice" (Koppich, 1992). When the school code provides for such choice, students may attend any public school that has openings. In Michigan, the school of choice must be within the county of the student's residence. Other requirements ensure an orderly process. For example, a school district must advertise in advance the number of openings in each grade.

### Opening up the System

At the time when this reform was implemented in Michigan, it seemed like a radical change to some people. However, one historian has suggested that school choice was common a century ago (Gross, 2014). Thus, it should not be seen as a major change. Parents choose to enroll their children in schools outside of their attendance area for a variety of reasons. A study in Wisconsin found that higher spending districts tended to attract more schools of choice students (Welsch, Statz, & Skidmore, 2010). Another research indicated the possibility of a racial motive (Possey-Maddox, 2016).

When the Michigan legislature amended the education code to allow for interdistrict choice in the public schools, not every educator in the state applauded. A number of school boards hesitated to get their districts involved. Administrators and board members alike were fearful that an influx of students from outside their own community might somehow damage their schools. A *Perspective,* written during that period of time, reveals my thinking on the topic.

> While no evidence of a great competitive advantage in school choice has been found, that may come eventually. As public schools see the benefit in the free enterprise system, they may find ways to market the aspects of schooling where they excel. Since state dollars follow the student, schools with unused capacity will find it financially advantageous to attract students from outside the district to fill those vacant seats. To do so they must offer a superior educational program in order to attract new students.
>
> When school leaders get competitive everyone benefits. Private schools have faced this situation for many years. They not only have to compete with each other, but also must convince parents to pay high tuition when the public schools are free. This is a tough sell, but private schools all across America have done very well at it for many years. Now they are facing a new challenge as schools of choice in the public sector has re-energized the public schools. The choice plan, along with the public school academies, introduces a new competitive spirit into the educational marketplace. (*Perspective*, 1997, May 21)

## Let's Compete

During most of my professional career as an educator, I have heard the statement made several times, "We should run schools like a business." At first I resisted the idea. Classroom teaching seemed a more sacred calling than a mere business would deserve. I felt that running a school like a business would demean the profession. Then one of the business professors at the university where I was teaching suggested to me that any time an economic exchange occurs, you have a business. In the private schools, parents pay money to the school in return for the service it provides in educating their children. That certainly met the professor's definition of a business. Likewise, in the public arena, taxpayers provide funds to public schools in exchange for education for all children in the community.

When the option came to open the doors of the school district where I served on the Board, I realized I needed to rethink my whole position on the administration of schools, both public and private. Schools should not try to mimic the manufacturing model of business. The service industry provides a better pattern for education. Even the profit motive is beneficial in keeping schools in a financially sound condition. When the matter was presented to the Board, I had no hesitation in voting "yes."

When school personnel expressed concern about the potentially destructive result from competition among the public schools, I could honestly give them reassurance. I encouraged them to look at this as an opportunity. The school district already had the necessary human resources available to compete with most of the other districts. The major need was a change in mindset on the part of the board, administration, and professional staff.

That change occurred much faster than I expected. The Board included several small business owners who did not need convincing. Administrators understood that attracting more students would bring more revenue. In Michigan, the public schools get most of their income from the state in the form of a per pupil allowance. Thus, more pupils result in more allowance from the state. The professional staff was already performing at a reasonably high level. Most of the things necessary to compete in the marketplace of public education were already in place. Our school district was ready to do business.

### A School of Choices

How successful was this foray into the rough and tumble world of competitive business? It started with small successes. A new superintendent with an eye for aesthetics upgraded the buildings and grounds. At almost every meeting of the Board, someone mentioned the need to keep our district competitive with other school districts. The number of transfer students increased yearly. Most importantly, the reputation of the district spread throughout the county. The administration and professional staff scrambled to live up to that reputation. The Board supported those efforts.

The result was far beyond anything I expected. The most recent count showed nearly five hundred students from other school districts had chosen to attend our public schools (Schulz, 2015). With the arrival of the new superintendent, the district's competitive edge took a giant leap forward. At this point I observed that in every instance where a change was needed, it was the district superintendent who led the process. I realize that several components were part of the success of our venture into the marketplace. However, above all others, the leadership skill of the superintendent made the ultimate difference. My observation is consistent with the scholarly literature (Petersen, 2011).

The superintendent had a vision that the district should be, not just a school choice, but also a school of choices. With the Board's support, he implemented a number of different options for those who chose to attend the schools within the District (Michigan Public School Districts, 2015).

The school district is quite competitive with other school districts in Southwest Michigan. A total of 492 students transferred in from other schools. One hundred twenty-four students transferred out of the district. I am never discouraged when a student transfers out. That action indicates the success of public school choice,

The school district offers other choices for its students. The Virtual Academy provides a full curriculum for students who choose to do their class-work at a distance. Students that have a scheduling conflict or who desire to study a subject not offered in the regular curriculum find the Virtual Academy a real benefit in accomplishing their educational goals. Finally, the school district also offers a variety of services to parents who choose to school their children at home. During the 2015/16 school year, the district provided support to over 500 home-schooling students. A more complete description of the choices available to students can be found at http://www.homeoftheshamrocks.org/.

## THE HOME IS A SCHOOL

Every home is a school whether the parents like it or not. As soon as a child is born, learning begins. At first, children learn through the sense of touch. Eventually, when their eyes get adjusted, they see things that need to be explored. Children also learn by hearing. This is most critical for parents to know. Every sound that comes to the child's ears adds to their knowledge of the world around them. The parents are the first teachers a child will have and they lay the foundation for what comes later.

When the child is old enough to enter formal schooling, the parent must make a decision as to what should be the venue for their children to gain the accumulated body of knowledge that society expects of them. A small but growing number of parents choose to carry out that function themselves. At one time, it took a good bit of courage to provide schooling at home for one's children. A compulsory school attendance law in a number of states mandated that children attend either a public school or an approved private school between the ages of six and sixteen. Few states made provision for home schools. Public school administrators took a dim view of home schooling as an alternative to the schools they operated. Some public educators viewed it as an insult that parents implied they could do a better job of teaching the children then certified teachers.

Bruce Cooper, (2005) in the preface to the book on home schooling that he edited, suggested that public school personnel make peace with homeschoolers, and even offer some services to them when it is possible. He recommends a pragmatic acceptance of homeschoolers by public educators. "It is to the advantage of every educator to know and understand the causes, needs, and goals of homeschool children and parents," he states. "After all, the families are taxpaying, voting, active, and well organized citizens of their community" (p. xi). In the section immediately above, I provide an example of a public school district that follows that prescription with positive results.

Several years ago, I attended a research convention on the West Coast. The convention is too big to be of value in any practical sense, so small groups of scholars with narrow research interests, form Special Interest Groups (SIG) of like-minded attendees. I maintained membership in three SIGs groups, including one focused on research on private education. We included home schools under the general meaning of private schools. A *Perspective* describes one moment that stuck in my memory.

We had several new members in the private school research group, and they were as interested in getting to know the old timers as we were in getting to know them. Several of the new people were especially interested in this matter of teaching children at home. "What is the best method of home schooling a child," one asked a colleague who specializes in research on home schools? His reply was very instructive. "First, you should consider the child," he said. "What are his interests, what are his needs and in what way does he learn best? No one best way to do home schooling has been found. The method must be made to fit the child." (*Perspective*, 2006, May 17)

From my perspective, that is good counsel for all types of schools.

The subject of home schools is of special interest to social science researchers. How do those who have been homeschooled in their childhood turn out when they become adults? This research question has resulted in a growing body of literature on the topic. One recent study indicated benefits to adults that had been home schooled as children when compared with adults who had attended traditional schools. The condition under study included factors necessary in the development of intrinsic motivation. (Riley, 2015)

## NONPUBLIC SCHOOLS

Private schools sometimes referred to as nonpublic schools, have been in existence since before the Republic was formed. With the emergence of the common school concept and compulsory school attendance laws, a shift to public school dominance occurred. Then came the waves of immigration that included people from countries where the dominant religion was Catholic. As children from these families enrolled in the school, they discovered a definite Protestant orientation in the classroom instruction. Eventually, the Catholic bishops became concerned about the education of their children and maintaining allegiance to the Catholic faith. As a result, Catholic schools soon became a dominant force within the Church (Walch, 2014). Schools sponsored by the Lutheran and Seventh-day

Adventist faith communities soon followed suit with their own system of religious schools. A variety of other types of non-public schools developed during the years since the Republic was founded. Diversity seems to be the best general description for the nonpublic schools. They include not only the religiously affiliated schools, but also private religious schools without denominational support. Secular private schools of many varieties offer their services to the public. All of these nonpublic schools provide options to parents as they choose schools for their children. Most private schools charge a tuition fee to cover the cost of operating the school. In some instances, the school receives a subsidy from a sponsoring organization, such as a church. Proceeds from an endowment also provides for a significant portion of the operating costs in elite private schools. Such schools usually have relatively high tuition rates. This results in a form of self-selection that helps the school maintain a student body with desirable characteristics. Eventually, public school leaders noticed that private schools were a major competitor for students. Their response was to seek enactment of regulations for the nonpublic schools. Much variation in regulation occurred from state to state. Some states allowed the nonpublic schools a great deal of freedom in their operations. Other states enforced a regulatory regimen that seemed to private school leaders to be overly constricting. These states claimed it was necessary to keep a close eye on private schools to ensure that all the children of the state got an adequate education.

In an intensive study of private schools and their relationship to the need for an educated population, Randall (1994) expressed doubt on the states' claim. He stated, "Besides the lack of any substantial benefits, most regulations exact a high cost from private schools. Just as important, research conducted in connection with this study did not discover a single documented case in which attendance at a private school had harmed a child in any way" (p 119).

My experience as both a teacher and administrator in private schools tends to support the conclusions of Randall's research. There might be times when parents do not exercise the best judgment regarding what is best to meet their own children's educational needs. However, those are unusual instances. Most parents demand that the nonpublic school provide a quality education for their children.

Schools do not need government regulation to make that happen.

Private schools, while competitive with public schools, are at a disadvantage when the cost of tuition is entered into the formula. Public schools are free to parents yet, if they enroll their children in a private school, they still have to pay property tax to support the public schools. Still, nonpublic schools should have a place in the menu of school choices. Nationally recognized authority on nonpublic schools, Bruce Cooper, (1994) sums up the topic with a short statement, "In summary, then, private schools have made a significant contribution to America's school reform effort, supplying ideas, concepts, dedication, and productivity" (p. 188).

## SOME FINAL THOUGHTS

This chapter explored a number of options provided to parents as a part of the educational reform agenda. I strongly support the efficacy of freedom of choice in deciding the optimum venue for schooling one's children. The free market can be a severe taskmaster for school administrators. However, I am convinced it is the best chance we have to bring lasting improvement to the nation's schools. The only choice I have been hesitant to support is the voucher plan. That is because I fear the heavy hand of the state bureaucracy will jump at the opportunity to impose restrictive regulations on participating private schools. Such an event would have a negative effect on the value of private schools.

Some educators fear that the rough and tumble of the business world would destroy the democratic values taught in the public schools. I do not discount that possibility. A *Perspective* published a decade ago speaks to that issue.

From my perspective, no benefit accrues when supporters of the three approaches to schooling feud among themselves. They should consider that they all have the same goals—the education of children. Thus, if they see themselves involved in education rather than schooling, they will find much common ground.

Public school people should be thankful for the tax dollars that are saved when parents home school their children or send them to a private school. Private school supporters should recognize the advantage they have in being able to select their student body while the public schools must provide services to all children.

Home-school parents must acknowledge that more formal approaches to education are best for many if not most children. Rather than attacking public schools they should admit that universal home schooling is bad public policy as evidenced by the experience of Afghanistan. That country's four years of home schooling did not provide any benefit to the nation. (*Perspective*, 2005, June 22)

## LIST OF *PERSPECTIVES* REFERENCED

Published in *The Journal Era,* Berrien Springs, Michigan

1996, November 20. A Quick Look at the Voucher Plan
1997, May 21. Some Thoughts on Choice
1998, March 11. Choice of Education
1998, June 24. Engler's Attack on Public Schools
2000, October 11. Examining the Myths About Vouchers
2000, October 18. More Thoughts on Vouchers
2005, June 8. A Quiet Week and the Future Ahead
2005, June 22. More Thoughts on Schooling
2006, May 17. Consider the Child
2008, February 20. Choice in Public Education
2011, April 27. The Problem with School Vouchers
2012, January 4. Some Thoughts on Charter Schools

## REFERENCES

Austin, M. J. (2015). Schools' responses to voucher policy: Participation decisions and early implementation experiences in the Indiana choice scholarship program. *Journal of School Choice, 9*(3), 354–379.

Boston, R. (2015). Despite sketchy schools and disappointing results, Washington D.C.'s private school voucher continues to stumble along. *Church & State, 68*(11), 4–5.

Chandler, K., Fortune, N., Lovett, J. N., & Scherrer, J. (2016, February). What should common core assessment measure? *Phi Delta Kappan, 97*(5), 60–63.

Chubb, J. E., & Moe, T. M. (2001). Better schools through new institutions: Giving Americans choice. In *The Josey-Bass reader on school reform* (pp. 279–280). San Francisco, CA: Jossey-Bass.

Cooper, B. (1994). Privatization, policy, and private schools: The irony of recent school reform. In C. E. Greenwalt II (Ed.), *Educational innovation: An agenda to frame the future* (pp. 172–199). Lanham, MA: University Press of America.

Cooper, B. S. (2005). Preface. In Bruce S. Cooper (Ed.), *Home schooling in full view: A reader* (pp. ix–x). Greenwich, CT: Information Age Publishing.

Fleming, D. J. (2014). Learning from schools: School choice, political learning, and policy feedback. *Policy Studies Journal, 542,* 55–78.

Furst, L. G. (1996, January 26). The short but vary curious legal history of Michigan's charter schools. *West's education law reporter, 125*(1), 1–13.

Gross, R. N. (2014). Public regulation and the origins of modern school choice. *Journal of Policy History, 31*(2), 509–533.

Kahlenberg, R. D. (2001). *All together now: Creating middle-class schools through public school choice.* Washington, DC: Brookings Institution Press.

Koppich, J. E. (1992). Choice in education: Not whether, but what. *Social Work in Education, 14*(4), 253–257.

Merrifield, J. D., & Gray, N. L. (2013). School choice and development: Evidence from the Edgewood experiment. *CATO Journal, 33*(1), 127–142.

Michigan Public School District. (2015, October 7). *Headcount & F. T. E. totals by building.* Berrien Springs, MI: Michigan Public School District.

Petersen, G. J. (2011). Superintendent leadership. In S. Conley, & B. S. Cooper (Eds.), *Finding, preparing, and supporting school leaders: Critical issues, useful solutions* (pp. 137–154). Lanham, MA: Rowman & Littlefield Education.

Possey-Maddox, L. (2016). Beyond the consumer: Parents, privatization, and fundraising in US urban public schooling. *Journal of Education Policy, 31*(2), 178–197.

Randall, E. V. (1994). *Private schools and public power: A case for pluralism.* New York: Teachers College Press.

Ravitch, D. (2010). *The death and life of the great American school system: How testing and choice are undermining education.* New York: Basic Books.

Ravitch, D. (2013). *Reign of error: The hoax of the privatization movement and the danger to America's public schools.* New York: Alfred A. Knopff.

Riley, G. (2015). Differences in competence, autonomy,and relatedness between home educated and traditionally educated young adults. *International Social Science Review, 90*(2), 1–27.

Schulz, S. (2015, October 7). *Pupil accounting auditor. Count Day: October 7, 2015, 1.* Berrien Springs, MI: Berrien RESA.

Smrekar, C. (1996). *The impact of school choice and community: In the interest of families and schools.* Albany: State University of New York Press.

Walch, T. (2014). The past before us: Historical models for future parish schools. In P. A. Bauch (Ed.), *Catholic schools in the public interest: Past, present and future directions* (p. 376). Charlotte, NC: Information Age Publishing.

Welsch, D. M., Statz, B., & Skidmore, M. (2010). An examination of inter-district public school transfers in Wisconsin. *Economics of Education Review, 29*(1), 126–137.

Woods, P. A., Bagley, C., & Glatter, R. (1998). *School choice and competition: Markets in the public interest?* London, UK: Routledge.

# CHAPTER 9

# STATE AND FEDERAL CHALLENGES TO LOCAL CONTROL

## MY GREAT FRUSTRATION

To say that I was frustrated would be a gross understatement. As a member of the local public school board, I was asked to serve on a small ad hoc committee tasked with revising the school district's entire policy manual. It was woefully out of date and desperately needed the work we were doing on it. The

Board had talked about this need for several years without any action. Eventually, the Superintendent recommended a consulting firm to give us guidance as we tackled this onerous undertaking. They sent a retired public school superintendent in their employ to give us assistance.

While I did not relish the thought of spending many hours in discussion about the fine points of school district policy, I did not protest the assignment. In my experience, I have observed that when organizations get their policies right, the management tends to be much more effective. I have distinct ideas regarding the governance process in schools, and I saw this as an opportunity to see that the policy manual was properly constructed.

*Helping Parents Understand Schools: A Different Perspective on Education and Schooling in America,* pages 145–163.

I soon discovered that the consulting firm had a template already in place for every part of the policy manual. It contained much legal language that the average person would not automatically understand. In some instances, the proposed statements contained sentence structure that was so convoluted that I feared it would be an embarrassment if it were published as an official document of the school district. The consultant usually responded to my objection over the proposed language with the simple statement, "You have to. The law requires it."

That was the source of my frustration. I felt that it restricted any variation among school districts in what policies would apply for their day-to-day operation. Eventually I began to doubt the veracity of our consultant. He made it easy for me to check on him because every policy in his template cited the specific law that required it. In doing a little fact checking, I discovered that he was mostly correct. The law on the books specified the statement that had to be made in the school district's voted policy.

That was not the end of my frustration over the higher levels of government intruding into the operation of local schools. As I stated in Chapter 7, some things should be decided at the local level. Not all children are the same throughout the United States, and a policy that may be very effective in one place might be disruptive in others. Certainly, we should be secure with a locally elected school board making some decisions about the day-to-day operation of the schools. In response to the No Child Left Behind Act (NCLB) that took a major step in expanding federal control of the nation's public schools, a *Perspective* emerged. The concluding paragraph is presented here.

> From my perspective, the framers of our Constitution were wise to leave some matters of public life to local levels of government. Some things, such as making war, fit well at the Federal level. However, schooling should stay with the states. The states and especially school districts here in Michigan are closer to the students who are served by the schools and have a better sense of what individual kids need in the classroom. Bureaucrats in Washington do not necessarily understand what is needed in the millions of classrooms throughout the country. Certainly much variation is present in those needs. One size does not fit all. Unfortunately, the attempt at accountability by the new federal legislation will in fact leave lots of children behind in the matter of schooling. Our federal lawmakers would do well to stay by the Constitution in matters of public schooling. (*Perspective*, 2003, April 2)

## THE ROAD AHEAD

Education and schooling have been local functions since the Republic was formed. The founders of the nation had no idea that eventually public schools would come under the heavy hand of the federal government. They made no provision for such an event in the Constitution, or the amendments to it. Yet, for the last few decades of the twentieth century, the federal government has played an increasingly intrusive role in the operation of the public schools. This resulted in a polarization between educators who see the school as a national function and those who support local control of local institutions. At this point, it appears that those who would increasingly centralize public education are in the ascendancy. This chapter explores the dynamic tension that results from efforts to decentralize educational policy with those who feel it should be increasingly centralized.

This chapter is divided into three major sections: The first section, The Centralization of Public Education, lays the groundwork for the rest of the chapter and especially exposes the federal intrusion into public education. Next comes a section dealing with the state's control of public schools. The third section presents my view on the proper role for federal involvement in public education. The chapter closes with a lighthearted look at the policies imposed on public schools as applied to the healthcare profession.

## CENTRALIZATION OF PUBLIC EDUCATION

Early in his first term in office, President Obama turned his attention to matters of public education. Apparently he had not been well briefed on contemporary issues in education, because he quickly stepped into the quagmire of merit pay. The pros and cons of that topic were discussed in Chapter 7. The issues and problems of public education look different from the vantage point of Washington DC, than to those who actually work in the schools. Inevitably, politicians try to find a simple answer to the questions of how to upgrade our education system. In response to the continuing quest to "fix" the schools in America, a *Perspective* was published. The concluding paragraph is presented here:

> So, what is the real answer to this? How do we improve poor performing schools so they are as good as high-performing schools? That is a really complex problem and cannot be solved with a simple answer. Some schools have found ways to become more effective in helping their students score high on statewide exams. But, no one simple answer has been found that works everywhere. Some things work better in one setting than another. That is one of the reasons I believe that public schooling should be controlled by the states and local communities *rather* than the federal government. My recommendation to President Obama is: do not try to control educational policy on the national level. Leave that up to the states as the Constitution provides. Then, let the local public schools devise the best educational program for the children in their community. (*Perspective,* 2009, April 15)

Without question, a good argument can be made for the centralization of policy making and control of the public schools. It makes for a much more uniform system of schools than occurs when schools are operated in a decentralized mode.

Lance Fusarelli (2009) sums it up quite well at the close of his chapter on the topic: "Increased state control and federal involvement in education are, on balance, a good thing, which will, over time, lead to a more coherent, tightly coupled, more organized, and more equitable system of schooling for all children than does the current system of educational governance and control" (p. 264).

While Fusarelli makes a good point about the advantages of centralized control over the public schools because of the uniformity it requires, some thought leaders suggest that innovation tends to flourish best under local control (Berube, 1994). The last paragraph of a *Perspective* agrees with that concept.

> From my perspective, not all wisdom emanates from Washington DC or even from Lansing. The best thing President Obama could do in his Race to the Top approach to education is to let the teachers be free to make their own race to the top. They do not need a bureaucrat from Washington telling them what to do in the classroom. They do not need a preplanned curriculum that is imposed throughout the entire nation to get a standardized educational product. Nor do they need a continuous round of standardized testing mandated by the state or national authorities. What they need is some degree of freedom to do what they have been trained to do. Let the teachers teach! (*Perspective*, 2011, March 16)

## Counter-Revolution in Education

Other observers also maintain that innovation will flourish better when it is encouraged close to the classroom. O'Brian (1994) concurs with his insightful statement: "Real improvement of classroom instruction requires that teachers buy into the reform. When they make reforms their own business and become energized by changes in the classroom, they can energize their students" (p. 52).

On the next page, he further states, "Americans would be wise to accept the notion that there is no magic wand in the hands of state leaders, teachers, business leaders, or educational researchers" (p. 53). There seems to be a confrontation brewing between those who favor innovation at the classroom level and those who support the centralization of education (Woods, Bagley, & Gatter, 1998, p. 213).

America was born in revolution. The whole idea behind our Constitution was a revolutionary concept at the time. This notion—that groups of ordinary people gathered together in a geographic area could govern themselves without the nobility or even the landed gentry to guide them—was unique among the nations on our planet. Public schools in America were among many governmental units that emerged throughout the nation. Yet there seems to be a reaction to the decentralization of governance in so many areas of life (Lane & Epps, 1992, p. xi). This counterrevolution threatens to sweep away some of our freedoms including the freedom of local control over public schools. The final paragraph of a *Perspective* sounds a warning for those desiring to maintain some degree of local control over the public schools.

> From my perspective, Americans of all political persuasions should view with alarm the progress of the counterrevolution and the subsequent loss of freedom. While we do need national policy for some broad issues such as defense, issues that can be decided at the local level should be left there. The same goes for the State. Not all wisdom resides in Lansing. Maybe it is time for ordinary people to wake up and

reclaim the freedom of local control that was won at great price some twenty-three decades ago. If we do not do that soon we will be saddled with the old world style of overly centralized government. (*Perspective*, 2005, October 26)

It is a popular pastime in America to bash the public schools. A few years ago, I read in a nationally distributed magazine, an article on the sad state of affairs in America's system of public education. The solution given was quite typical of professionals outside the field of education who have a mechanistic view of the teaching/learning process. His solution was to give more power over the schools to the national level of government. That is the way they do in other countries, he claimed. My reaction was predictable, as seen in two paragraphs from a *Perspective* at the time.

> Further, centralizing the control of education in the federal government is not the solution to any problem that might exist within the public schools. Of course we have a hodgepodge system of rules, regulations, procedures, and practice among the 50 states in their operation of public schools. We fought a long war some 200 years ago just so we could have such a system. The American Revolution was about getting rid of centralized government. Why should we go back to that?
>
> Achieving effective schools does not require rigid national standards, more centralization of control, or even more national testing. What it does require is strong leadership that keeps the work of the school focused on learning. Fortunately, our local schools, both public and private, seem to have adopted that formula and appear to be getting on about the task of becoming even more effective than what they already are. Hopefully, those who keep proposing more centralized control over education will fade away into the sunset. (*Perspective*, 2009, April 29)

For most of our nation's history, the federal government had little if any involvement in the primary and secondary schools. That changed when Congress passed the Elementary and Secondary Education Act (ESEA) in 1965 (Peterson, 2010, p. 74). At first, the federal footprint was very light with only a minimum of regulations impacting the schools. Funds provided by the federal government were in the form of categorical aid, rather than being designated to the general fund. The funding mechanism did not impinge on the authority of locally-elected boards in the operation of their public schools.

## Federal Intrusion

It did not take long for all that to change. Just after the turn-of-the-century, the No Child Left Behind (NCLB) act during the Bush administration—followed by Race to the Top (RTT) from the Obama administration—gave the federal government a great deal more power over the operation of public schools. As Ravitch (2013), noted regarding this shift in control to the federal level, "Its powers expanded far beyond the imaginings of the legislators who passed ESEA in 1965, or who created the Department of Education in 1979" (p. 281). Two paragraphs from a *Perspective* comment on this major step in centralizing control over American public schools.

> At the same time that the state of Michigan took a giant leap forward in the process of centralizing public education, a nationwide effort to establish the Common Core Standards, which would dictate a common curriculum for all public schools throughout the nation, is moving at full speed (Hartong, 2016). While acceptance of these standards is voluntary on the part of states, 42 of them have already signed on. We are fast on the road to a one-size-fits-all curriculum throughout the United States. From my perspective, this does not augur well the future of schooling in our beloved Republic.
>
> The Common Core Standards are based on the erroneous assumption that all children are alike and have the same needs and that all communities have a similar sociological makeup. This is a faulty assumption. I find it puzzling that among the prime movers behind the centralization of American public education are conservative politicians who deplore European socialism. What they are giving us is essentially a socialist system of centralized education such as what we might find in many European nations. Unfortunately, there seems to be no stopping this movement. (*Perspective*, 2011, June 1)

## *The Ultimate in Centralization*

A multitude of challenges to local control of public education are ever present throughout the nation. Those arising from the federal government are most serious in my mind. In the previous section, I noted that it was the confluence of two federal programs (NCLB & RTT) very early in the 21st century that made a major change in the locus of control over the public schools.

During the 2008 presidential election cycle, Senator John McCain, the Republican candidate, announced his proposal for federal involvement in public education and operation of the schools. I found it very strange that he was running as a conservative, yet proposing a liberal educational policy. I did not favor his proposed change in federal policy for the public schools. The last two paragraphs from a *Perspective* tell the rest of the story.

> Having considered McCain's proposal on education, I then turned to Barack Obama's recommendations for federal policy. I must admit that I was greatly disappointed, for he also sees an expanded role for the Federal government in education. I suggest that both candidates get a copy of the Constitution and read Amendment 10 which provides that functions not delegated to the federal government by the Constitution are reserved to the states. Since education and the operation of schools is not one of the functions listed in the Constitution as belonging to the federal level, it by default belongs to the states.
>
> It is true that Article 1, Section 8 allows Congress to provide for the general welfare of the United States, which might be interpreted to include funding public education. However, nothing that allows the operation and management of schools at the

federal level can be found among the enumerated powers listed in the Constitution. Thus, the federal government's role should be limited to providing funds for specific programs that cannot be adequately funded at the local or state level.

However, the kinds of control over public schools proposed by both candidates is clearly outside the intent of the Constitution. From my perspective, the federal role in public education should be a very limited one. Both candidates should rethink their current proposals on this issue. (*Perspective*, 2008, August 13)

Several years earlier, I became alarmed over the possibility of greater federal incursion into the domain of public education. During the presidential election campaign of 2000, both candidates promised to pour significant amounts of federal money into the public schools. President Bush delivered on his promise by pushing an education bill through Congress. At that time, I thought it was a bad plan and would not be beneficial to either America or its children. The following paragraphs from the heart of a *Perspective* identify my concerns.

The Bush education plan requires that schools test children every year in core subjects. Those schools where children do not meet the federal standard will lose their federal money. By one report teachers at such failing schools would have to be either fired or assigned elsewhere. The federal government does not give large sums of money to the public schools—somewhere between seven and ten per cent of total revenue.

Most funding comes from either state or local sources. Further, in the Constitution education is not within the purview of the federal government. But that is just one reason why the new education plan is bad for the country.

In addition to encroaching on the states' powers over public schooling, the federal education bill is defective in its attempt to hold schools accountable. Federal funds for public schools are quite limited.

Yet, as Kahlenberg (2001), notes, school's dependence on federal funds "gives the federal government a potent tool to use in leveraging education reform" (p. 185). When they take federal money, the federal mandate will dictate to states and local school boards how the schools should be run. It is the states and local boards that should hold the schools accountable not the federal bureaucracy. Under the new plan the agency that gives the least financial support has the most to say about school operations.

Public and private schools alike are expected to deliver a wide variety of services to the children they serve. Of course instruction in academic subjects is the primary function. However, other tasks are required of school people such as health services, job training, sex education, civic responsibility, breakfast and lunch, reporting of child abuse, recreation and entertainment, and many others too numerous to list here. We demand these services of the schools yet the only measure of their success is a narrow test of student's academic skills. From my perspective, this one test is not a valid measure of school performance. (*Perspective*, 2001, June 20)

Two years after the previous *Perspective* was published, I again expressed concerns about what I viewed as problematic portions of the federal education law. While attending a workshop focused on the various provisions of the federal law, I became keenly aware of the accountability provisions imposed upon public schools. Accountability is "bureaucratic speak" for testing. Two paragraphs from a *Perspective* on this topic show my deep concern:

> Current education law also assumes that all children possess the same mental capacity. All children must be tested no matter their ability. Kids with low intelligence are expected to score as high on standardized tests as those with a high level of intelligence. Physical handicap is no excuse for not getting a high test score. If the child is sick with the flu on test day, s/he is still expected to score high. If s/he does not come to school, the test is graded as zero and that score goes into the average for the school. Even students with limited English ability must take the test and have their scores as part of the computation for the school average.

> Some schools that are populated by very bright students will look good when the school report cards are made available to the public. Schools lacking such advantage will not be so favored and the public will be led to believe that it is because the teachers are doing a bad job. What the public must remember, if they are to make any sense of the report, is that children are not all the same. Some have more capacity to learn than others. Some are easier to teach than others and some are better test takers than others. It is this natural variability among people that the Federal government seems to have ignored. As a result, they will bring severe score high on the flawed tests that are used to grade the schools. *(Perspective*, 2003, April 2)

## *Large Scale Reforms*

As I see it, a major problem with the ultimate in centralization, where controls over the public schools are largely housed in the federal government, is that those who make and enforce the regulations, tend to ignore the individual differences among children they serve. A great deal of variation exists among the human species. Federal programs in education that are implemented on a nationwide basis tend to ignore that fact. It has been my observation that large-scale reforms generally fail rather quickly (Hoff, 2001, pp. 435–6). The ineffectiveness of so many large-scale educational programs can be explained by a lack of awareness regarding the value of the personal touch.

In designing the components of any educational program there must be built in to it allowance for human variability. However, in doing so the seeds of failure are planted. It is very difficult to maintain adequate controls if too much freedom is given to on-site program directors. Near the end of the Bush administration's first term, a *Perspective* was published that expressed my concerns regarding public education being centralized in the federal government.

> Of continuing worry to me is the basic assumption by the NCLB Act that all children can not only learn but they can learn the same amount and during the same amount

of time. Under the guise of high standards, all children must be proficient in basic subjects by the year 2014. If they do not make adequate yearly progress toward this goal, severe punitive actions can be taken against the school they attend and the personnel who serve them. In other words, all children must be above average or else!

From my perspective, the new Secretary of Education needs to go back to school. She needs to learn that children are all different and have different capacities for learning. They do not all learn at the same rate and no amount of punitive measures on the part of the federal government will change that fact. Mrs. Spellings can close all the failing public schools, fire all the teachers and administrators, put all the money into vouchers, violate the Constitution to her heart's content, and take any other punitive action she desires, but she cannot change the simple fact that some children will remain below average. Try as she might, I seriously doubt that there will come a time when all children in middle school in America will learn to solve the quadratic equation. Some will be doing well if they can learn to tie their shoes while others may master calculus but they will not all be proficient in math and learn at the same pace. Certain laws of human nature exist that the federal government, with all its magnificent power, cannot violate. (*Perspective*, 2004, November 24)

While I agree that the federal Department of Education plays an important role, it should do so with a very light touch. The United States is such a large nation that programs affecting individual people are not well handled at the national level. This is obvious from a review of how regulations have put a stranglehold on innovation at the local school level. The bureaucracy in

Washington tends to view children as interchangeable parts in the machine shop of learning. As Peterson (2010) noted, programs imposed by the federal government "turned the eyes of local administrators away from their immediate constituency of parents and taxpayers toward rules and procedures designed by those to whom they reported" (p. 227). From my perspective, regulations affecting individual children are best developed at the local or state level of government. The final paragraph from a *Perspective* sums up my thinking on this topic.

I agree that some things are best handled at the federal level. Other things are best decided locally. The operation of schools is one of those that should be handled locally. One size does not fit all when it comes to classroom teaching. If people from other countries, which have a highly centralized educational system, can see the advantages of American decentralized public education, one wonders why our leaders in Washington can't see the same thing. Hopefully they will eventually come to their senses and keep their hands off our public schools. (*Perspective*, 2010, January 13)

## STATE CHALLENGES TO LOCAL CONTROL

It is not only the federal government that interferes with local control of schools but states also present challenges to local decision-making on school policy (Fusarelli, 2009, p. 254). The State has the right to control the public schools. It has plenary power in this aspect of governance. However, most states have delegated much of the responsibility for day-to-day operations and decision making to local units of government, known in Michigan as school districts. On some occasions only one school is in the district. However, in the more populous areas, a large number of schools might be found in a single district under the control of an elected Board and administered by a superintendent at the district office.

The state of Michigan provided for a great deal of local control of the public schools early in its history. It has been difficult for many people to accept the notion that the state has the right to control the schools any way it wants. From my perspective, just because the state has the right to control public schools does not mean it should exercise such power. It might be well for states to protect the community ethos that develops when the local school is not overly dominated by regulation from higher levels of government (Foster, 2004).

Several years ago political leaders in Michigan publically discussed several ideas for improving public education. Since we live in a technological society, it was suggested that the state require all schools to have a curriculum that was heavy in math and science. A school district that was getting state aid would be required to comply. One paragraph from a *Perspective* illustrates my response.

> These are all good ideas, but from my perspective, not every good idea should be required. We live in a sufficiently advanced society that ordinary citizens should be trusted to make decisions for themselves as to what course of action they should follow. Local school boards, which have been elected by the public, should be able to determine how much math and science is needed by the children in the local community. That answer might vary throughout the state. Not every child in Michigan can profit by taking a course in calculus. Some might only be able to handle the basics of arithmetic. Local boards are better able to decide that than the state legislature or even the state board of education. (*Perspective*, 2005, December 14)

Several years later, the movement to make kindergarten required of all children came under discussion by the legislature. At present, kindergarten is optional. Some school districts offer both full-day and half day programs for kindergarten age children. This allows parents to make decisions as to what is best for the child. Two paragraphs from a *Perspective* written in response are presented here.

> When the state mandates a specific educational program for all children in an age cohort, it presents a challenge to the philosophical foundations of our Republic. As James Clark McReynolds so cogently wrote some 90 years ago, "The child is not the mere creature of the state; those who nurture him and direct his destiny have the right, coupled with the high duty, to recognize and prepare him for additional obligations." *(Pierce v. Society of Sisters*, 1925)

> While the state has the responsibility to provide adequate education to all children within its boundaries, it certainly does not have unrestrained control over those children. Parents should be the primary source of information regarding the proper time for their children to enter the formal academic setting. The state legislature with all of its collective wisdom is still not smart enough to make that important decision

by a broad sweep of its lawmaking power. In my view, parents are best suited to determine the appropriate level of schooling for their young children. We do not need any state mandates intruding into the sanctity of the home. (*Perspective,* 2015, December 16)

## Providing Information to the Public

Several years ago, the state legislature in Michigan pushed a bill through that required school districts to provide a variety of information to the public. I support the idea of keeping the public well informed about school operations. However, not all information is easily assembled, and further much of the reports required by Lansing (The state capital) would not be of much use to the public. Publishing the school district's check register, for example, gives the public very little useful information regarding the financial status of the schools. It seems that the legislators did not trust local school district administrators to provide sufficient information.

From my perspective, local school districts, under the control of locally elected boards, should be trusted to provide whatever information the public wants. If the public is not satisfied with the Board, they can always vote them out of office. In response to the lawmaker's misguided challenge to local control, a *Perspective* was published. One paragraph shows my agitation about the situation.

> Local public schools are already providing a wide variety of school information. The test scores are reported in the local media as are financial data including employee salaries. Local voters have ample information to determine if local boards are doing the job. They also have recourse at election time to challenge individual members of the board. And, if they are really in a rush they can always ask for a recall election. They do not need any help from the big government people in Lansing. (*Perspective*, 2000, April 12)

## The Unanswered Question

During the 19 years I was a member of the public school board, I was invited to attend a "Legislative Breakfast" that occurred a few times each year. The locally elected state and federal legislators were present to update school board members on potential legislation impacting public schools. It was usually an informative session. After the speeches had been made, the politicians fielded questions from the audience. I was generally satisfied that our representatives at the higher levels of government were doing their best to advance the best interests of public education. Instead of asking a question about the minutia of pending legislation, I decided to query our politicians about a more global issue. A *Perspective* tells the rest of the story, beginning with the question I asked.

> During the 19 years that I have been on the school board, I have noticed a continual centralization of authority over the public schools by both the state and federal government. During the recent revision of the policy manual in our district I found that

most of our policies are mandated by a higher level of government. We can't even decide on when the first day of school will be. My questions are:

1. Is there any hope that some semblance of local control can be restored to locally elected Boards of Education?
2. What do local boards need to do to restore faith at the state and federal levels, that we have the ability and wisdom to operate the public schools in the best interests of the public?"

At the end of my question a moment of dead silence occurred. None of the politicians rushed to the microphone to give an answer. Finally, our State Senator said that he would respond to the issue of setting the first day of school. He extolled the virtues of the state government in trumping decisions by local school boards on that matter when it mandated that school could not begin until after Labor Day.

This increased the customer base for the resorts in our state by extending the vacation time for a week or two. The result, he said, is that the resorts make more money and therefore pay more taxes to the state which results in the state giving more funds to the local schools. It is to the local school's benefit, he indicated, for the state to take this authority away from local boards. It was obvious to me that the answer to my first question was a resounding "No! We have no hope that local control can be restored to locally elected school boards."

From my perspective, it is time for our politicians in both Lansing and Washington, DC to loosen the reins of power a bit and give local school boards more control over the operation of the public schools. We have had too much of a move toward the old world education system of centralized curriculum, centralized testing, and centralized administration.

Over 200 years ago we threw off the shackles of European centralization with a revolutionary idea that "we the people" are capable of governing ourselves. It has worked pretty well for two centuries but more recently the conservative interests in our state seem intent on moving back to the centralized the governance system that is so popular in the old world countries of Europe. So here's a call for a return to the American Revolution: let's restore local control to the governance of our public schools. (*Perspective*, 2007, October 24)

## PROPER PLACE FOR FEDERAL INVOLVEMENT

Several years ago, in the early days of the Internet, I joined a listserv (an electronic discussion group) that focused on school administration. As I far as I could tell, over 1000 people subscribed to this group. In one discussion, an elementary principal from a southern state expressed great disappointment because the federal government was discontinuing a program that assisted impoverished children. A member of the group, who was a frequent contributor to the discussion, went by the name Sharon. "Why should taxpayers be robbed of their hard-earned money to help poor kids in Arkansas?" She asked. "The local community should take care of such cases. The federal government cannot do everything."

The listserv went what has become known as "viral" with a wide variety of responses. They consisted of such things as, "What tree did you fall out of? Why do you hate children? Get a life! Eat more fiber in your diet!" Not a single one of them had a serious answer to Sharon's question. I began to realize why she did not provide her true identity. She used the code name Sharon, instead.

From my perspective, good reasons exist for providing special assistance to children with special needs. Likewise, good reasons exist for placing the funding mechanism for such programs at the federal level rather than the state or local level. Four paragraphs from one of the earliest *Perspectives* provide the rationale for these statements.

> First, we live in a mobile society. Those poor children from Arkansas probably will not be living in their home town as adults. They could well be living in California, Nebraska, or New York. The results of poor education in Arkansas become a nationwide problem and needs a nationwide solution. Second, local communities have seldom been responsive to the needs of disadvantaged or dis-empowered people.

> Local communities would not provide local resources to educate the children of migrant workers even though those workers are essential to the local economy. Nor would they designate the necessary funds to provide schooling for physically handicapped children. In the extreme is a local community in Virginia that refused to fund public schools at all if they had to admit children who were not white. Only at the higher units of government is there any willingness to commit funds for the education of disadvantaged children.

> Economic reasons exist for funding education for such children. The success of America's businesses depends on a continuing supply of educated workers. Such workers are more productive and earn more money than uneducated workers. Higher wages are pumped back into the economy and everyone benefits. Children who fail to get an adequate education become adults who are a drag on the economy. As an example a majority of the prisoners in America are lacking the educational skills to be productive citizens. In Michigan it costs about $30,000 per year to house a prisoner while it costs around $5,000 to educate a child. Education pays much higher returns and is a much better investment.

> Yes, Sharon, good reasons exist for why taxpayers should spend their hard earned money to educate poor children in Arkansas or where ever they might live. The whole nation benefits by such an expenditure. (*Perspective*, 1995, June 21)

In general, I have observed that citizens in small units of government seldom are willing to spend tax dollars on children who are outside the mainstream of the community. In some cases, sufficient resources are not available within the community to meet the special needs. Thus, these programs are best handled at the federal level.

During the Clinton administration, the federal government put in place a program to provide local school districts with financial assistance in updating their facilities. I supported the proposal even though I have a natural inclination to be suspicious of anything coming from Washington, D. C. I felt it was appropriate for America to invest in upgrading its aging infrastructure. Many school districts still had buildings that were constructed during the Great Depression. Two paragraphs from a *Perspective* provide a defense for what was seen by some observers as inappropriate federal intrusion into the public schools.

> In this respect, schools should function like business. While I agree that educational policy should be made primarily at the local level, capital investment should be augmented at the state or national level. The educational function in an advanced society such as the United States is absolutely essential to maintaining its international competitiveness. To leave the funding of school construction to the chance of local property values, which have huge disparities throughout the nation, just does not make good business sense.

> I realize that conservatives throughout America shudder at the prospect of any new intrusion by the federal government into matters that have been by tradition under local control. I think they can rest easy on this one. I doubt that having the federal government pay some of the interest on locally voted bonds will result in much more intrusion than we already have. Clinton's school construction plan is a good one even if it is politically motivated. The cost will have minimal impact on the federal budget but will spur the economy not only with increased construction activity but decreased millage rates for local taxpayers. The best economic benefit will be the increased educational potential which will keep America competitive in a global economy. (*Perspective*, 1996, July 17)

Criticizing the public schools is a favorite pastime of the American people. Every four years, when the presidential election is held, it seems that any candidate who intends to be taken seriously must have a plan for reforming the public schools. In the year 2000, both candidates developed serious proposals for making major changes in federal education policy. Both George Bush and Al Gore had plans to increase the federal control over the operation of public education. My response is contained in three paragraphs from a *Perspective* published at the time.

> The framers of our nation's basic document had a rather novel idea for the time. They believed that some aspects of life exist that a national government is not well suited to dabble in. Some things are best left to smaller units of government such as the states. And in some states the same plan was followed by delegating some powers to even smaller units such as counties, cities, towns, and townships. In some states, such as Michigan, special units of government called school districts are given power over educational policy. The idea that policy relating to the operation of schools should be close to the people is still unusual in much of the world. Most countries have such matters decided at the national level.

While Americans are very adept at criticizing their own public schools, the rest of the world marvels at our system of public education. They envy the involvement parents have in the operation of the schools. In many parts of the world, school management is dictated by the Ministry of Education in the nation's capital. School administrators simply relay orders from the central government to the teachers and report on their obedience. Local control is only a far-fetched dream.

Michigan has found a reasonable balance between state education policy and local control. So have a number of other states. We do not need the federal government telling classroom teachers how to teach reading as Bush would do, or dictate teacher salaries as Gore would do. Enough federal regulations are already in place. The schools do not need any more bureaucrats from Washington watching over them. From my perspective, both Bush and Gore should leave education policy at the state level where it belongs. (*Perspective*, 2000, October 4)

## A Modest Proposal

Throughout this chapter, I have expressed my concerns about the overreach of the federal government in public education. I point out a few places where the federal is better suited to provide services than local agencies. Nevertheless, most of the policy issues for the operation of public education are best handled at the state or local level. So, how can public policy be framed to differentiate which level should be in control? During the presidential election campaign of 2012, I pondered this question in response to the policy President Obama had implemented during his first term in office, in contrast to proposals by his opponent Governor Romney. Two paragraphs from a *Perspective* published just prior to Election Day summarize my thinking at the time.

I would not favor the elimination of the federal Department of Education as Governor Romney has suggested at various times. Good public policy would include a definite role for such a department. Especially important is the dissemination of information and research findings to the public schools, which was the original purpose of the Office of Education before it became a department. Also, federal funding is needed to support children who are not well served at the local level, including those who are physically or cognitively handicapped, and other special needs students.

However, any regulations accompanying funding for federal programs should be restricted to the program in question and not broadly applied to the operation of the entire school district. Only a few other things that can be more effectively accomplished at the federal level than at the state or local level come to mind. From my perspective, they are very limited. While I am somewhat like Mitt Romney in that my thinking is in a constant state of flux, these are my current thoughts on what would be effective educational policy at the federal level. (*Perspective*, 2012, October 17)

## A Glimmer of Hope

I had about given up hope of ever seeing a reversal of the trend toward centralizing educational policy, when Congress surprised everybody by voting, with bipartisan support, an enactment entitled, Every Student Succeeds Act (ESSA). The final paragraphs of a *Perspective,* reveal my guarded excitement resulting from that event.

> Then it happened. A hopelessly divided Congress cast aside many of their political animosities and put together an education law that reduces the power of the federal government over the local public schools, while maintaining an appropriate level of funding. Monies made available for the public schools will now come through block grants to the states. Imagine that! Federal funds but limited federal oversight.
>
> From my perspective, on December 11, when the President signed the "Every Student Succeeds Act" (ESSA) federal education policy made a major step forward. I have not seen the details yet, but it appears that when it comes to public education, the politicians finally got it right. (*Perspective,* 2015, December 24)

ESSA removed some federal controls previously imposed on public schools and returned at least a portion of the oversight function to the state level—which is now responsible for enforcement of the rules and regulations. My reaction was guarded as indicated by the last two sentences of another *Perspective* published on the topic.

> While I remain cynical about anything coming out of Washington, ESSA, is a major step in the right direction. However, from my perspective, more work remains to be done in getting the federal involvement in education in the right relationship with the states. (*Perspective,* 2015, December 30)

### SOME FINAL THOUGHTS

One of the major flaws in just about every educational program that originates in the federal government is the uniformity that is required in its implementation. No recognition of individual differences—among children or even groups of children—is recognized. They are considered interchangeable parts in the vast territory of United States. That is probably a major reason why neither No Child Left Behind (NCLB) nor Race to the Top (RTT) reached their goals.

Just as a spoof, I decided to apply the basic principles of federal regulations controlling education to healthcare providers. What initiated my journey into the realm of foolishness was a report that residents of the county where I live fall far below the state and national averages on several indicators of health. Mimicking the critics of public schools, I noted the high cost of healthcare. The public has a right to expect at least average health for the people in our county. Maybe Congress and the State Legislature should mandate the development of new and more rigorous tests to determine the level of the citizen's health. Everyone who seeks the services of a healthcare provider must take the same test regardless of their medical condition. That will allow a comparison of the relative effectiveness of each healthcare facility.

The rigorous testing will provide the data to hold healthcare professionals accountable for the services rendered just like we have in public education. At the end of the year each medical facility must publish the average test scores of all clients that have been given care. The public will then be able to see where they can get the best health care. The rest of my silly plan is described in three paragraphs from a *Perspective* that was published.

> For example, since obesity seems to be a major health problem, my plan would require that everyone who seeks care at a hospital, dentist office, nursing home, mental health clinic or doctor's office will be weighed with exacting weight scales. The record of such weighing will be kept and the average weight of all clients of that facility will be published at the end of the year. Those facilities where the average exceeds the standard for healthy weight will be given a warning. If they do not make adequate yearly progress (AYP) toward the goal of good health for their clients, they will be required to pay the cost of healthcare for any of their clients at another facility that does meet the national standard.

> Weight is only one of the health problems we face, so the same process will be implemented for other indicators of good health. Each client at a health facility will be tested for blood sugar, high blood pressure, arthritis, and propensity to smoke and drink. Every healthcare facility will be required to show AYP for all those indicators of good health or face the same penalty as described above. Of course each facility is required to provide care for anyone who seeks its service. They cannot just choose clients who are already healthy. Eventually, those healthcare providers who are not able to meet the good health standards for their clients would lose their license to operate here in Michigan. This is another form of accountability which is so essential to meet the health crisis we face.

> Further the state legislature should require that each healthcare provider implement a high quality health plan for each client under its care. Since obesity, which leads to Type II diabetes, is a major problem in our nation as well as here in Berrien County, it only stands to reason that everyone seeking health care should be placed on a low calorie diabetic diet. I realize that people who tend toward thinness might protest but they have to remember that we have a national health crisis and we must deal with it. The good health of America depends on us taking drastic measures to meet this serious situation. (*Perspective*, 2006, August 16)

I may have overstated the case in my attempt at satire. However, many of the regulations imposed upon the public schools are just as foolish as what I have suggested for the healthcare industry. From my perspective, it is bound to be that way as long as the decision making process is centered in the federal government. This chapter ended on a positive note with hope for the future. If other programs are able to shift major control to states or local level, I believe there will be a great improvement in the public schools in America.

## LIST OF *PERSPECTIVES* REFERENCED

Published in *The Journal Era,* Berrien Springs, Michigan

1995, June 21. Code Name Sharon
1996, July 17. Clinton's School Repair Program
2000, April 12. Another bad idea from Lansing
2000, October 4. Bush and Gore on Education
2001, June 20. More Trouble for the Schools
2003, April 2. No Child Left Behind
2004, November 24. All the Children Are Above Average
2005, October 26. Counterrevolution in America
2005, December 14. Every Good Idea
2006, August 16. No Person Left Unhealthy
2007, October 24. An Unanswered Question
2008, August 13. Federal Education Policy
2009, April 15. Another Simple Answer
2009, April 29. The Only Way to Fix the System
2010, January 13. RTT is Bad Policy
2011, March 16. Not All Wisdom Emanates from Washington
2011, June 1. Centralizing Public Education
2012, October 17. Some Thoughts on Education Policy
2015, December 16. When Mandating a Good Idea Is Bad Policy
2015, December 24. The Politicians Finally Got It Right
2015, December 30. Still More Work to Do

## REFERENCES

Berube, M. R. (1994). *American school reform: Progressive, equity,and excellence movements, 1883–1993.* Westport, CT: Praeger.

Foster, W. P. (2004). The decline of the local: A challenge to educational leadership. *Educational Administration Quarterly, 40*(2), 176–191.

Fusarelli, L. D. (2009). Improvement or interference? Reenvisioning the state in education reform. In B. C. Fusarelli & B. S. Cooper (Eds.), *The rising state: How state power is transforming our nation's schools* (pp. 243–264). Albany, NY: State University of New York.

Hartong, S. (2016). New structures of power and regulation within 'distributed' education policy—The example of the US common core state standards initiative. *Journal of Education Policy, 31*(2), 213–225.

Hoff, D. J. (2001). With 2000 looming,chances of meeting national goals iffy. In *The Jossey-Bass Reader on School Reform* (pp. 434–439). San Francisco, CA: Jossey-Bass.

Kahlenberg, R. D. (2001). *All together now: Creating middle-class schools through public school choice.* Washington, DC: Brookings Institution Press.

Lane, J. J., & Epps, E. G. (1992). Introduction and overview. In J. J. Lane & E. G. Epps (Eds.), *Restructurng the schools: Problems and prospects* (pp. ix–xvi). Berkeley, CA: McCutchan Publishing Corporation.

O'Brian, T. V. (1994). Educational reform movements among the states in the last 10 year. In C. E. Greenwalt, II (Ed.), *Educational innovation: An agenda to frame the future* (pp. 31–58). Lanham, MD: University Press of America.

Peterson, G. J. (2011). Superintendent leadership. In S. Conley & B. S. Cooper (Eds.), *Finding, preparing, and supporting school leaders: Critical issues, useful solutions* (pp. 137–154). Lanham, MA: Rowman & Littlefield Education.

*Pierce v. Society of Sisters,* 268 U.S. 510 (1925).

Ravitch, D. (2013). *Reign of error: The hoax of the privatization movement and the danger to America's public schools.* New York: Alfred A. Knopff.

Woods, P. A., Bagley, C., & Glatter, R. (1998). *School choice and competition: Markets in the public interest?* London, UK: Routledge.

CHAPTER 10

# SCHOOL FINANCE AND FINANCIAL MANAGEMENT

## THE FAILURE OF FEDERAL FUNDS

"It was not time to panic yet, but it soon would be." That was one of the thoughts going through my mind. As I peered through the little window into the University Boardroom, I could see six men around the big conference table in animated discussion. The purpose of their discourse was to determine if my doctoral dissertation was acceptable, and if I had defended it well enough so that I was worthy of being granted the advanced degree. I thought I had answered their questions quite well, even deflecting the long, entangled, and deeply philosophical inquiries of the Dean of the School of Education. He was not a member of my committee but was, by University policy, allowed to sit at the defense with a full vote in the decision.

My impression was that the document was reasonably well constructed and further that my defense was more than adequate. The research topic was public school finance and especially the impact of federal aid to schools in the state of California. This was in the early days of federal involvement in the financing of the public education and I wanted to help shape public policy by determining if

*Helping Parents Understand Schools: A Different Perspective on Education and Schooling in America*, pages 165–180.

federal money was disbursed to the schools in such a way as to achieve one of its major purposes: to equalize the disparities in the funds available to finance the operation of public schools in the state. Much to my surprise, the research findings indicated that it did not. Federal funds were not distributed to public schools in a manner that significantly affected the financial inequalities that existed in the wealth available for school operation in the state of California. Wealthy districts were getting about as much federal aid as poor districts. Federal-aid did not assist in closing the gap that existed in financial support for the public schools in California (Furst, 1974). As I glanced through the little window into the somber chambers of the Board Room, the chair of my committee suddenly looked up and saw me with a worried look on my face. He immediately rushed to the door and apologized for the length of time I had been kept waiting. "We agreed to pass both your dissertation and the defense in the first five minutes of our discussion. We just got involved in talking about sports and forgot what our purpose was for being here." We both had a good laugh at the situation, and then all the other members rose to offer their congratulations for a successful defense.

## THE ROAD AHEAD

This chapter takes a look at the matter of money and education from two different vantage points. The next two sections deal with policy issues at the state level regarding the method by which public education is funded. First is the short history of changes in the method used by states to provide financial support for its public schools. This is followed by a rather long section that considers the experience of the State of Michigan as it grappled with the problem of finding an equitable method of financing public education. Because each of the 50 states has its own structure for public education, it is hard to find answers to the school funding issue that can be generalized across the whole country. Michigan's story provides an interesting look at the financial and political forces that impact attempts to change school funding formulas. The rather bizarre political fight in Michigan's legislature will probably not be replicated in any other state. However, it resulted in an improved policy on school funding that other states would do well to consider.

The third section turns to matters of financial management. It considers the oft-heard recommendation that schools should be run like a business. Some specific management procedures that are appropriate for public education are recommended. The final section introduces some advanced ideas on financial management. A short section on Some Final Thoughts ties the chapter together.

## A SHORT HISTORY OF SCHOOL FINANCE

Since early in the last century, discussions among educational leaders in America have considered the matter of financing the public schools. The tradition in America has been that a local tax on real property was the major source of revenue for local schools. That was in the days when ownership of property was considered an indicator of personal wealth. However, many things have changed over the years and real estate is no longer the best measure of a community's wealth nor is it an adequate source of revenue for many school districts within an individual state. This problem was made public when Elwood P. Cubberley (1905) published his doctoral dissertation in book form early in the 20th century. With the title of "School Funds and Their Apportionment," he documented the wide variation in funds available to finance the operation of America's public schools.

Tradition again had an overwhelming influence in perpetuating the contemporary belief that public schools are, and should be, under the control of local school boards. This was paramount in the minds of much of the voting public.

Funding should be provided locally, without any outside meddling (Arocho, 2014). However, as educational leaders began to express concern about the uneven education available to students throughout the state, legislatures in many states sought to remedy the problem by providing what was known as a foundation grant. This would guarantee every school district at least a certain basic amount of revenue for each student (Ramirez, 2003). Beyond that, it was up to the local taxpayers to provide sufficient financial support for the school.

It wasn't long before it became apparent that the foundation plan would not be sufficient to provide every district the funds needed to operate a modern school.

Various schemes were proposed by the so-called experts on school finance, one of which is known as district power equalizing (Verstegen, 2012). Under this plan the state would guarantee that when local districts set the tax rate for real property, each mill would generate at least a specified amount of funds for the district. In property-poor districts, the state would make up the difference between the guaranteed amount and actual revenue that was generated by the rate of taxation imposed on property. Thus, local districts maintained their independence and at the same time could be rewarded for their effort when they imposed a high rate of taxation (Mattoon, 1995).

This plan seemed to work for a while but it soon became evident that there were continuing wide disparities within the state regarding the funds available for school operation. Per-pupil revenue that was available for a child's education was dependent on value of the property within the geographic location where the child lived. People in property-poor districts had to impose a higher rate of taxation to generate sufficient income than those in property-rich districts, which could get the same amount of revenue with a much lower rate of taxation. It must be noted that poor people do not necessarily live in property poor districts. Property rich districts are those that have commercial and manufacturing ventures within their territory.

Districts that are primarily residential housing tend to have a lesser value and thus would be considered property poor. Over time, this dependence on the taxation of real property to support public education became problematic.

As costs of schooling rose faster than the value of property, public school boards soon discovered that the revenue raised by the tax rate they had imposed on the community began to decline relative to costs. Using the state of Michigan as an example, the financing formula put limits on the rate of taxation that school boards could levy without approval by the voters in the district. Thus, many of the school districts in the state faced difficult choices when it came to meeting the increasing revenue needs of the schools. They could either make radical cuts in expenditures or increase the rate of taxation, known as a millage rate. However, local boards did not have the authority to impose tax rates beyond a specified level. If they felt the need for additional revenue, they had to submit a proposal to the electorate to do so (Van Beek, 2010).

## THE MICHIGAN EXPERIENCE

The result in my home state of Michigan is a prime example of the conflict that developed in many communities throughout the nation. In general, people tend to support the public schools, but when it comes to reaching into their own pockets for the funds to do so, their support for the schools is not quite so strong. In the school district where I reside, the school board's public plea for help was met with cold indifference. However, when the board scheduled an election to ask for a higher millage rate, formal opposition arose and the community quickly descended into a hostile environment as far as public education was concerned,. The district's financial operations came under rigorous scrutiny to determine places where money was being wasted. Several millage elections went down to defeat causing a major crisis for the local school board. The tax rate allowed by law without a millage election was simply not enough to operate the schools at any level of academic integrity.

Meanwhile, a few school districts that had a concentration of commercial and industrial property were able to raise large sums of revenue with a low rate of taxation. The resulting inequity generated a good deal of political turmoil throughout the state of Michigan.

The governor and the legislature faced an intractable problem with continued demands for the state to impose controls over the amount of property tax local voters could impose on the residents of the district. Arriving at a solution was made particularly difficult by the almost equally divided legislature. Control shifted from one party to the other as each jockeyed for position. Republicans proposed a considerable cut in the rate of taxation on real property. Because property tax formed the majority of funds available to school districts, that proposal would have been financially devastating to a majority of the public schools in the state. The fight between the two parties over this issue waxed hot and heavy. At one point they engaged in a game of political "chicken" when leaders of one party proposed to completely eliminate property taxes as a source of funds for public schools. The other party took the dare and suddenly there was no legal mechanism to provide for the financial needs of the public schools in Michigan with tax money (Green, 1994).

## Proposal A and Its Implementation

The Governor took advantage of this situation by insisting that the legislature come up with a plan that met certain goals he had for the public schools. One of these was to have some degree of equality in the amount of revenue per pupil available to each school district. Revenue generated by property tax was mostly replaced by an interesting mix of revenue sources. This new formula roughly approximated a full state funding mechanism for financing the public schools as it replaced the district power equalizing formula. In essence the state returned to the foundation program that it had abandoned some years before. However, this time the foundation was made sufficiently high so that a school district could provide an acceptable program of education to the children and youth within the district.

Some parts of the new public school funding scheme could be enacted by the legislature, but some parts required an amendment to the state Constitution. These were submitted to a statewide vote under the title of Proposal A. To make up for the major loss of revenue from property tax, voters were given the choice between an increase in the state income tax rate or an additional two percent added to the existing four per cent sales tax. The voters chose the sales tax. The law no longer provided the option for a local school district to seek additional operating revenue through a local millage election (Olson & LaFaive, 2007).

Districts that had formerly been property poor saw a marked increase in their revenue because state aid payments were designed to increase each year for those districts until they reached the basic foundation allowance of $5,000 per-pupil set by the state. Since the majority of the school districts in the state received considerably less than that amount from the tax rate they previously were able to impose upon property within their district, the increased per pupil funding from the state was spread out over three years. Property rich districts were held somewhat harmless in that their revenue per-pupil was not decreased towards the basic foundation (Addonizio, Furst, & Dayton, 1996) Four short paragraphs from a *Perspective* on the topic published two years after the enactment of Proposal A, provide a response to some wrinkles in the new school funding mechanism.

A number of public school administrators have complained to the media about the deleterious effects of Proposal A on public school budgets. For those of you who have forgotten, Proposal A was part of the school finance reform here in Michigan that shifted the burden for funding public education from local property tax to the State School Aid Fund. The primary source of revenue for that Fund was an increase in the sales tax.

While there is still a small amount of property tax designated to support local public schools, most of the operating funds come from the state and are based on the number of students enrolled. In the system replaced by Proposal A, funds for public schools were based primarily on the wealth of the real property within a school district. There was no relationship between the funds available and the educational or financial needs of the district.

The system created when voters overwhelmingly approved Proposal A seems so much more rational that one wonders why school administrators are now complaining about it. The public schools are no longer faced with those rancorous millage elections that threatened the tranquility of small communities with increasing regularity. Property poor districts are funded at a level that allows a good basic education without placing a hardship on local taxpayers, many of whom are on fixed incomes and find ever increasing property taxes an unreasonable burden.

Property poor districts, like Berrien Springs, have benefitted by the additional revenues they receive under the new finance system. It is primarily in the property rich districts that administrators complain. They were so used to feeding well at the public trough that they were not ready for the tough management decisions demanded by a rational approach to school funding. (*Perspective*, 1995, October 11)

## Continuing Issues in School Finance

As might be expected proposal A did not solve all the financial problems of Michigan public schools even when fully implemented. However, it did relieve many small towns from the hostile millage elections that had on occasion decimated the social structure of what was, at one time, a vibrant community, supportive of the public schools. Primarily, the school districts that experienced the most pain where those that were property rich. They were known as out-of-formula districts because they had been able to raise so much revenue with a low tax rate that they did not qualify for any state funds. While they still maintained their high per-pupil income, under the new law they could not augment the funds they now got from the state by increasing their low property tax rate. It is hard to get sympathetic with the formerly wealthy districts that now have to operate their schools with the same per-pupil income as other districts that are not property rich. Two paragraphs from a *Perspective* published nearly 10 years after proposal A was implemented, catch my lack of sympathy for administrators who complained about lowered state aid payments to public schools as a result of an economic downturn.

In reading about the public angst of a school administrator from one of the upscale communities in our part of the state, I remembered a conversation I had with another administrator from that same school district several years ago. In those days, tax on real property was the primary source of funding for public schools. The state did give some aid to school districts whose tax base was limited, but it was not enough in many cases to provide a quality education. School districts, like the object of our discussion, that had high property values could spend several thousand dollars a year more for each pupil with significantly lower tax rates than property poor districts such as Berrien Springs.

In our discussion, I mentioned to the administrator from the wealthy district, how unfair it seemed that his district with a low tax rate had more money to spend on the education of their children than our district did with a high tax rate. He was unimpressed with my whining about the situation. "Don't you know," he said with a bit of a sneer in his voice, "when it comes to education, money really doesn't matter."

He went on to lecture me on how his district was well run and that fact, not the additional money they had, was the reason why their students scored so well on state assessment tests. (*Perspective*, 2003, March 21)

It was an interesting experience to see the reaction from former out-of-formula districts as they experienced lower levels of increase in their funding each year while at the same time the poor districts were experiencing much larger increases in revenue from the state. For the formerly less wealthy districts, the change in the school funding formula, bought some time for public schools to get out of the limelight as far as local politics was concerned. No more highly emotional elections regarding operating funds for the public schools were necessary. That was not, however, the end of financial struggles by public school administrators as they grappled with budgets. The slow economic recovery took its toll on public education around the country (District spending, 2016).

Additionally, in Michigan everyone was aware that after Proposal A, many of the schools had more income at their disposal. Therefore, various interest groups within school districts began to lobby for the funds to be spent on their particular cause. First in line of course, were the employees' unions. Their remuneration demands skyrocketed in some areas of the state. Further, school districts that had delayed maintenance because of a shortage of funds, now discovered the high cost of catching up.

Eventually, the problem of an inherent flaw in any financing plan that is fully funded by the state (or nearly so) began to make its appearance. The state school aid fund, from which state aid payments were made to local districts had as its primary source of revenue the 2% increase in sales tax and also additional monies from the general fund of the state which were primarily derived from income tax. Sales tax and income tax are both economically elastic. That is, small changes in the economy can have a devastating effect on those two sources of revenue. Real property by contrast is quiet inelastic, that is, the condition of the economy has very little effect on the value of property. When school funds were primarily obtained from property tax, changes in the state's economy had relatively little effect on the income available for school operations (Mattoon, 2004).

However, it did have a negative effect on the people who had to pay the taxes during economically hard times. Such a condition is especially burdensome for those who are on fixed incomes. Fortunately, Michigan's funding formula for public schools included a good bit of property tax, which is now collected for the state rather than the local school district. This tended to blunt the dilatory effect of the economic downturn although the aid fund was not able to maintain the same level of funding as it had prior to the economy's collapse.

## A Challenge to Local Boards

How should local school boards, that are charged with operating their schools in an efficient manner while providing a high quality education, react to a downturn in the economy? Quite frequently a common response across the country is for school boards to begin lobbying the state legislature to find additional funding. Schools have quite large constituencies and, when organized, can be a formidable political force.

In response to the tight financial situation, educators, as well as politicians, made a variety of suggestions to give relief to the public schools. One proposal was for public schools to be guaranteed a stable income regardless of the state of the economy or the funds available to state government. In an economic downturn, other programs of the state would have to take the cuts while education funding would be guaranteed at its current level. A proposal to return to the use of property tax as a primary source of funding public education gained very little support.

At the time, I agreed with 'supporters of public education that there needed to be a greater degree of certainty in the funding process. One way to accomplish that goal would be to initiate the funding cycle earlier in the calendar year. School districts were required to have their budgets adopted by July 1, while the state did not announce its level of aid payments until October. This made it impossible for school administrators to develop budgets with any degree of certainty. I suggested that the state legislature should make its decision on funding levels by the first of May. Then administrators and school boards would be able to put together a budget based on real numbers rather than guesswork.

Another change that I suggested, related to the expense side of the financial process. The best thing the Legislature could do would be to rescind all of the unfunded mandates they voted over the years and agree not to enact any more of them. For those not knowledgeable about the intricacies of public finance, an unfunded mandate is a requirement the Legislature places on other government agencies without providing the funds to carry out the task required. The state legislature can add significant cost to local public schools without providing any increased income to cover those costs. In other words, they can control the schools without paying the price. Two paragraphs from a *Perspective* express my concern about several of the proposed changes in funding public education in Michigan.

> More recent suggestions look at the expenditure side of public school operation. Some have proposed that the state mandate cuts in school employee wages and salaries, decreased medical benefits, consolidation of school districts, integration of purchasing services, and other measures to reduce the cost of education. All of them have in common a concentration of decision-making authority over public education in Lansing. From my perspective, this is a bad idea. It is nothing more than a raw power grab on the part of the state. There has been too great a loss of local control in our state already.

> I have written previously about my concern over the desire on the part of our politicians, both at the state and national level, to concentrate power in central government. This is not good policy and is not consistent with the American tradition of governance. From my perspective, the best school finance reform in Michigan

would be for the Legislature to give some certainty to the budgeting process and at the same time stop enacting regulations that cost the schools money without providing the funds to cover those costs. That is real reform." (*Perspective*, 2010, January 27)

A year earlier, I published a *Perspective* entitled *What Is the Problem with Proposal A*? In that article I suggested that when schools, or any other organization, faces difficult financial times, there are only two approaches they can take if they are to remain solvent. They must either cut expenses or increase revenue. In publicly supported institutions, such as schools, very little opportunity is available to increase revenue beyond the per-pupil state aid payment set by the legislature. However, a superintendent who is a true entrepreneur can always look for ways to increase enrollment or sell services to some other school or school district, thus enhancing the district's revenue. A situation like this is seldom seen. Thus, it remains for the superintendent to recommend to the board, places where the budgeted expenditures can be trimmed to the point where there is some degree of balance in the financial operations (Hardy, 2009). Cutting programs and services is never a popular event. Two paragraphs from a *Perspective* add emphasis to the struggle that administrators face when finances are tight.

> Americans have gotten used to lots of services from their government. They take it for granted that they are entitled to such services and can be expected to howl in pain if those services are cut. From my perspective, we had better get ready to howl. The problem as I see it is not with proposal A. Rather it is with us. We have become so used to a high level of service from the government we feel abused when we get less than what we normally expect. Maybe it is time for Americans to get used to doing with less. Our public institutions can no longer cater to our every whim.

> I don't have a list of things the public schools should discontinue doing. That will have to be determined in each individual school district. I do know that our public schools provide a wonderful education as well as other services to parents and the community and no decision on cutting those services will be easy. Yet, until the economy improves in Michigan, there is just plain not going to be enough money to fund all the things that we've gotten used to. (*Perspective*, 2009, November 4)

Just one month later, I felt compelled to write on the topic again from a slightly different angle. The catalyst for my additional *perspective* was an article in a recent issue of a journal with a conservative editorial policy. While its following among those who have a bent toward a conservative viewpoint is well established, it took the unusual editorial position of supporting the federal government's attempt at stimulating the economy, even in light of the massive debt that was being accumulated as a result of deficit spending each year. Meanwhile at the state level, money for the school aid fund was in short supply. In response, several organizations that had a vested interest in public schools pressured the legislature to change the financial formula for distribution of financial aid to public education. They insisted that some scheme be found so that public schools would not get hurt no matter how low the revenue collected by the state turned out to be. Two paragraphs from a *Perspective* on that issue gives voice to my contrarian viewpoint.

> The public school organizations, including the Michigan Association of School Boards (MASB), to which I belong, have a strong lobby in Lansing. They are demanding that the legislature find a new way of funding public schools, which will result in a stable and increasing source of income for them. However, they have declined to identify what that source should be. Thus, they have only half a plan for the state budget, which includes spending but not income. Half a plan does not work.
>
> I have declined to support my colleagues in their effort because I am convinced that there is no perfect system that will guarantee a steady source of income regardless of changes in the economy. Schools, which have been the focus of my life for half a century, will have to function like every other public institution within the state. They have to budget within the existing economy. While I realize that this position will probably be met with outrage by my fellow educators, that is my current perspective on the situation. (*Perspective*, 2009, December 2)

## Further Thoughts on Public School Finance

In considering the story of Michigan's experience with reforming its school funding mechanism, it should be apparent that no perfect system for financing public education has ever been found. Every arrangement that has been tried, even those that seem to work quite well, eventually develop flaws that cannot be easily remedied. However, certain principles exist that do emerge regarding the overall financing of public education within a state. The purpose of telling the story of Michigan's school finance reform and of subsequent events is to give an example of one possible school funding mechanism that might be considered in other locales. The basic philosophy underlying a full state funding mechanism, which has a foundation large enough to operate a public school with some degree of effectiveness, looks at schools as a function of the entire state with responsibility for financing them retained at that level. With this philosophy, the problem of financial disparity among the schools within the state becomes much easier to solve. Where a majority of the taxing authority is at the state level rather than the local school district, a formula can be based on a per-pupil foundation allowance that is equal for each district. The major task that remains then is to determine the level of the foundation payment per pupil and make it equally distributed among the districts. While this brings equality, it does not necessarily bring equity, because some pupils require more services to get their basic education than others (Darby & Levy, 2011).

This is covered by a system of categorical funds where the foundation allowance is based upon the educational category within which a student is placed. For example, students with a hearing loss require a much higher level of service then those who have no such condition. Fortunately, there is a good amount of funds available from the federal government to assist states in providing the services that are essential to provide a basic education for special needs children. That topic has not been developed in much detail here in this chapter. The major caveat to be considered is the dangers of categorizing children which in some cases marks them as not being worthy of association with the rest of the children in the school. Students labeled "special education" sometimes find a stigma placed upon them by their classmates, other parents, and even some teachers. A humane school administrator will ameliorate this situation as much as possible.

## RUNNING SCHOOLS LIKE A BUSINESS

Vocal critics of the public schools frequently suggest that schools would not be in a perpetual state of financial crisis if they were operated more like a business. I have, on occasions, expressed serious doubts over the efficacy of schools being run by following the American corporate business model. I have noted the high management salaries, which the public schools could never be able to pay. In addition, the for-profit business sector operates with a lack of accountability to the general public. An example is the situation where top management's employment has been terminated because of incompetence or poor job performance. Usually they are provided a lucrative severance package, even though the performance has been much less than acceptable. Such a practice would not be possible in the public schools. Thus, the corporate model is not really a useful blueprint for public school financial management. However, some aspects of business management do apply to the not-for-profit sector, including public schools. A paragraph from a *Perspective* identifies applicable management principles.

> The administration of the public schools must be carried out with a high level of transparency. There must also be a high degree of responsiveness to the needs and desires of the institution's customers. In this, schools must model their management operations after small town personal service businesses. They must first and foremost serve the core customers—students, parents, and the local community. Schools must be managed both efficiently and effectively. And there must be some degree of accountability for those managers who are not able to achieve success under such constraints. (*Perspective*, 2009, January 14)

Some aspects of business management do apply to the operation of public schools. A previous *Perspective* (1996, March 6) spoke to the matter of capital improvement. "Successful business leaders know that it is very important to continually upgrade their company's capital investment," I wrote. "Keeping plant and equipment up-to-date pays good dividends." However, even in view of such a fact, the same *Perspective* noted, "Public schools have typically failed to consider this important business principle."

Many of the school buildings that are in America today were built 40 or 50 years ago. State-of-the-art buildings at that time were built to be functional for the type of education provided. Thus, they are, on the whole, woefully inadequate for the type of education that is currently offered in the American classroom. Thus, good financial management requires a certain level of investment in capital needs of the school district. Also, it is absolutely essential that maintenance not be delayed in times of budget cutting. Failing to maintain the buildings will come back to haunt the next administrator because it will be much costlier to fix the things that have been broken years earlier.

## Three Rules of Financial Management

For many people, the process of managing the financial aspects of the public schools is mostly a mystery. A *Perspective* published in 2007 spoke to that issue and attempted to simplify the process by reducing the mechanics of financial management to its core elements. The purpose was to give parents and other adults some tools that would help them assess the level of functioning of their public school administrators in managing the school's finances.

Even more importantly, the three principles that were developed, provide management tools appropriate for either for-profit or not-for-profit organizations. These three rules will not be found in a standard textbook on school finance, but arose from personal experience in both public and private schools over a number of years. They have been sharpened through continuous observation. While the rules may seem to be quite simplistic, yet they are much more complex than might be at first apparent. Two paragraphs from a *Perspective* are presented in support of that assertion.

> First, spend less than you make. Put the surplus in a savings account and draw on it only for emergencies or to tide you over during brief hard times. That rule seems so obvious but so hard to follow because the things we feel are necessary for our wellbeing are usually beyond the ability of our income to afford. In schools, the administrators could easily justify a thirty percent increase in expenditures and find support from parents for such an increase.

> The hard part comes when administrators must make a decrease in expenditures. Well managed schools have leaders who can make those hard choices and then convince the public that it is necessary to live within the income that is available to spend. That is hard to do in America, the land of plenty, but it is necessary for sound financial management. (*Perspective*, 2007, April 4)

## Count the Money

While rule number one can be a somewhat difficult part of financial management, rule two is more mechanistic in nature. It is simply this: count your money on a regular basis. It is absolutely essential to have accurate records of the status and flow of financial assets in any type of business operation. In the public schools, these documents must be made available to the public for their review. The wise administrator will not only distribute financial statements, but will also explain their meaning and discuss the key indicators most frequently used in analyzing the financial status of any organization (Bailban, 2013). The school administrator should also identify the potential impact of financial activity on the long-term financial security of the school or school district.

Finally, any organization including schools should have policies and procedures to make sure that the other two rules are carried out. Developing policy is a major function of the public school board (Mountoy, 2000). This also holds true in many private schools. Board members function best when they focus on policy and provide oversight to see that it is implemented. However, if they are utilizing a major portion of their time in micro-managing the school administration rather than setting policy and seeing that it is employed, they are not doing their best work. If those who lead our public schools followed these three principles, they would function well and be able to survive in the financial hard times that come to most schools at one time or another.

## WHAT TO DO WITH A SURPLUS

"With wise management school districts should end each year with a slight surplus." So stated a *Perspective* which was among the very earliest ones published in 1995 (June 14). Accumulating an operating surplus by budgeting for a small profit each year was not a common practice in those days. However, it, along with opposition to deficit spending, became a recurrent theme in the *Perspectives* over the next 20 years. The concept of a public school operating at a profit was a novel idea at the time, but the more closely the financial operation of public schools was observed, the more vigorous was the *Perspective's* response. As these surpluses accumulate, they provide a balance that funds cash flow needs and also produces interest income to purchase additional services. The fund balance furnishes a cash cushion in case of emergency needs. Organizations can afford to have budget deficits occasionally when there is an adequate fund balance. However, when deficit budgets continue over time the fund balance is wiped out. This is very costly because it requires borrowing money to fund cash flow with a simultaneous decrease in interest income (*Perspective,* 1995, June 14).

Several years later, a *Perspective* entitled Making Hard Decisions picked up on the same theme. After describing financial hardship that had fallen on Michigan's public schools, largely because of a nationwide downturn in the economy, the *Perspective* spoke to the issue of cash reserves, otherwise known as unrestricted fund balance.

> So, what is the basic problem that has caused this situation. How can such a crisis be averted in the future? From my perspective, this is part of the natural economic cycle of a free economy. There will always be both good times and not so good times. The best way to avert a real crisis is for local school districts to maintain fiscal discipline during good times and build up a reserve of funds to soften the blow when bad times come. (*Perspective*, 2009, October 7)

Three paragraphs from an earlier *Perspective* looked at this issue from a broader view.

> Not-for- profit businesses, such as schools, should maintain a sizeable fund balance as an operating reserve. Such reserves help maintain their services during the down times of the economic cycle. They also fund cash flow while waiting for state aid payments which do not come at the time needed for the normal expenditures required to maintain the work of the organization. Further the income from invested reserves helps augment the regular income of the district and thus enrich the program.
>
> When the reserves are used to fund normal operations it sets in place anticipated expenses that cannot be preserved when the fund balance is depleted. In such situations, cash flow can be maintained only by borrowing which, with interest payments, increases the costs to the district. In addition, the loss of revenue from invested reserves means a loss of ability to fund the existing program of the schools.
>
> Teachers as well as other employees would be wise to encourage the Board to engage in sound business practices rather than spend the district to the brink of bankruptcy. Teachers would find better working conditions in a system that has a sound financial basis than in one that is always in a financial crisis. In tough times as well as good times, it is smart to engage in good business practices. (*Perspective*, 2003, October 22)

## SOME FINAL THOUGHTS

The issue of accountability in financial management is one that is not considered often enough in the public schools. It is obvious that this is a primary function of the financial people hired by the district for that service, I take a broader view of the matter. A more recent *Perspective* described how one school sank into crisis mode because of stress brought about by a financial shortfall. The central point of the *Perspectiv*e is found in one paragraph:

> Whose job is it to oversee the finances of the public schools? From my perspective, that is a primary function of the elected members of the school board. But accountability for the operation of schools does not stop with the school board. They must hire competent personnel to manage the day-to-day operations of the school district. Further, the electorate should monitor the work of the school board to make sure it is doing its job properly. If it is not, then somebody else should be elected in their place. Thus, accountability for the financial mess in this particular school district rests with the administrators that were hired to manage the school district, the elected school board members, and the voters in the district who were not paying attention to what their elected officials were doing. (*Perspective,* 2011, January 19)

An old saw states it well, "eternal vigilance is the price of liberty." Thus, from my perspective, all citizens need to be aware of the financial condition of the schools and hold the elected boards, as well as the administrators employed by the board, accountable to properly maintain the financial strength of the school district.

That's the only way we can keep the public schools strong.

## LIST OF *PERSPECTIVES* REFERENCED

Published in The Journal Era, Berrien Springs, Michigan

1995, June 14. The High Cost of Deficit Spending
1995, October 11. Proposal A Reconsidered
1996, March 6. Running Schools like a Business
2003, March 21. Money Does Not Matter
2003, October 22. Good Business in Tough Times
2007, April 4. Three Rules for Financial Management
2009, January 14. Run Schools Like a Business
2009, October 7. Making Hard Decisions
2009, November 4. What Is the Problem with Proposal A?
2009, December 2. Half a plan Does Not Work
2010, January 27. Reforming Michigan School Finance 2011
2011, January 19. The Price of Maintaining a Liberal Democracy

## REFERENCES

Addonizio, M. F., Furst, L. G., & Dayton, J. (1996). Blowing up the system: Some fiscal and legal perspectives on Michigan's school finance reform. *Education Law Reporter, 107*(1), 15–35.

Arocho, J. (2014). Inhibiting intrastate inequalities: A congressional approach to ensuring equal opportunity to finance public education. *Michigan Law Review, 112*(8), 1479–1505.

Bailban, J. L. (2013). Young lawyer focus: Financial statement analysis in determining solvency. *Bankruptcy & Insolvency Litigation, 18*(4), 5–11.

Cubberley, E. P. (1905). *School funds and their apportionment* [Nook ]. New York: Teachers College Columbia University Press.

Darby, D., & Levy, R. E. (2011). Slaying the inequality villain in school finance: Is the right to education the silver bullet? *Kansas Journal of Law & Public Policy, 20*(3), 351–387.

District spending. (2016, February 10). *Education Week, 35*(20), 5.

Furst, L. G. (1974). *The equalizing effects of federal aid among California elementary and Unified School districts.* Stockton, CA: University of the Pacific.

Green, D. (1994). Engler's angle. *Reason, 26*(4), 28–35.

Hardy, L. (2009). Hard lines, tough steps. *American School Board Journal, 196*(4), 22–25.

Mattoon, R. (2004). School funding 10 years after Michigan's proposal A: Does equity equal adequacy? *Chicago Fed Letter,* (203), 1–4.

Mattoon, R. H., & Testa, W. A. (1995). Midwest approaches to school reform. *Economic Perspectives, 19*(1), 2–20.

Mountoy, J. J. (2000). Education accountability. *Spectrum: Journal of State Government, 73*(3), 1–4.

Olson, R. S., & LaFaive, M. D. (2007). *A Michigan school money primer: For policy makers, school officials, media and residents.* Midland, MI: Mackinac Center for Public Policy.

Ramirez, A. (2003). The shifting sands of school finance. *Educational Leadership, 60*(4), 54–58.

Van Beek, M. (2010). *School funding in Michigan: Common myths.* Midland: Mackinac Center for Public Policy.

Verstegen, D. (2012). New study finds Inequities in state education funding formulas. *District Administration, 48*(1), 14.

# PART IV

SENSITIVE ISSUES IN PUBLIC SCHOOLS

# CHAPTER 11

---

# ISSUES OF RACE

---

### SURPRISING PREJUDICE

As I looked at the group of professional people sitting around the conference room table, I instinctively knew they would be very shocked if they could discern the thoughts churning through my mind right at that moment. They had just revealed themselves to be racially prejudiced, bordering on bigotry. I would certainly never call them that to their face. In fact, coward that I am, I never did let them know how I viewed their behavior that day.

I was serving as a consultant to a medium-sized private school in the Midwest. The current school principal had resigned—effective the end of the school year—and the personnel committee of the board requested my assistance in the search for a new principal. Because of the religious and cultural orientation of the community served by the school, the candidate pool was quite small.

Economically, the school's clientele was primarily from middle and upper middle- class families. I did a nationwide search and found a number of qualified people who were willing to have their names on a list of possible candidates for the principal's position, and submitted their resumes.

I did a perfunctory background check on each one and checked with the references each had provided. I settled on five persons who had the necessary educa-

*Helping Parents Understand Schools: A Different Perspective on Education
and Schooling in America,* pages 183–195.
Copyright © 2017 by Information Age Publishing

tion and experience and who potentially would be acceptable to the board of the school. I gathered as much information as I could about each person and then notified the Chair of the Personnel Committee that I was ready to give my report.

At the meeting, we sat around the conference room table where I circulated the resumes I had chosen. I indicated that each one was, in my view, qualified to be principal of their school. After an hour's discussion had indicated to me that they were satisfied with the pool of applicants I had assembled, I tried to get a consensus from the group as to their choice for top candidate for the position. One resume was far superior to the others. The individual had more experience, and more education, as well as a number of other factors that clearly indicated he had, on paper at least, qualifications that were a good bit higher than the other potential candidates.

The members of the committee gave evidence of more than a little excitement about the possibility of having such a high quality principal for their school. That is when I dropped the bombshell on them. "I need to tell you," I said with more than a little fear and trembling, "that he is an African-American." As I observed the members of the committee, I saw a look of dismay and disappointment. I gave it a little time to let the shock wear off. Then, I asked if they thought this person was still a viable candidate. The response greatly disappointed me.

One of the committee members seemed to speak for the whole group when he said, "I do not have any problem with a Black principal, but I do not think the rest of the community is ready for that." Another member spoke up and said, "We have never even had a Black teacher at this school, so I do not think a Black principal would work in this community." Finally, a third member stated, "I am not prejudiced against those people, but I think we should not move too fast in that direction. After all, we are dealing with people and their children, and we must keep that in mind."

Without letting them see the contempt that was raging in my soul over their prejudice, I quickly removed the resume of the most qualified person and helped them work through the other four resumes until they arrived at consensus regarding one they wanted to interview.

## THE ROAD AHEAD

The vignette I just presented happened several years ago, and I hope the members of that community have been able to come to grips with some of their inherent racial prejudice. In my view, there will always be some degree of racial animosity in society and especially in the setting of the public schools. Educators need to be prepared to deal with racial issues as they bubble to the surface in the community and among the students in the schools. Parents play a key role in helping their children come to grips with racial distrust.

The remainder of this chapter is divided into four parts. The first has to do with the legal response to racial discrimination in the schools. This is followed by a discussion of "affirmative action." The third section makes suggestions for confronting racial animosity. The final section, entitled "Not So Evident Prejudice," deals with subtler aspects of racial discrimination. Some Final Thoughts ties it all together.

## LEGAL RESPONSE TO ISSUES OF RACE

During my lifetime, I have seen a great deal of change in the relationship between and among people of different racial or ethnic backgrounds. America is not yet completely free from racial division and discrimination. However, looking back on the predominant culture following World War II, the American people have made great progress considering the racial tension that prevailed at the time I was in school. In those days, several states had laws that made it illegal for people of different racial and ethnic groups to intermingle in public. This meant that schools for children of color were required by law to be separate from those designated for White children.

Eventually, the laws were changed so that it was no longer in violation of state law for people of different colors to associate in public. It was not an easy transition. In some situations, attempts to break down the color barriers were met with violence. This is not a part of American history that we like to talk about. However, it helps us understand current events and reactions of various people to the organization of public schools, when we recall the long, hard process it took to get where we are today in racial relationships.

I had lived all my life in the North and had not seen the impact of legally mandated segregation. In fact, during my days in college, I began to seriously doubt the validity of stories I heard about the indignities people of color were forced to endure in Southern states. I thought it was probably just propaganda used for some political purpose. During one of the breaks in the academic year I traveled by automobile to the South with two of my friends, just to see for myself what it was really like.

Imagine my surprise when, arriving in a Southern state, we stopped for fuel and something to eat, and discovered the restrooms labeled Men and Women inside the facility, and then a wooden outhouse behind the building with a sign, Colored. I soon discovered that was not the worst of the indignities heaped upon this segment of the population right here in America.

The Supreme Court ruled, in a landmark decision (*Brown v. Board of Education*, 1954) that a state's requirement that schools must be racially segregated violated the Constitution. This seemed to catch everyone by surprise. A tremendous effort ensued in which the predominant White population resisted all the legal requirements for dismantling the system of *de jure* segregation (Epps-Robertson, 2016).

The efforts to dismantle the entrenched segregated school system in southern states seemed slow and torturous. Half a century after the Court's landmark decision, four paragraphs from a *Perspective* provides a brief analysis of the court's decision in *Brown*.

The question before the Court in *Brown* related to state laws that mandated racial segregation in the public schools or permitted local school districts to segregate students based on race. Those pressing the case claimed that such laws were in violation of the Equal Protection clause of the 14ᵗʰ Amendment to the Constitution. Those who defended such segregation pointed to a long-standing tradition of the Court that determined that if segregated facilities were equal, they met the Constitutional requirement (*Plessy v. Ferguson*, 1896).

This separate but equal doctrine had met the test of time through numerous decisions of the courts. However, the Supreme Court in *Brown* changed all that when it ruled that separate educational facilities are inherently unequal. What distinguished this case from others that had been before the courts was that the school buildings in Topeka, Kansas, were in fact of equal quality.

The school designated for Black children was as nice and well equipped as the one for White children. So, *Brown* was a clean case in that there was no question about the equality of the school buildings. The only question was the constitutionality of legally required racial segregation.

The Court in *Brown* decided that legally mandated (*de jure*) segregation in public schools was unconstitutional. Its decision did not require integration or that students of different races should have equal facilities. It did not mandate equal teaching, curriculum, or learning outcomes. The *Brown* decision did not even deal with school segregation based on housing patterns (*de facto* segregation). The decision merely forbade school segregation based on race that was required by law. Thus, the promise of *Brown* was very narrow, indeed. (*Perspective*, 2004, June 2)

The question naturally arises, why did it take so long for the Court's declaration regarding the unconstitutionality of racially segregated schools, for a remedy to become reality? Nationally recognized scholar on the legal aspects of education, Charles J. Russo, posits that, while courts were quite active in the first twenty- five years following the *Brown* decision, they were mostly absent from the battle during the next quarter century (Russo, 2004).

By contrast, Turner (2015) offers a more theoretical view of the situation with his discussion of discretionary originalism. Writing more recently, Strauss and Lemieux (2016) suggest that the difficulty with *Brown* is there are two ways to interpret it. Those hostile to the desegregation required in *Brown*, view the decision rather broadly. Thus, even today, vestiges of segregation in the public schools are still to be found in some parts of the country.

In a *Perspective* written just a year ago, I responded to concerns I had heard regarding the federal holiday designated as Martin Luther King Day. Two paragraphs give support to desegregation of public schools.

During that year, (1971) the city in which I resided, attempted to racially integrate the public schools. In some cases, this required busing students from one community to another based on their race. At first there was a great deal of angst, especially among the White community, regarding the integration process. I had my own doubts about the effectiveness of such a plan.

Then I talked to the principal of one of the recently integrated schools. He told me of a fascinating thing that was taking place among the children under his care. Both Black and White children had a great deal of misconception about what life was like for each other. For example, children in both races discovered that their fathers had to work and many worked at the same kinds of jobs. The Black students had always pictured White families with the father at home because he was so wealthy he didn't need to work. Conversely, the White students just assumed that all the Black fathers were on welfare and so they didn't have to work. What an amazing discovery they made when they found that having a job was essential to families in both communities. (*Perspective*, 2015, January 21)

## AFFIRMATIVE ACTION

It has been my observation that in any organization nothing happens unless some individual makes it happen. Changes in operation do not magically appear out of the sky. Someone must cause the change to happen. As Americans became aware of the deleterious effect of forced separation of the races, particularly in schools, educators who are determined to deal with this situation developed a system to include qualified minorities. Thus, "affirmative action" came into play for both the placement of students in school and in employment decisions.

Very few attempts to overcome the vestiges of racial discrimination have generated as much anxiety on the parts of the majority as has affirmative action.

Some years ago, Senator Trent Lott, a political leader in Congress responded to legal challenges to admissions policies at a major public university. He strongly opposed affirmative action by suggesting that it would be unconstitutional for race to have any part in the application process. He, along with his political colleagues, insisted that applicants should be admitted on the basis of merit alone. In a rather strong reaction, a *Perspective* cast doubt on the validity of their reasoning. Two paragraphs are presented here.

From my perspective, opponents of affirmative action have gotten religion a little late in life. They seem to have forgotten that in the good old days that Trent Lott longs for, it was against the law for Black children to attend the same schools as White children in many states. Southern governors enforced these laws with armed troops. Going a few decades farther back in history, it was against the law for people of color to have any education at all. Severe criminal penalties were meted out to Black people who tried to learn to read or write.

As far as higher education is concerned, merit has never played more than a passing role in the admission decision. If it did, neither George Bush nor Al Gore would have been admitted to their Ivy League schools. Affirmative action in those days meant that sons of the rich and famous were assured entrance while those with merely high-test scores had to take a chance that there would be enough room for them. Of course people of color need not apply no matter how high their test scores were. Opponents of affirmative action, such as Senator Lott, remember those days with fondness. (*Perspective*, 2002, December 18)

Affirmative action plans have been successfully implemented in a number of places. For example, the Chicago public school is reported to have achieved some degree of success in its efforts to provide racial, ethnic, and socioeconomic equity as it offers education and schooling to the young people in that school district (Miretzky, Chennault, & Fraynd, 2016). However, other observers cast doubt on the efficacy of affirmative action, especially when it is attempting to offer schools of choice to the parents in the attendance area (Kojima, 2012). An earlier *Perspective offers* a slightly different view of the issue.

> What seems to make opponents most angry about affirmative action is, not only do minorities have a chance to get into the mainstream of American life, but that some organizations have adopted a quota system as part of the policy. For example, a state college might have a policy to employ minorities in the same ratio as the racial make-up of the student body. If ten per cent of the students are Black, the school will have as a target a faculty that is ten per cent Black. In hiring practices this will result in preferential treatment for Black applicants at least until the quota has been met.
>
> The very mention of a quota enrages those who remember the "good old days." It is discriminatory, undemocratic, and unconstitutional they say. Why can't all decisions be made on the basis of merit alone? Pick the most qualified candidate regardless of race, gender, ethnicity, or age. In a perfect world they might be right. But the world is far from perfect and ever will be. There has always been a quota system in America and always will be. Not long ago the quota for Blacks at the University of Alabama was set at Zero (0). The governor himself stood in the door trying to enforce that quota. Most corporations in America have the same quota for Black, Hispanic or women executives. Zero.
>
> Business leaders argue that they choose the most qualified person for the job. However, the definition of "qualified" is a person who looks just like the ones who are there now. Job skill has nothing to do with the employment decision. This past year the top executives of a large American corporation were secretly recorded in a criminal conspiracy to practice racial discrimination in hiring. They were merely applying the most popular quota to their company's policy. Zero. (*Perspective*, 1998, January 21)

When it comes to the public schools, it is well documented that education available to children in schools with mostly Black students is significantly inferior to the quality of education provided to children in schools with predominantly White students (Kozol, 1991). When such reports first became public, support for dealing directly with the issue of inequality in education was in general supported by the general public. However, time marches on, and eventually the notion that racial discrimination no longer exists became widespread. This was especially true following the election of America's first Black president. Soon the concept of a "post-racial" world appeared in the literature (Powell, 2013). A great divide of opinion continues to this day, regarding the efficacy of affirmative action. One author even justifies affirmative action as needed in private schools even though they are not under legal obligation (Lee, 2007). From my perspective, as long as people are placed in categories based on physical features, a need for affirmative action will exist. We all benefit when opportunity is available to all the population.

## CONFRONTING RACIAL SENSITIVITY

Racial sensitivity has two sides to it. Some people are overly reactive to anything that makes life somewhat difficult for them. It is easy to blame it on racial bigotry. From my perspective, such an attitude is not productive even when the discrimination is genuine. The other side of the issue is where members of one race truly discount the human value of people of another race. No question can be legitimately raised that racial animosity and discrimination exists within our society. Of special concern to me is discrimination that exists within the public schools (Welch & Payne, 2010). Two paragraphs from a *Perspective* provides my viewpoint on the nature of racism in our current society.

> Racism has been defined as the honest belief that there are genetic components in the human make up that can be used to differentiate between people of the various races. While science does not support the concept, there are those who truly believe that distinct racial differences are inherent in the human species. (Painter, 2010) This forms the basis for racial discrimination in all aspects of society. People are judged by the racial group in which they are placed, not on the basis of their individual qualities. While there has been a marked advance in public understanding regarding the true nature of racial differences, discrimination still exists, although it is carried out in much subtler ways these days.

> Our nation, as well as some others, has confronted matters of racial discrimination by eliminating laws that required the differentiation of people based on their racial designation. In fact, such things as affirmative action attempted to reverse the negative effects of previous public policy. It was hoped that racism would eventually cease to exist in modern America. To some the election of Barack Obama to the presidency is an indicator that racism has been defeated. Yet, Americans remain very touchy on the subject of race and any slight hint of racism, especially in the form of statements which include some degree of racial overtone, results in a great outcry condemning the individual uttering offending words, who is then labeled a racist. (*Perspective,* 2013, August 21)

Several years ago, I had the privilege of attending a graduation ceremony in a Midwestern city of some size. It was an awe-inspiring event, conducted in the big stone church of early Gothic architecture. Of the 145 men and women who were graduating that day, the one I had come to see was easily identified because she was the only person of color in the entire line-up of graduates. I know only a part of her story, but the part I do know has a vital message for Americans of all racial and ethnic backgrounds.

Her parents survived a fierce dictatorship in their home country on the continent of Africa. However, the new regime did not seem to be much better, so they packed their meager belongings and headed for that great land of promise, the United States of America. Shortly after arriving in this country, the father abandoned his wife and four young daughters for reasons not known to me. The mother survived, based on the old-fashioned formula for success in America: hard work and frugal living. Now, as a reward, this African immigrant single parent would witness the first of her four daughters to graduate with a college degree.

I have long pondered the situation this daughter of Africa faced as she pursued higher education at an institution that catered primarily to students of European heritage. She was not an affirmative action student, but earned her way by accumulating a solid academic record. One unique trait that seemed to be common to this family was they grabbed every opportunity that presented itself. The rest of the story is contained in three short paragraphs from a *Perspective*.

Did she ever face discrimination as a child of color? Of course she did. I witnessed her expulsion from elementary school for a petty offense that would ordinarily require only some amount of time after school as punishment. When the school administration was reminded of the little matter of due process, she was quickly readmitted. She took advantage of the opportunity and graduated first from elementary school and then high school. Blatant discrimination was no deterrent to her.

From my perspective, America is still the land of great opportunity. Some see America as a land of discrimination while others see it for its potential. Others deal with discrimination by pretending it does not exist and press their advantage every chance they get. True, discrimination of all sorts is ubiquitous throughout the land but there are still possibilities for those who will take advantage of them. And those who do will eventually participate in the good life America makes possible.

So, here's to my young friend who made us all proud when she graduated from college. And, here is to her sisters who still journey in the halls of academe. They too are taking the opportunities America presents to them. And here is to that African mother who turned personal tragedy into an American success story providing inspiration to us all. And, here's to America, still the land of boundless opportunity. (*Perspective*, 2005, May, 11)

The experience described in the *Perspective* above is probably not representative of a typical person of minority status in America. Yet, I think it is instructive as to what might be a positive message for the future generations. The young woman determined not to be a victim of race discrimination, even though it seemed at times the system was weighted against her. She realized that education was essential for achieving the American dream.

Unfortunately, opportunity is not equally distributed among the population in America. Khatri and Hughes (2002) stated the implication of this inequality of opportunity based upon racial characteristics quite succinctly: "Achieving the American dream for all our citizens must guide the public policy agenda for the foreseeable future" (p. 107). Two short paragraphs from an early *Perspective* support that conclusion although from a different point of view.

> Discriminating against people because of their minority status, while emotionally gratifying, is an economic detriment to the nation. It is well known that people who are more highly educated tend to be more productive and have higher incomes. Both productivity and high income spent on consumer goods act as a catalyst to the economy and the entire country benefits. When people of minority status are blocked from educational and professional advancement both productivity and income drop resulting in a declining economy.

> Human skills are the most valuable natural resource we have. When these resources are not utilized to the fullest, the economy misses a great potential. Imagine how stupid it would be if we refused to produce iron just because the ore is black. We engage in the same economic stupidity when we refuse to allow minorities into the mainstream of commercial activity because of their minority status. (*Perspective*, 1995, August 2)

## NOT SO EVIDENT PREJUDICE

Racial animosity is frequently just below the surface and not readily identified. There are many subtle ways that discrimination and bias against people of minority races emerge in the public schools. These schools are especially vulnerable to the deleterious effects of racial animosity. The fact of such attitudes on the part of majority race teachers and students is often quite subtle. Frequently, the catalyst for such attitudes is a growing belief that racial minorities, and more particularly African-Americans, have the advantage because of their race (Ford, 2011). A personal experience related to this issue is told in a single paragraph from a *Perspective*.

> Many years ago when I was pursuing an advanced degree at a university in California, I applied for a position as a research assistant at the University. I was informed that I had all the qualifications for the job but they already had a White person among their researchers and needed to reserve this position for a minority. A fellow student, who was Hispanic, got the job. I was a little perturbed at the fact that race was the deciding factor. However, I did get work as a substitute teacher in an upscale school district nearby. They would never have given a job to a minority such as my Hispanic classmate. So I quickly got over my angst regarding the University's discrimination against me because I could see that discrimination worked both ways. (*Perspective*, 2013, August 28)

It is very difficult to get a full understanding of the various types of race related discrimination that people, including children, of minority status are subjected to in society, especially in schools. Pollock (2008) notes the changing definition of racial discrimination: "Today, rather than defining discrimination generally as race-conscious policies designed to *deny* opportunities to students of color, many now redefine discrimination generally as race-conscious policies designed to *provide* opportunities to students of color" (p. 102).

It is very easy for members of the majority to fall into the trap of feeling victimized by a system that tends to give special notice to persons of minority status. The redefinition of discrimination identified in the previous paragraph tends to provide some degree of credence for such a reaction. One paragraph from a *Perspective* seems to find me arguing with myself on this point.

> I am not so naive as to think that racism is nonexistent in modern society. While racial animosity is seldom openly displayed, I know that beneath the surface there is much more racism in most communities than people would like to admit. The solution to that certainly is not helped by such a big hullabaloo being made over a very minor item. When one segment of the population is overly sensitive on the topic, it tends to trivialize more severe racial prejudice. Everyone loses when that occurs. It would be more productive if people would save their outrage for really outrageous behavior and not insignificant matters such as the teacher's word usage. (*Perspective*, 2012, March 28)

It is a difficult balance between accepting the tragic results of racial discrimination and using the race card for every petty inconvenience. I have no question but most schools in America have some degree of discrimination against people of color (Keith & Monroe, 2016). Determining the root cause of such a condition is a never-ending search. There are multiple factors that need to be considered to get the true picture (Monroe, 2016).

From my perspective, school systems are wise to seek a diverse group of instructors for their classrooms, making it possible for the adults to get used to people from different cultures and races. As they get to know each other, they can learn which subtle words are offensive to children of the other culture. Schools do their best work when they function as true learning communities. There will be a time when we can afford to ignore variations in the cultural aspects of children from different racial and ethnic groups (Michie, 2007). In searching for that delicate balance between subtle racism and overemphasizing complaints of discrimination in the schools, one small paragraph at the end of an early *Perspective* gives my summary viewpoint.

> Most of us are so rigid in our cultural perspective that we seldom recognize the contributions of those who are racially different. However, as we integrate our economic and social activity we become more perceptive of our need for each other and our prejudices tend to dissipate. During this season of peace on earth, we might consider how we can express good will toward those who are different than us and show respect for the contribution they make to the larger society. (*Perspective*, 1997, December 24)

## SOME FINAL THOUGHTS

Racial differences within the public schools have been, and will continue to be, a touchy issue for long in the future. But, that is not a matter that should make us despair. Tension is a normal part of life. From my perspective, the public schools and their leaders should attempt to find some natural balance between the extremes that have existed for many years in our society.

Two factors had a significant influence on my thinking on racial relationships in the schools. First, the public and private schools in the community where I live have a student body marked by a great deal of racial and ethnic diversity. I have a large amount of respect for a community that works together to make outsiders feel welcome in the village, especially in the schools, both public and private. The faculty and staff, along with the administrators, view the presence of so many minority students as a strength of the school district. The resulting positive atmosphere has provided a rich learning environment with academic advancement, accompanied by cultural awareness, preparing the students for the world community they will enter at the onset of adulthood.

The other factor is the experience of my own children and grandchildren. As they have grown up in this culturally diverse community, their minds tend not to focus on a person's racial characteristics. Of course they can see color because it is around them every day. However, it does not seem important to them, nor has it been an issue regarding the racial or ethnic makeup of their circle of close friends.

As parents of the students get acquainted with each other and become friends, it makes a big impression on the young people. In fact, I have noticed that children and youth are sometimes the main factor in bringing families from different racial and ethnic groups together in social activities. The school can assert a positive social function in its role as a community center.

It appears then that parents are a key factor in bringing racial harmony to the school community. They are the first teachers of their children and their influence is ever present in the child's life. Parents are well advised to exercise a degree of care about subtle expressions of racial antagonism. Children are very quick to pick up on the signals adults send and make them a part of their own persona. A short paragraph from an early *Perspective* brings this chapter to a close.

> I believe we all need to lighten up a bit. We can enjoy humor and still show concerns for the racial sensitivities of all Americans. We need to stop looking for an excuse to label every little misstatement "racist." And we especially need to stop letting the media do our thinking for us. We need to make more progress in improving race relations. America is a multiracial society and we might as well learn to live with each other. (*Perspective*, 1997, April 30)

## LIST OF *PERSPECTIVES* REFERENCED

Published in *The Journal Era*, Berrien Springs, Michigan

1995, August 2. Affirmative Action Revisited

1997, April 30. What is Wrong with Fried Chicken?

1997, December 24. Some Thoughts on the Race Issue

1998, January 21. Some Thoughts on Affirmative Action

2002, December 18. A Lott of Action to Affirm

2004, June 2. *Brown v., Board of Education:* Promise and Hope

2005, May 11. Land of Opportunity

2012, March 28. Perspective on a Sensitive Issue

2013, August 21. Perspective on a Truly Touchy Topic

2013, August 28. More Perspective on the Touchy Topic

2015, January 21. A Brief Primer on Race Relations

## REFERENCES

*Brown V Board of Education*, 347 U .S. 483, (1954).

Epps-Robertson, C. (2016). The race to erase Brown v. Board: The Virginia way and the rhetoric of massive resistance. *Rhetoric Review, 35*(2), 108–120.

Ford, R. T. (2011). *Rights gone wrong: How law corrupts the struggle for equality.* New York: Farrar, Straus and Giroux.

Keith, V. M., & Monroe, C. R. (2016). Histories of colorism and implications for education. *Theory into Practice, 55*(1), 4–10.

Khatri, D. S., & Hughes, A. O. (2002). *American education apartheid—Again?* Lanham MD: The Scarecrow Press, Inc.

Kojima, F. (2012). School choice: Impossibilities for affirmative action. *Games & Economic Behavior, 75*(2), 685–693.

Kozol, J. (1991). *Savage inequalities: Children in America' schools.* New York: Crown Publishers, Inc.

Kuklinski, J. H., Sniderman, P. M., Knight, K., Piazza, T., Tetlock, P. E., Lawrence, G. R., & Mellers, B. (1997). Racial prejudice and attitudes toward affirmative action. American Journal of Political Science, 41(2), 402–420.

Lee, S. H.-Y. (2007, Spring). Justifying affirmative action in K–12 private schools. *Harvard Blackletter Law Journal, 23*(Spring), 107–136.

Michie, G. (2007). Part II: Advancing the conversation: Seeing, hearing, and talking race: Lessons for White teachers for teachers of color. *Multicultural Perspectives, 9*(1), 3–9.

Miretzky, D., Chennault, R. E., & Fraynd, D. J. (2016). Closing an opportunity gap. *Education and Urban Society, 48*(1), 48–76.

Monroe, C. R. (2016). Race and color: Revisiting perspectives in black education. *Theory Into Practice, 55*(1), 46–53.

Painter, N. I. (2010). *The history of white people* (Nook ed.). New York: W. W. Norton & Company.

*Plessy v. Ferguson*, 163 U.S. 517, (1896).

Pollock, M. (2008). *Because of race: How Americans debate harm and opportunity in our schools.* Princeton, NJ: Princeton University Press.

Powell, C. M. (2013). Critiquing neutrality: Critical perspectives on schools, the First Amendment, and affirmative action in a "post-racial" world. *University of Louisville Law Review, 52*(1), 105–111.

Russo, C. J. (2004). One step forward, half a step backward? *Journal of Negro 21 Education, 73*(3), 174–181.

Straus, R. M., & Lemieux, S. (2016). The two Browns: Policy implementation and the retrenchment of Brown v. Board of Education. *New Political Science, 38*(1), 44–60.

Turner, R. (2015). On *Brown v. Board of Education* and discretionary originalism. *Utah Law Review, 2015*(5), 1143–1199.

Welch, K., & Payne, A. A. (2010). Racial threat and punitive school discipline. *Social Problems, 57*(1), 25–48.

CHAPTER 12

# RELIGION IN PUBLIC SCHOOLS

## DRAMA IN THE COURTROOM

It promised to be a moment of high drama. All the key players were in place. While it was a rather ordinary proceeding, it appeared to have all the ingredients of a full-blown Hollywood production. The high ceiling courtroom had a somber effect on those in attendance at such a proceeding for the first time. The well-organized, well-dressed, and very articulate yuppie attorneys were ready to engage each other in severe legal combat. The sloppily-dressed teenager slouched in his chair at the table beside his attorney. His blank stare seemed to indicate some degree of boredom with the adult's penchant for nitpicking every little detail. At the other table, the lawyer was accompanied by a middle-aged man dressed in casual business wear. The small group of observers became instantly quiet as the curmudgeon, who presided as judge, entered the room. The drama was about to begin and I, with my front row seat, could watch every bit of it from close range.

At issue in the case was a complaint by the high school student that a picture of Jesus, posted prominently in his public high school, was a violation of the First Amendment to the Constitution that states in part, "Congress shall make no law respecting an establishment of religion. . ." This protection from actions of the federal government was extended to protection from actions by the state govern-

*Helping Parents Understand Schools: A Different Perspective on Education and Schooling in America*, pages 197–206.
Copyright © 2017 by Information Age Publishing
**197**

ment, through the 14th Amendment. The applicable words from the amendment are, "No state shall make or enforce any law which shall abridge the privileges or immunities of citizens of the United States." Thus, schools, being a part of the state government, are forbidden from taking actions that might be seen as an "establishment" of religion. The court had to decide in this case if the picture of Jesus affixed to the wall in a public high school resulted in "establishing" the Christian religion.

As soon as the events in this case were published in the newspaper, I knew an important legal decision would result. I also suspected that whatever the decision was, the losing side would appeal, probably all the way to the U. S. Supreme Court. This was confirmed later by my private conversations with each of the attorneys involved.

I just could not miss the opportunity to see in person, the beginning of what I thought might be a landmark case. Reading the written decision is much more instructive when augmented by a personal observation of the proceedings. The judge, as I expected, ruled in a written opinion that the picture of Jesus prominently displayed on the wall of a public high school, did indeed violate the First Amendment establishment clause (*Washegesic v. Bloomingdale Public Schools*, 1993). Just as he had told me, the lawyer for the defendant school district appealed the decision to the Circuit Court. In the meantime, the District Court Judge ruled that the picture should not be removed until the Circuit Court made its decision. The reason for this is that the picture was permanently affixed to the wall and removing it would result in severe damage. Thus, the picture may be protected until the High Court has the last word.

## THE ROAD AHEAD

The topic of religion is indeed a sensitive matter. A general unwritten rule prevails: that polite people do not initiate discussion of either politics or religion in public places. It seems that these topics are too sensitive for most people to engage in rational discourse about them with any degree of equanimity. While I strongly disagree with the rule, I do accept that it is necessary to take notice of its application. My goal is to remove some of the obstacles to conversing on the subject by exposing the source of some unfortunate misconceptions on the topic

The subject of religion in the public schools was tackled in the very first *Perspective* written (1995, February 15). It treats one aspect of religious ritual in public schools. The first section of the chapter deals with that topic, including both prayer and Bible reading. Next comes a section on the challenge of science from a religious point of view. This is followed by Written on Tables of Stone, which deals with attempts to display the "Ten Commandments' in public schools.

The Supreme Court's decisions, misunderstood by both the public and school personnel, are explained throughout the various sections. In answer to critics of public education, a section is devoted to teaching about religion. The emphasis is on appropriate ways to provide instruction in religious studies in public schools. Some final thoughts bring the chapter to a conclusion.

## RELIGIOUS RITUAL

A great deal of angst can be found throughout the nation regarding the issue of religion in public schools. In some respects, the public schools have become a cultural battleground over the issue of separation of church and state. "They have taken God out of the public schools," is a common mantra that can be heard in conservative circles. An increasing number of people believe that religion, especially Christianity, has been removed from the curriculum and a religion of secular humanism is being forced on the children. Parents are in a quandary as to what to do about schooling for their children, partly because they realize that Americans are very proud and protective of the religious freedom they enjoy. Public opposition can be expected whenever encroachment on the freedoms granted under the First Amendment to the Constitution is suspected.

A large minority of conservative Christians strongly believe in a "conspiracy theory" regarding public education. It appears that the government is actively engaged in displacing the Christian religion in the country, especially in public schools. Typical of their fear is a statement by Wick (2011) "Through the public and higher education system, they have excluded, criticized, and satirized faith while encouraging moral relativism. Once God has been excluded from the equation, someone or something else must take His place. The Supreme Court banned prayer in public schools in *Engel v. Vitale* (1962) though Bible study and Christian education had been part of the system since the nation's founding" (p. 7). It is the "Statists," claims Wick, who are undermining Christian faith in their rebellion against God and church authority.

### Ceremonial Prayer

The first *Perspective* published took issue with that line of thought. For starters, prayer in public schools has never been ruled illegal by any court or legislature. The Supreme Court decision simply declared unconstitutional the requirement by the state of New York that each teacher in the public schools must begin the day by leading students in reciting what was known as the "New York Regents prayer." The words of that prayer are, "Almighty God, we acknowledge our dependence upon thee and we beg thy blessings upon us, our parents, our teachers, and our country." In this case the state not only allowed children to pray in school, it required them to pray; and to make sure they got it right, the state dictated the exact words the children were to say in their prayer.

Unfortunately, this decision is cited as being the first step in the government's rebellion against God by taking religion out of the public schools. In my view, the Court did religion a favor by removing the banality of this statement from masquerading as a prayer. Such substitute for real spirituality casts doubt on the seriousness of Christian believers. It is merely a ritual and has no significant meaning regarding the relationship between the believer and the Creator.

In response, numerous attempts to amend the Constitution to allow prayer in public schools have been initiated (McCarthy, 2009). What has caused a great deal of angst in the aftermath of the *Engel* decision is that traditional prayer in public school ceremonies is now considered unconstitutional. This includes such events as graduation, football games, and other student gatherings where the tradition has been that prominent clergy would offer a prayer as part of the ceremony. In my view, that is just the kind of activity that should be viewed with alarm by those who cherish religious freedom. School administrators should not become the arbiters of what kind of a prayer is acceptable for school-sponsored events. The closing paragraph from the firs*t Perspective* published provides a summation of my thoughts on the effort to amend the Constitution to allow prayer in public schools.

> An amendment to allow voluntary prayer in the public school is neither wise nor necessary. Students already have the right and the ability to pray privately at any time during the school day. Some have joked that as long as there are examinations in school, there will be prayer. Further, it is well established that student groups have the legal right to meet during free time to pursue extracurricular activities. A prayer group is an acceptable extracurricular activity (Mawdsley, 2004). With all the rhetoric and emotional discussion that has taken place about the need for prayer in public schools as a way to strengthen the moral fiber of the nation, one might consider that other institutions are better suited for such a task. If there were more prayer in the home under the sponsorship of the parent, certainly the religious strength of the nation would be enhanced without disturbing either the legal or political climate of the school. Conservative religionists might better consider that venue for their crusade. (*Perspective*, 1995, February 15)

In another *Perspective* published several years later, I expressed a bit of cynicism of the respondent to the outcry against courts for supposedly taking God out of the public schools: "From my perspective, we do not need prayer in the public schools. We need prayer in the churches and in homes. Ritual prayer should be led by pastors and parents, not school principals." (*Perspective,* 2000, February 2) I believe there is value in personal prayer. Yet, I do not think public school is the right place to be organizing or managing the prayer life of young Americans. As far as their ability to pray in the public schools, one can pray without making a noticeable sound.

Lofaso (2009) states it well as she defines the act of prayer:

> In simple terms, prayer is talking to God or a god. During the conversation, the person praying may use his or her own words to talk to a god, may use 'a set order of words,' such as the Lord 's Prayer to speak to God, may request or wish something from a god or may attend a ceremony that invokes such conversations with a god. That conversation may be vocal or silent. (pp. 25–6)

With that definition in mind, no one can be stopped from praying in a public school. While I have presented a separationist point of view, I do acknowledge that a case can be made for a view that is more accommodating toward religion in public schools. (Russo,1999)

## Bible Reading

Just a year after the Supreme Court decided the school prayer case, it issued another controversial decision regarding religion in the public schools. It consolidated two separate cases that were before it because they had similar legal questions. In *School District of Abington Township v. Schempp & Murray v. Curlett* (1963) it was required that reading of the Bible was added to the list of forbidden religious activities in public schools. As with the decision on school prayer the year before, a great outcry arose against the Courts as a result of the High Court's rulings. New accusations against the government for taking God out of the schools were brought to the surface.

The Christian Bible has within it the seeds of much controversy. Introducing it into formal ritual of public education may cause more friction among the student body then it tends to subdue crude behavior. Yet, many the individuals sincerely believe that there is value in having some degree of awareness of what might be included in the Biblical narrative. Emerging adults who knew nothing of the Bible when they graduate from public high schools have a serious knowledge deficit. The impact of religion, especially Christianity, on modern society cannot be denied (Kreamelmeyer, 2014).

Two aspects of the Christian Bible have been especially problematic in the public schools in America. Of long-standing issue is the biblical story in the book of Genesis on the origins of the earth. There, the story is told of an omnipotent Being (God) who, through tremendous power, spoke the word and this world and all that is in it suddenly came into existence. Scientists tend to overwhelmingly disagree with that description and offer the theory of evolution in opposition to the biblical story. There is a clash of religion and science on that point in the public schools.

## THE CHALLENGE OF SCIENCE

Numerous attempts have been made to have the creation story taught in the public schools as an alternative to evolution. Resistance from the scientific community came quickly and forcefully. One opponent of giving any recognition to creation theory in the science curriculum, (Eldredge, 2000), seems to claim the topic is not worthy of discussion: "The tired old creationism debate—mired as it is so thoroughly in the nineteenth century—simply has not prepared us for the kind of positive interaction between science and religion that I see as eminently possible as we enter the new millennium and grapple with tough environmental issues" (p. 168).

I would take issue with the scientist. I believe that public schools must inform students regarding the existence of alternative ways of interpreting the evidence upon which evolutionary science is based. While I have no question that the theory of evolution has strong support behind it, the traditional creation story from Genesis can also muster evidence in its support (Brand, 2009). Likewise, some factual evidence can be interpreted to support the theory of intelligent design (Beckwith, 2003).

From my perspective, no damage is done to the scientific knowledge children acquire in school by being made aware of alternative interpretations of the data that are consistent with their religious beliefs. Unfortunately, in some public schools the controversy has grown far bigger than it is healthy for the school and surrounding community (Romero & Temple-Raston, 2008).

## WRITTEN ON TABLES OF STONE

Exodus, the second book of the Bible, tells the exciting story of how the descendants of the patriarch Abraham escaped enslavement in a foreign land and trekked across a barren wasteland to the place that had been promised to their forefathers. At one point in their long trek, when they stopped at the base of a mountain for a little rest and recuperation, Moses, their leader, left the crowd and climbed up to the top of the mountain. He was there for several days. During this time mysterious flashes of lightning and peals of thunder emanated from the mountaintop. When he returned, Moses was carrying two slabs of stone on which had been written 10 rules that were to be foundational to the happiness of human kind.

Now, those rules are the source of controversy in public schools and many other public places where they have been displayed. With the goal of supporting the moral fiber of the nation, well-meaning people have long campaigned to have the 10 Commandments prominently displayed in the public schools. In one instance, the words of the commandments were engraved on a stone slab in an attempt to replicate the original and to provide some degree of permanence to the display.

Such religious icons exhibited on public property are in violation of the First Amendment' Establishment clause. Restricting display of the Ten Commandments is seen as more evidence that "They have taken God out of the public schools." Both sides of the issue pressed their positions in the courts (Spencer, 2011). Three short paragraphs from a *Perspective* indicate my reaction to the issue.

> From my perspective, the Supreme Court did us all a favor many years ago with their ruling that disallowed the incursion of overt religious ritual and instruction in the schools. Even the current move to place the Ten Commandments in public schools is fraught with danger. There are different versions and different interpretations of each version. Which one should prevail? The answer to that question will be determined through serious conflict.
>
> It is not all as simple as it seems. The four little words, "Thou shalt not kill" have wide interpretations. To some it is an absolute. To others it is relative. Is it ok to kill

animals for food? What about killing animals for pleasure? Is killing in war a violation of the commandment? How about killing those convicted of crimes? Or those with deviant lifestyles? Or those not yet born? Or those who want to be killed? What is a classroom teacher to do when confronted by one who will kill to have the right interpretation of that commandment taught in school?

We have enough problems in our country without further fanning the flames of religious strife. If religious leaders feel the need for greater influence, I suggest they lead by example and overtly obey the Ten Commandments rather than campaign to post them in the schools. Children will learn more by their example than by the writing on the wall. They certainly will not benefit by any more religious strife among the adults. *(Perspective*, 2000, March 8)

It is very difficult for me to give parents suggestions regarding what side of the issue they should be on, because I have vacillated on this topic for many years. At one moment, I tend to lean towards strict separation between church and state. At other times, I move towards accommodating religion in the public schools. It is a tough issue and sometimes there is not a clear answer. Two paragraphs from a *Perspective* published nearly two decades ago summed up my position at that time.

From my perspective, it is time for religious leaders and concerned politicians to get honest on this subject. They need to discontinue the public attacks on the government, public schools, and the courts. They need to admit that the decline in prayer and Bible reading is caused, not by government edict, but because of their own lack of power in the pulpit. When religion depends on government agencies to enforce the performance of its rituals, it has no moral power. Churches and families should not expect the public schools to do their job in teaching the youth to read the Bible and pray. They should be honest about their own shortcomings in these matters.

If conservative leaders want to make a significant contribution to the moral climate of the country, they should forget about forcing children to pray at school. Instead, they should encourage parents to be people of prayer. The Bible should be read in the church not in the public schools. Pastors, who themselves know the Word, can expound its truths far more effectively than the classroom teacher. Parents who pray and pastors who preach the Bible will fill the nation's moral vacuum much more effectively than any amendment to the Constitution. *(Perspective*, 1998, May 27)

## RELIGIOUS INSTRUCTION

The real struggle comes when public school teachers provide instruction in subjects that intersect with some aspect of religion. The social studies are particularly problematic in that religion is so intertwined with historical events that it is difficult to ignore the topic and still be able to give a complete view of the subject. Without the inclusion of religion in the curriculum, students would likely have a distorted view of the world.

It is more than just a knowledge base that students obtain during their time in public school. The school years are times when character is developed and individual attitudes towards others become solidified. Haynes (2011) suggests a structural model for the appropriate inclusion of religion in the public schools. He identifies a major goal in his closing paragraphs:

> In order to live with our deepest differences in the United States, we must get religion right in public education, the institution primarily responsible for preparing young people for citizenship in a pluralistic democracy. If we cannot get this right in public schools, we have little hope of getting this right in the public square of what is now the most religiously diverse nation on earth. (p. 14)

Thus, much is at stake when public schools accept the challenge of religious instruction.

Nothing in the Supreme Court decisions would prohibit teaching courses in religious studies in public schools. Such instruction must avoid advocacy and be free from any appearance of proselytization. The strategy is more teaching "about" religion than teaching religion as an advocate. While this attitude of accommodation is becoming more popular among educational leaders, Passe and Willox (2009) identify an important concern regarding teaching religious studies in the public schools. American teachers lack the skills required to teach the content appropriately. "A single preservice course in social studies methods is insufficient for teachers to develop instructional techniques that promote tolerance, sensitivity, non judgmental expression of beliefs, and an in-depth grasp of the nuances of major world religions" (pp. 104–5). They note special concern for elementary teachers who are likely to have gaps in their knowledge of basic social studies.

McCarthy (2009) outlines the challenge quite succinctly. She notes the vulnerability of children in their care, in alerting educators to their duty:

> Educators overriding concern should be to protect students from religious indoctrination by school personnel or classmates and to ensure that school policies do not unduly interfere with students practice or expression of their beliefs. Balancing the competing interests can be daunting at times, but it is an important responsibility. (p. 718)

## SOME FINAL THOUGHTS

This chapter has tackled a very touchy issue in American public education. I am certain that it has not answered all the questions; in fact it has not even identified all the questions. Rather, the goal was to provide a broad view of the place of religion in the public schools. It has opened up some of the issues and provided a brief analysis of key court decisions so a parent should get some idea of an appropriate response when events at a public school impacts their own children.

The courts have neither taken God out of the public schools nor have they forbidden children to pray in school (Flowers, 2005). The result of the court action has been to restrict religious rituals as a function of the school. The chapter also identified the appropriate approach to instruction in religious studies. While that does not remove all the controversy in the public schools over the place of religion, it does give parents some general guidelines on how to react in different situations that they might encounter in dealing with schools.

A major problem is that in many cases school personnel have misinterpreted and misapplied court decisions affecting religion (Fraser, 1999). This raises a great deal of concern among ordinary citizens, especially parents, when they feel their right to freedom of religion is being overly restricted. Some parents are very assertive to see that religion of any sort is kept out of the public schools. Even the Pledge of Allegiance that contains the phrase "under God" has been subjected to litigation because of opposition by those who interpret that simple clause as establishing religion (Russo, 2004).

It is my goal that through the perspective presented in this chapter, those who, like myself, have a strong separation of church and state viewpoint can find common ground with those more willing to accommodate religion in public schools. It might be that both sides need to moderate their stance a bit. From my perspective, we should be able to do so without compromising our basic principles. It is to that end that I have dedicated this last chapter of the book.

## LIST OF *PERSPECTIVES* REFERENCED

Published in *The Journal Era*, Berrien Springs, Michigan

1995, February 15. Prayer in The Public School
1998, May 27. Filling the Moral Vacuum
2000, February 2. The Forgotten Commandment
2000, March 8. The Coming Religious War in America

## REFERENCES

Beckwith, F. J. (2003). *Law, Darwinism, and public education: The establishment clause and the challenge of intelligent design.* Lanham, MD: Rowman & Littlefield.

Brand, L. (2009). *Faith, reason, and Earth history: A paradigm of earth and biological origins by intelligent design* (2nd ed.). Berrien Springs, MI: Andrews University Press.

Eldredge. (2000). *The triumph of evolution and the failure of creationism.* New York: W. H. Freeman and Company.

*Engel v. Vitale,* 370 U.S. 421 (1962).

Flowers, R. B. (2005). *That godless court? Supreme Court decisions on church-state relationships* (2nd ed.). Louisville, KY: Westminster John Knox Press.

Fraser, J. W. (1999). *Between church and state: Religion and public education in a multicultural America.* New York: St. Martin's Griffen.

Haynes, C. C. (2011). Getting religion right in public schools. *Phi Delta Kappan, 93*(4), 8–14.

Kreamelmeyer, K. (2014). Religion and the increasing impact on America's schools: How religion impacts society and schools in post-911 America. *Culture and Religion Review Journal, 2014*(4), 8–17.

Lofaso, A. M. (2009). *Religion in the public schools: A roadmap for avoiding lawsuits and respecting parents legal rights.* Americans United for Separation of Church and State.

Mawdsley, R. D. (2004). Access to public school facilities for religious expression by students, student groups, and community organizations: Extending the reach of the free speech clause. *Brigham Young University Education & Law Journal, 2004*(2), 269–299.

McCarthy, M. (2009). Beyond the wall of separation: Church-state concerns in public schools. *Phi Delta Kappan, 90*(10), 714–719.

Passe, J., & Willox, L. (2009). Teaching religion in America's public schools: A necessary disruption. *The Social Studies, 100*(33), 102–106.

Romero, A. D., & Temple-Raston, D. (2008). *In defense of our America: The fight for civil liberties in the age of terror.* New York: Harper. Russo, C. J. (1999). Prayer at public school graduation ceremonies An exercise in futility or a teachable moment? *Brigham Young University Education and Law Journal, Winter, 99*(1), 1–23.

Russo, C. J. (2004). The Supreme Court and Pledge of Allegiance: Does God still have a place in American schools? *Brigham Young University Education & Law Journal, 2004*(2), 301–330.

*School District of Abington Township v. Schempp & Murray v Curlett,* 374 U.S. 203 (1963).

Spencer, D. (2011). What's the harm? Nontaxpayer standing to challenge religious symbols. *Harvard Journal of Law and Public Policy, 34*(4), 1071–1097.

*Washegesic v. Bloomingdale Public Schools,* 813 F. Supp. 559 (W. D. Mich. 1993).

Wick, J. (2011). *Public education: The final solution in the conquest of America's ideals.* Enumclaw, WA: Wine Press Publishing.

# EPILOGUE

Children are a heritage from the Lord, or so said the ancient Muse. The premise of this book rests solidly on that statement, that parents have a privilege that originates at a much higher level than any agency on this planet. Along with that privilege, however comes a parallel responsibility. The descendants of the patriarch Abraham provide a case in point. They were finally approaching the land of promise after wandering in the wilderness for forty years. Before they crossed the border, into the Promised Land, some instructions were provided to guide them as they established new communities in a new homeland.

The new nation was to be protected in perpetuity by following a plan for the education of their children. While rather primitive by today's standards, it was a clear plan for schooling the children in the new nation. No compulsory school attendance laws provided the force to support the plan, and no high-stakes testing imposed an evaluation system on the citizens of the new nation. Also, no, common core curriculum guided their way. The instructions to parents were very clear—that the education of their children was to be an all-encompassing experience.

As expressed by a modern English translation of the Torah (the first five books of the Old Testament), the charge to parents stated, "These commandments that I give you today are to be upon your hearts.

*Helping Parents Understand Schools: A Different Perspective on Education and Schooling in America*, pages 207–209.

Impress them on your children. Talk about them when you sit at home and when you walk along the road, when you lie down and when you get up. Tie them as symbols on your hands and bind them on your forehead. Write them on the door frames of your houses and on your gates."

This challenge to parents is found in the book aptly named Deuteronomy, which means a "repetition of the law."

A major purpose of this book is to help parents understand schools and the education of their own children. Nothing could describe parental responsibility for the function of education as cogently as the statement above taken from the ancient writings. Parents carry the major burden as directors of their children's education. While they employ professional instructors who have expertise in teaching groups of children in the formal school, these professionals should never be expected to supplant the work of the parents.

The first section of the book presented a defense of public education. In America we have a marvelous system of schooling, even though it is not highly functional in parts of society that are highly dysfunctional. Yet, the public school is a haven of refuge for many children. In some areas of America—both urban and rural—the public school is the only institution offering an opportunity to escape poverty and grasp the American dream. In my view, there is no educational cure for the social problems of America's inner cities or other areas. That teachers and administrators can function at all—in the midst of social upheaval—is nothing but a miracle. The schools cannot be reformed until the society is reformed.

In Part Two of this book, five chapters provide parents with a look at contemporary schooling, including suggestions on how parents can collaborate with the professional educators for the benefit of their children. At no point do I concede responsibility for the child's education to the school. It always remains in the hands of parents to determine the general direction of their child's schooling and life. While not conceding their duty, parents are best advised to seek counsel from the professional educators. When parents and teachers form a team, they together provide a much better education than if they function in isolation from each other.

To many parents who have not been close to their children's schooling experience, it will come as a surprise just how different the classroom is when compared to their own experience in school just a few years ago. Children today are expected to carry much more responsibility for their own learning experience they have in the formal school setting, then at any time in the history of public education. Parents need to be alert to the burdens their children bear as far as the schooling experience is concerned.

Part Three of the book is concerned with public policy. Most parents are not aware of how public policy is made or how it affects them and their children. In my view, parents can be a valuable resource to the professional educators and political leaders as policy matters are considered at the higher levels of government. The four chapters dedicated to public policy barely scratch the surface. However, some of the major issues are identified and an initial analysis provided. Parents can take what is presented in the book as a starting point and exercise their influence in the support of positive changes in public education.

Part Four tried to bring some clarity in discussing two sensitive issues in public education. First, the matter of race is still a challenge in many schools. This is another one of those problem areas on which the school can have, in many cases, only minimal influence. The home life of the child sets the standard. Therefore, a great burden for racial harmony rests with parents. The school, of course can greatly enhance positive attitudes towards racial and ethnic diversity that have been instilled in children prior to their arrival at school.

Finally, the place of religion in public schools brings the book to a close. I have dedicated this book to parents—and all those who carry a parental role. I place a strong emphasize on the responsibility of parents in the schooling process. Some might be discouraged because they view the parent's role as quite overwhelming, especially if they expected the school would carry most of the burden. A more positive way to look at the function of parenting in the education of their children is that mothers and fathers have been given tremendous opportunity to perpetuate the race and pass on to future generations the traditions and values that parents treasure as part of their life on this terrestrial globe. Children are indeed a heritage from the Lord. May God bless parents and their children!

# AUTHOR'S PAGE

**Lyndon G. Furst** (known as Jerry to his friends) is Dean Emeritus of the School of Graduate Studies and Professor Emeritus of Educational Administration at Andrews University. Furst served as Professor of Educational Administration prior to his work as Graduate Dean. He also worked in the Seventh-day Adventist school system for 21 years as elementary teacher and principal, principal of a coeducational secondary boarding school, and Educational Superintendent for the Adventist schools in a two state region. Furst holds an Ed. D. in educational administration from the University of the Pacific. Furst was elected to the Board of the local public schools in 1994. The voters returned him to that position several times for a total of 19 years.

**Bruce S. Cooper** is Emeritus Professor at Fordham University Graduate School of Education where he was a professor for 33 years; he also taught at University of Pennsylvania, the University of London Institute of Education, and Dartmouth College. His research focuses on policies, politics, and programs in education. He has written 44 books—and over 200 articles and editorials—including the *Handbook of Education Politics and Policy* (2 editions) and has a particular interest in private and religious education, as well as public school policies and improvements. He resides in New York City near the 13 members of his immediate family.

*Helping Parents Understand Schools: A Different Perspective on Education and Schooling in America,* pages 211–212.

**Heather L. Beals** is a homeschooling mother of 3, living in Vancouver, WA. She designed the front cover of this book using an original water color she painted for that purpose. She also designs and produces children's clothing which she markets for online sales. Beals' latest venture includes production of scented bath salts and sugar scrubs which are retailed in the Vancouver area. She is the grand-daughter of the author.

# ACKNOWLEDGMENTS

Any written work of this size requires a substantial amount of resources and assistance. I do appreciate all those who helped me along the way as I worked on this book project. Three individuals were especially supportive of, and deserve credit for the completion of this book.

First, there is Reva, my wife of 57 years who is now, because of my physical handicap, also my caregiver. She has shown a tremendous amount of patience with me as I struggle to overcome the ravages of physical and technological dysfunction. She frequently found lost items for me, and picked up things off the floor that I, in my clumsiness knocked off the table or had slipped out of my hands. Her sweet spirit and continuous encouragement has been essential to maintaining my own mental health, as I encountered one problem after another with the computer or misplaced things I needed as I worked on the project. Reva deserves much credit for the finished work.

My longtime friend and colleague Dr. Bruce Cooper originated the idea of this book some years ago when he encouraged me to take my published newspaper articles and combine them into a book about education. I told him no, that with my declining physical condition, I just did not have the energy to take on a project of that magnitude. But, he would not let the idea die a natural death as I desired. For several months every e-mail he sent had at least a hint about the book. "How is that best seller coming along?" he would inquire. At first, I would protest that

*Helping Parents Understand Schools: A Different Perspective on Education and Schooling in America,* pages 213–214.

I just could not do it. I had all kinds of good reasons why I should not even think about it. Still, he persisted. "Just checking to see how you are doing on the great book you are going to write," he would put in an e-mail.

Finally, I tired of the game and in exasperation I responded to his needling with words of surrender. "Okay, you win. I will write the book." At first I could not conceptualize how to integrate the *Perspectives* into the narrative of a book. I made several different attempts at it but nothing seemed to work. Bruce could always find something either missing or redundant when I sent him a copy for review. I was about to give up when Reva looked at one Bruce's comments. In puzzlement, she asked me, "Isn't that the same thing you required of your doctoral students at the University?" That is when it all came together in my mind. And the rest of the story is history. Bruce Cooper certainly gets much credit for the origin and completion of the book.

The third person that should get credit for the completion of this book is Kathy Pullano, publisher and editor of our hometown weekly newspaper *The Journal Era.* The story of how she encouraged me to start writing the *Perspectives* is told in the first section of the book in the chapter entitled Genesis. For 20 years Kathy has kindly published my written work. Seldom has she ever exercised her editorial prerogative on something I have written. She has given me mostly an open field in choosing topics for my commentary each week.

When I sat down to seriously consider writing the book, I had nearly a thousand essays already written. That gave me a depth of material to draw upon for the book. I owe a great deal of gratitude to Kathy for getting me started on writing the *Perspectives* in the first place, and for her encouragement to continue the process. Kathy Pullano deserves much credit for the completion of this book.

Numerous other people have generously assisted me in various parts of the book. Long-time friend and colleague Dr. Charles Russo from the University of Dayton provided valuable editorial assistance on several chapters. Dr. Jimmy Kijai, from Andrews University, provided consultation for the chapter on testing. Timothy Chung, who is known to me only via the Internet has been so kind to provide editorial assistance as needed. Jenifer Daly, brought me up-to-date on the changing technology of word processing. She serves as Adjunct Professor in the School of Business at Andrews University while doing advanced studies in systematic theology. Finally, a word of appreciation to Andrews University for keeping my account open at the James White Library. That gave me access to data bases needed for research on the book.

45178666R00131

Made in the USA
San Bernardino, CA
03 February 2017